THE LIFE OF PEACE

Also by Martyn Lloyd-Jones

I Am Not Ashamed
Preaching and Preachers
The Life of Joy

THE LIFE OF PEACE

PHILIPPIANS, VOLUME TWO
CHAPTERS THREE AND FOUR

Dr Martyn Lloyd-Jones

HODDER AND STOUGHTON
LONDON   SYDNEY   AUCKLAND

British Library Cataloguing in Publication Data

A Catalogue record for this book is available from the British Library

ISBN 0-340-59520-5

Published by Hodder and Stoughton, a division of Hodder and Stoughton Ltd, Mill Road, Dunton Green, Sevenoaks, Kent TN13 2YA. Editorial Office, 47 Bedford Square, London WC1B 3DP. Typeset by Watermark, The Old Hall, Crostwight, Norfolk NR28 9PA. Printed in Great Britain by Clays Ltd, St Ives plc.

Contents

	Note	6
1	True rejoicing	7
2	True worship	20
3	All in Christ	32
4	The Christian life	44
5	The righteousness of God	56
6	Paul's great ambition	68
7	The ultimate goal	79
8	The one thing	91
9	Belief and conduct	103
10	Citizens of heaven	116
11	The life and work of the Church	128
12	Rejoice always	141
13	Moderation	153
14	The peace of God	165
15	The Hebrew and the Greek mind	178
16	How to know God's peace	190
17	Learning to be content	202
18	The final cure	215
19	All our need supplied	228
20	My God	240
21	The fellowship of the saints	250
22	The grace of the Lord Jesus Christ	261

Note

Readers of Dr Lloyd-Jones' books will realise that Chapters 14, 17 and 18 of this volume are also published in *Spiritual Depression* (1971). The reason for this is that he preached those sermons in his Philippians series, but realising how appropriate they were to the subject of spiritual depression he included them in that book. However this volume would clearly be incomplete without these chapters, so with the kind permission of the publishers Marshall Pickering we have put them again in the series in which they were first preached.

Chapter 1

True rejoicing

Finally, my brethren, rejoice in the Lord (Phil. 3:1).

There can be no question but that in these words we come to a point of transition, or a turning point, in this letter written to the church at Philippi. From the very earliest days of the Christian Church there has been much discussion and disagreement about just what this injunction means. We need not enter into that in detail here, but it is interesting, from the standpoint of a study of the Scriptures, to attempt, by analysis, to arrive at the precise idea that was in the Apostle's mind. There are those who think that Paul was about to end his letter here, that he really had said everything he had set out to say, but that as he was writing the words, 'Finally, my brethren, rejoice in the Lord,' he suddenly thought of something else he wanted to say. So he went on to say it, and hence the whole of chapter 3 and the first part of chapter 4, for you notice that in the fourth verse of that chapter he returns to the same theme and says, 'Rejoice in the Lord alway: and again I say, Rejoice.' These interpreters, therefore, would regard the entire argument of chapter 3, and the first part of chapter 4, as a kind of afterthought which Paul incorporated in the letter instead of making it a postscript.

Well, it is not necessary for us to discuss that question, for ultimately, of course, it really does not matter; the mechanics of this letter, while they have their interest, are the least important part of it. But for myself, I find it difficult to accept that analysis as an explanation of what the

Apostle says at this point. It seems to me, rather, that Paul is merely resuming here the theme we tried to indicate in our introductory study* when we took a general view of the whole epistle. Paul wrote this letter in order to teach the Philippian people how to rejoice in the Lord – that is the theme, that is the message. And because he is such a practical man, he talks about various things which are likely to rob them of that joy; he deals with the difficulties one by one, and shows how they are to be surmounted. You remember how, in the first chapter, he talks about his imprisonment. This was tending to depress the people at Philippi and he puts them right about it, by dealing with various facts about his own state. He says, You need not worry about me, 'to me to live is Christ and to die is gain'; it was immaterial to him whether he be put to death or not.

Then Paul talks about the trouble which was caused by certain false brethren, and he says that in spite of that the Philippians can rejoice, for, although the false brethren preach Christ with the wrong motives, Paul will still rejoice because Christ is preached. He goes on next to talk about the persecutions which they were experiencing, and he shows them how to deal with these, too, still in order to maintain their joy. Then there was the tendency, perhaps, for the Philippian Christians to experience a certain amount of jealousy and envy with respect to one another, and Paul deals with this at the beginning of the second chapter, where he produces that amazing antidote, giving his wonderful description of the incarnation. He says, 'Let this mind be in you . . .', for if that mind is in them, then their joy will be maintained. Then he takes up once more the question of his absence from them, and points out that they need not be dejected or troubled because of this; he knows that the work will go on, because 'it is God which worketh in you both to will and to do of his good pleasure' (2:13); and he shows them how to work that out. And, lastly, he comforts them over the illness of Epaphroditus, and he says: I am sending

---

* See chapter 1 in Volume 1, *The Life of Joy* (Hodder & Stoughton).

him back to you, and not only that, I am hoping to send Timothy too.

All along, then, in various ways Paul is showing these people how to maintain their joy and now here in verse 1 of chapter 3 he comes to the end: 'Finally' – or, if you prefer it, you can translate it, 'For the rest' – 'Finally, my brethren, rejoice in the Lord. To write the same things to you, to me indeed is not grievous, but for you it is safe.' He has something else to bring to their remembrance, and, like the excellent teacher, the profound psychologist that he is, he thus reminds them, in passing, about the joy, and we are back again with the great theme of rejoicing in the Lord. It is as if he were saying, 'Now that we have dealt with these matters, let us continue; the big thing is to rejoice' – and then he talks about the things which were tending to cause trouble, namely, the work of the Judaisers and those false teachers who followed him around and caused intellectual and theological confusion in the infant Christian churches.

That, it seems to me, is the most natural way of regarding this point of transition in the epistle. It is merely a continuation and a reminder of the same central theme. We can illustrate this from the realm of music. In a symphony, for example, there is one predominant theme, and again and again the composer just throws in that theme; he may wander off in his variations, and it would seem that he has forgotten it, but he always comes back to it. That is what you find Paul doing in this, the most lyrical of all his epistles. So here once more he is reminding us of the major theme in the light of which all these other particular matters must always be considered.

That, then, is the setting, and it is important for us to bear it in mind. But I am also anxious now to concentrate on the positive exhortation itself. All along Paul has been inclined to suggest it; it has been there in different forms, but here he puts it explicitly. It is an exhortation, a command – 'Finally, my brethren, rejoice in the Lord . . .' I suggest that the obvious way to approach this is to divide it into three parts. First of all we must consider what it means to rejoice in the Lord. Then we must ask the second obvious question: why should we rejoice in the Lord? And thirdly: how are we to do this?

Now as we look at that first question and ask what it means 'to rejoice in the Lord', the first thing that strikes us is that it is, as we have said, a command. It is not a description of the state in which we find ourselves so much as something which we are exhorted to do. The tendency is always to think of joy as some subjective state or condition, and, of course, ultimately it is, and yet the very fact that Paul commands us or calls us to rejoice is proof positive that it is not something which we experience in a purely passive or subjective manner. We are not to sit down, trusting and hoping that we shall suddenly begin to rejoice! No, we have to do something in order that we may rejoice and it is something that we are capable of doing. These words are not just an intimation that we should passively expect or hope that something will happen or take place in us and that then we shall suddenly feel tremendously happy.

This whole question of joy in the Christian life has often caused a great deal of confusion. If I may so put it, many Christian people are unhappy because they are not experiencing joy. Their whole idea is that joy is the result of things that happen to us. They believe that we have no control over it, that we are not capable of making ourselves rejoice, that joy and rejoicing are the end result of the interaction and inter-operation of a number of forces and factors, most of them without, but some of them within ourselves. And, they say, as a result of all this, we are either happy or we are not. But that, it seems to me, is an error which is constantly exposed and denounced in these New Testament epistles, and here it is exposed by the very fact we are given a commandment – we are to rejoice, it is something we can do.

But having said that, I must again point out that two dangers arise immediately. The first is the danger of trying to produce this state of rejoicing by making a direct attack upon the emotions. I need not elaborate this, it is perfectly obvious, is it not? Some people will say that as rejoicing and happiness belong to the realm of the emotions, then, if we are commanded to rejoice, we must begin to do things to ourselves emotionally in order that we may get into this happy state. And, of course, we are familiar with the various methods that people will persist in employing to this end. For instance, in a public meeting, or in a public act of worship, think how often something like this happens: the leader of the meeting, or someone else, says, 'Well now, the first thing is to get this congregation or gathering into a good mood. Let's put on hymns or tunes or choruses of a certain type – we must get them happy, we must get them to rejoice. They have come in cold and miserable, let's get them into a good, happy state.' So, they put on bright, cheerful hymns to get the people to rejoice. That is what I mean by a direct attack upon the emotions, an attempt to produce joy by doing things to our emotional life which are calculated to lead to that result.

Now I want to show you that that is not the teaching of the Apostle here, as it is not the teaching of the New Testament anywhere. Indeed, I think I can demonstrate that such a direct attack upon the emotions is, according to the New Testament, one of the most dangerous things that we can ever do; that it is the high road to false teaching and the various cults. There are many ways in which people can make themselves feel happy: by taking drugs, by manipulating circumstances, or by groping in the realm of make-believe, fancy and fantasy, for example. There is an almost endless variety of ways, and, from the Christian standpoint, that is the major trouble of the world today. The world is full of troubles and unhappiness, terrible things are threatening life today, but instead of facing these things realistically and adopting the Christian way of surmounting them, people deliberately turn their back upon the troubles and, in their search for joy, happiness and peace, create an artificial sense of happiness and pleasure. And if that is wrong for the world, it is wrong also for us as Christian people. The principle is that we must never try to become happy and be full of rejoicing by doing something immediately and directly to our emotional nature.

The other danger which we must avoid is the pose of being bright, happy and cheerful Christian people. I think there are a number of people who have rightly seen and understood that Christians are meant to be men and women who rejoice. There is a type of Christian – a type that was perhaps far too common in the last century – who gives the impression that being a Christian means being mournful and miserable. This is the sort of person described by Milton as one who 'scorned delights and lives laborious days'. But people have now seen that that is a false representation of Christianity and of New Testament teaching, and that really the Christian is the only one who can know true happiness in a world like this. So, because of that, they adopt a bright and cheerful pose, and are always trying to give the impression that it is a wonderful thing to be a Christian.

That, it seems to me, is the second form that this error of the direct approach tends to take. I do not know what your experience is, but, speaking for myself, the most depressing people I think I have ever met are those who try to give the impression that they are always cheerful and happy. Is there not all the difference in the world between a person who is trying to give that impression and the one who really is happy? If a person is truly happy everybody can see it, it needs no explanation because you cannot help noticing. But you never feel that about these other people; you feel they are playing at being happy, it is the thing to do and therefore they are trying to do it. You see through them. You feel their joy is only skin deep, for it lacks some vital and essential quality.

But we are not exhorted by Paul to be exponents of what we may call 'mechanical' Christianity. No, it is unbelievable that the Apostle Paul was ever like that himself or would teach anybody else to be like that. He was a man who knew a joy greater than most people have been privileged to know in this world, and yet, at the same time, he said, 'We that are in this tabernacle do groan, being burdened' (2 Cor.

5:4); and that element must never be absent.

So when we are told to rejoice in the Lord, we must avoid the error of trying to do so by a direct attack upon our emotional nature. How, then, is it to be done? Well, first of all, our rejoicing is always something that results from a realisation of our position in Christ. My joy is the product, almost the by-product, of my concentration upon my relationship to God in Jesus Christ. That will become more clear as we work out these other points. Let me sum up this first point by saying that we do see very clearly that as Christian people we should rejoice; and I suppose that there has scarcely ever been a time in the history of the Church and of the world when this exhortation has been more important than it is today. The world, in spite of outward appearances and the various drugs with which it is drugging itself in an attempt to be happy, is profoundly unhappy, and what it is looking for is the secret which will bring it to this position of rejoicing. Now our whole case is that no one but the Christian can truly rejoice, and it is here, therefore, that we can bear the most striking witness at this present time. Are we giving the impression in practice that the words which our Lord spoke to his disciples are literally true: 'In the world ye shall have tribulation, but be of good cheer [rejoice]; I have overcome the world' (John 16:33)? And we are called to show that we do believe that to be true in our experience, that we do overcome the world.

The Apostle Paul expressed exactly the same thing on many occasions. He said to the Roman Christians, 'I am persuaded, that neither death, nor life, nor angels, nor principalities, nor powers, nor things present, nor things to come, nor height, nor depth, nor any other creature, shall be able to separate us from the love of God, which is in Christ Jesus our Lord' (Rom. 8:38–39) – that is the position, and you and I are called to it. We are commanded to this and it is our privilege just to shock the world, to convict the world and to lead the world to Christ by showing that even as things are today and in spite of everything, we still rejoice. But if that is true, it is also true to say that this is a very thorough-going test of our profession of faith. Are we rejoicing? We claim to be Christians – well this is one of the results of being a Christian, this is one of the things to which the Christian is inevitably exhorted. The Christian is actually commanded to rejoice – are we experiencing joy and is this great statement true of us?

But let us leave it at that and go on to my second question. Why should we rejoice in the Lord? And here again the Apostle gives us abundant answers to the question. There are many reasons why we should rejoice in the Lord. The first is the one we have already considered – that we have been commanded to rejoice. But that is not all. We should also rejoice in the Lord for the Lord's sake. This great salvation, that is in this world in the person of our Lord Jesus Christ, is something that has been worked out by God, it is God's plan, God's scheme, and he has sent his Son into this world. We are told that even the angels in heaven are looking out over the parapet, as it were, to see how this work of God is being conducted in this world. If you read Ephesians 3:10 you will find Paul's description of this: 'To the intent that now unto the principalities and powers in heavenly places might be known by the church, the manifold wisdom of God.' The principalities which appear in heavenly places are given an insight into the manifold wisdom of God by what they see in the Church; salvation is God's handiwork; salvation, the whole Christian gospel, is something that God has sent into life and into the world.

And so, since it is God's action, this is the greatest reason why you and I should be rejoicing. What credit to God is a miserable Christian? What credit to God and his great salvation in Christ are people who seem to be always apologising for their faith – does that manifest the manifold wisdom of God? There is the reason for rejoicing – for God's sake. In 1 Peter 2, Peter says the same thing when he tells us that God has called us out of darkness into his marvellous light that we may show forth his praise and his glory – that is the object. You and I have this inestimable privilege, therefore, of manifesting the glory of God, and the way we do so,

supremely, is by showing that this Christian life of ours is
one that enables us to overcome this world and rejoice even
in the midst of tribulation. That is the second reason.

The third reason is obvious. It is for the sake of others. I
have already dealt with this so I do not need to stay with it,*
but it is our bounden duty at a time like this to rejoice in the
Lord for the sake of the men and women who are around us,
in their misery and unhappiness, seeking and searching for
an answer, going from disappointment to disappointment,
sometimes even contemplating going out of life through that
back door that should never be opened. For the sake of
others, then, who are defeated and frustrated by life, it is
our business to stand out and radiate this new life, this
different life that calls for rejoicing, so that they, seeing it,
may say, 'There is hope for me after all.'

But let me show you also how the Apostle shows us that
even for our own sake we ought to rejoice in the Lord; and
that, in a sense, is the one big theme of this epistle. He has
already been emphasising the point so I need only summarise it. There are two reasons why I must rejoice for my
own sake. Do you know that rejoicing in the Lord is one of
the greatest safeguards against most of the dangers that con-
front us? 'The joy of the Lord is your strength,' says
Nehemiah (Neh. 8:10), and that is an obvious, psychological
principle. When we are happy we can do our work very
much better than when we are unhappy; the happier you are
the more easily you can do things and that is equally true in
the Christian life. The Christian who really rejoices in the
Lord has many fewer difficulties in this world and life than
the one who does not, because, if you are not centrally
right, you already have problems before you begin to deal
with other people. So that the way to live the Christian life
smoothly and freely is to be right at the very foundation.

But not only that; look at the various dangers with which
the Apostle has already dealt in his letter. To rejoice in the
Lord is the greatest safeguard, says the Apostle, against

---

*See Volume 1, *The Life of Joy*.

those brethren who are preaching Christ falsely. If I were rejoicing in myself and my own preaching, says Paul, their attacks upon me would be very hurtful; but thank God I do not preach for my own sake or reputation, I do it for his sake, so that though they are trying to hurt me they are not touching me at all. I rejoice in the Lord, therefore I cannot be attacked at that point. Is it not obvious that what makes us all so sensitive is our self-consciousness and our self-esteem? And it is these things that make us vulnerable to the attacks that are made upon us. The one thing needed is to rejoice in the Lord, just to forget yourself; you are not working for yourself, you are working for him. Paul talks about it in the second chapter: 'Let nothing be done through strife or vainglory; but in lowliness of mind let each esteem other better than themselves. Look not every man on his own things, but every man also on the things of others' (vv. 3–4), and if you only do that, says Paul, even if you lose all things, you will not be dejected because you have already been regarding yourself as a steward. He says, I am holding them in trust for the Lord, they are not mine, therefore if I lose all, I have not lost anything in that personal sense.

To rejoice is a safeguard against something else, too. The Philippians, you remember, were unhappy and wondering how they were going to do without Paul; they were tending to look a little too much to Paul as their guide and instructor. So Paul says in effect, 'Don't rejoice in me, rejoice in the Lord; and then, whether I am alive or dead, it does not matter, the Lord is always with you.' True rejoicing is a safeguard against such a danger, and as we go on to deal with the third chapter, you will see another very great reason. The Judaisers were boasting about their nationality and about the fact that they had been circumcised. They were boasting about their morality and various other things, and the result was, ultimately, that they had arrived at a state of wretchedness and misery and the only cure was to rejoice in the Lord. True rejoicing is a safeguard from the attacks that come from every direction.

The fifth great reason for rejoicing in the Lord is that it is the only joy that can never fail us. That is literally true. Whatever else you and I may try to base our joy and happiness upon will finally fail us, whether it be ourselves, our success, our ability, our worldly learning, our home, or our children. It does not matter what it is, every one of these things is finally going to be removed and we shall all be left in isolation. A moment will come when we will find ourselves going out of life, and out of the world, and we will realise that there are things which we cannot take with us. Then our souls will be suddenly stripped and made bare, and we will awaken to the fact that we have been depending upon things that cannot go with us across the river of death – that is the loneliness of death.

In John 16:32 our Lord says, 'Behold, the hour cometh, yea, is now come, that ye shall be scattered, every man to his own, and shall leave me alone: and yet I am not alone, because the Father is with me.' Ultimately, we are all coming to this. The test will come when we find ourselves stripped of all the world offers, then we will find that this joy is the only joy that abides – that it will never fail us or leave us. His promise is: 'I will never leave thee, nor forsake thee' (Heb. 13:5), so if my rejoicing is in him I am in an invulnerable position, for nothing can come between me and the love of God which is in Christ Jesus our Lord. They could throw Paul into prison, but they could not rob him of his Christian joy. They could persecute and strip him and malign him; they could try to rob him of his character and of everything else, but it did not matter. Here is something that can never be touched, that is beyond the reach of man and all his machinations and efforts to destroy; it is a joy that never fails and of which we can never be despoiled.

How, then, are we to rejoice in the Lord? That is the most practical point of all and yet it is perfectly simple. Let me put the answer in three propositions. The way to rejoice in the Lord, as we are commanded to do here, is, first and foremost, to be able to control every other source of joy. That is a negative proposition but it is essential. If I find that my joy is dependent upon anything which can be taken from

me, I must correct it. As a Christian I am in this life and
world, but though I must be in it, I am not of it; I must ride
loosely to it, and to all that it can give. I must be very careful
that I am not brought under the power of any one of these
things. They are quite permissible and legitimate in their
place, many of them have been ordained by God, but I must
look at the very centre of my joy, and must always be watching and correcting it. I must expose it to myself and realise
the danger, and I must refuse to build the whole of my ener-
gies upon any insecure foundations.

The next aspect, a positive one, is this: I am to meditate
upon him. You cannot rejoice in the Lord without thinking
about him. I must deliberately turn my eyes from the other
things that tend to charm and fascinate me and I must dwell
on him. Is that not the great reply of the author of the epistle to the Hebrews: '. . . let us lay aside every weight, and
the sin which doth so easily beset us, and let us run with
patience the race that is set before us, looking unto Jesus
. . .' (Heb. 12:1–2). Contemplate him, keep your eyes fixed
upon him. You have to look at him before you can rejoice
in him.

And then the third and last thing is this: we must consider
and meditate upon what he has done for us – his great, his
marvellous, his glorious work. We must go back and look at
the cross; we must see all the suffering that led to the cross,
and contemplate the meaning of the cross to him. As we
read the Bible, we must say, 'This is not a philosophy, this
is not an idea, or a fable.' We must go right over the whole
story of how he left the courts of heaven and humbled himself, of how he staggered up Golgotha and went to the cross.
We must consider all that he endured, and we must say, 'He
did all that for me.' That is the way to rejoice in him. We
must contemplate what he has done for us, and then go on
to remember what he is doing for us now. Paul has already
told us that he works in us 'both to will and to do' (Phil.
2:13). He has not only started this work, he is continuing it
– 'he which hath begun a good work in you will perform it
unto the day of Jesus Christ' (Phil. 1:6).

My dear friends, is it not amazing and wonderful, the way he comes into your life, changes your circumstances and raises hope and assurance in you? These are the ways in which he is working and continuing to work by the Holy Spirit, and the more you realise it, the more you rejoice. Then you look forward to the end and see the final consummation of it all. You take a grand view of history and see the world in all its confusion, its chaos and trouble, the warring factions and all the muddle of it all. Then you suddenly remind yourself that his work is going on and that he is working towards a goal. There is to be a final, grand consummation when Christ will come and rout all his enemies and set up his kingdom. Then there will be the glorious 'new heavens and a new earth, wherein dwelleth righteousness' (2 Pet. 3:13), and we who believe on him and rejoice in him shall reign with him for ever.

Is that not the way to rejoice – to contemplate that? That is what is meant by this exhortation. You do not sit down and hope you are going to feel joyful; you do not try to work up these feelings by some artificial stimulus. The way to rejoice in the Lord is to meditate upon the Lord and upon his salvation; it is to see what he has done and is doing and is going to do. If you truly see this, you cannot but rejoice. He will raise you to your feet; he will enable you to smile at the world and all its troubles; he will enable you to smile even in the face of death, because death will be nothing but the opening of that little door which will lead you into glory and into the presence of your beloved Lord. 'Finally, my brethren, rejoice in the Lord.'

Chapter 2

True worship

For we are the circumcision, which worship God in the spirit, and rejoice in Christ Jesus, and have no confidence in the flesh (Phil. 3:3).

In this verse the Apostle gives us one of the many definitions of the Christian which are to be found scattered so freely throughout his various letters. He found it necessary to give such definitions constantly. The people to whom he was writing had heard and believed the gospel; they had been converted and were made members of the Christian Church, but that did not necessarily mean that they perfectly understood the teaching and the doctrine. Most of the heresies that subsequently troubled the Church arose during its first years. Throughout the remainder of his career, the Apostle had to fight a great battle against heresy and that was why he had to keep on repeating these definitions of the Christian. In effect, he was constantly saying, 'If you believe this, or if you do that, then, of course, you are not a Christian: to be a Christian is this' – and then he gave a definition. And that is just what he does at this point.

I think you will find that every time you get one of these definitions in the Apostle's writings, it is always a matter of great interest and profound instruction to note the exact way in which he came to give the definition. In this verse, his reason for giving a definition of the Christian is that he is concerned about the joy and the happiness of these Philippian people. When we dealt in chapter 1 with Philippians 3:1 – 'Finally, my brethren, rejoice in the Lord' – we

20

pointed out that that is the theme of the whole epistle and that Paul wrote this letter in order to help the Philippians not only to have this joy, but to hold on to it and to maintain it. He has been dealing, as we have seen, with the various problems that were attacking them and threatening their happiness and here he takes up another trouble which was tending to interfere with the joy of the church at Philippi.

This time the problem was not something that was happening to him, or to them, it was the devastating false teaching and error which must be attributed to the people who are called Judaisers. Here were people who were going round those early Christian churches presenting a teaching and doctrine in the name of Christ which the Apostle goes on to show is entirely and utterly subversive of everything that constitutes true Christianity, and that is why Paul takes up this matter with such vigour. Let me make it plain that his primary interest is not mere controversy – Paul was never interested in controversy qua controversy, he did not delight in argument for its own sake, and he never argued, unless something of great importance was at stake. He takes up this point here because, in his view, if the members of the church at Philippi were to believe this other doctrine that was being offered to them, then their whole standing in Christ would be destroyed.

You notice how he shows us the all-importance of this subject. He does so in at least four different ways. First, he tells the Philippians that he is going to repeat something that he has already told them: 'To write the same things to you, to me indeed is not grievous . . .' Now the learned commentators exercise themselves very much over that statement. What does Paul mean by it? Has he written another letter which has been lost? Is he referring to something he has written in two or three other letters? Theologians show their learning in trying to settle that question.

But to me the obvious explanation seems to be that Paul is referring to something he had already told them while he was with them; it is, indeed, something that he is always repeating, you find it in almost every one of these letters.

'Therefore,' he says, in effect, to these people, 'I am going to tell you again something you have heard from me many times before, but I make no apology for repeating myself because "for you it is safe". This thing is so important and vital that at the expense of repeating myself I must say it again.' And that is something which displays Paul as a profound and wise teacher. There is no more subtle temptation for Christian people than the temptation to imagine that they are perfectly right and clear in the fundamentals of the faith. In one of his other epistles Paul said he was writing because the people were not certain of their principles. They seemed to be perfectly sound in their beliefs, but their behaviour revealed very plainly that they were wrong about some primary things. And there are people still who say, 'Oh yes, of course, I have been a Christian now for years, I understand the message of justification by faith and all that,' and yet it is at that very point that they have gone hopelessly astray. Let us never assume that we have arrived at a position in the Christian life where we do not need to be frequently reminded of the first principles of the gospel of Jesus Christ. This repetition is necessary; there is always the danger of slipping away from the truth and of assuming that we are right on fundamentals when sometimes we are not. Paul repeats himself and he makes no apology for doing so.

Then the second way in which he emphasises the great importance of this subject is by the repetition, three times over, of the word 'beware': 'Beware of dogs, beware of evil workers, beware of the concision.' Now this is not just undue exaggeration on the part of the Apostle. This matter is so vital that no pains are too great for him to take in his attempt to rouse these people to an awareness of their terrible danger. So Paul puts up this placard, this notice – beware, beware, beware – and by repetition impresses it upon their minds.

And then the next way in which he does it is by the violence of language with respect to these false teachers. Now by nature Paul was not a violent man. When you read his speeches in the Acts of the Apostles you see what a gentlemanly man he was, how unfailingly courteous in his addresses; he was not a man who would easily abuse others, and when he uses strong language, as he does here, there must be a very good reason. Because he sees the terrible danger of what was being taught by these false teachers, he calls them 'dogs'. They had claimed that they were preaching the true gospel and that Paul was not, and they had referred to all others as dogs, so Paul is saying that they are the dogs; they are behaving like dogs, tearing and destroying with this kind of talk.

And then he calls them 'evil workers', men who are doing evil things, upsetting churches, upsetting Christian people and causing schisms and divisions. It is evil work, says Paul. That is his estimate of the doctrine which they were preaching. Then, finally, he calls them 'the concision'. That is almost a pun. These men are talking about the circumcision, but what they really mean, what they are really interested in, is the concision: some mutilation of the body. But, Paul says, we, by contrast, are the circumcision. The violence of this language is again striking proof that the Apostle regards this matter as of the greatest importance.

And then, fourthly, Paul impresses this upon us by the way he gives his positive statement as to what does constitute a Christian, and here we come back to the point I was making earlier. Paul is writing to Christians; he is writing to people to whom he has said the noble and wonderful things that are to be found in chapter 1:4–10 and in the second chapter, too. Yet this man is such an expert in the spiritual life that he knows the subtleties of these teachers; so, once more, he says to the Philippians, Let me tell you what a real Christian is. Then he gives his three-fold definition.

There, then, we have seen the all-importance of this subject. Let me summarise it like this. According to the Apostle, our whole position in time and in eternity depends upon our clear understanding of what constitutes the Christian – of what are the basic elements of the Christian position. And Paul is so concerned about this, because, according to his teaching, if we are wrong about this, our whole future in eternity will suffer. How vital it is, then, that we should avoid those false teachings which are always ready to lead us astray.

But there is a second reason, and that is the one that Paul is so concerned about here. True joy in the Christian life also depends upon a correct understanding of doctrine. I know of nothing that so tends to rob us of our joy as Christians as uncertainty about doctrine. Alas, how many people there are who truly believe they are Christians but have never known the joy of the Lord about which Paul is speaking, simply because the teaching they have received has been false. There are those who think that it is almost sinful to rejoice as Christians. They think that the Christian walks with his head down, and goes mourning through life, and this in spite of the exhortations to joy which we find in such profusion in the New Testament. Such people are looking at themselves so much that they forget to look at the Lord; they have not understood the foundation. And that is why I maintain that it is so important for us to be perfectly clear and certain about this matter; it is the only way really to rejoice in the Lord and to have the full benefit of all that is offered us in Christ.

How urgently important this is for us! We are living in a world that is full of uncertainty. Many Christian people today do not worship in peace and safety and liberty; they are in circumstances where they seem to have been bereft of everything on which they have depended in the past, and the one thing that matters to them now is to know God and to be able to pray. And if you want to be able to do that you must be certain about your position. If, when you get on your knees, you begin to ask yourself whether you are a Christian, or whether you have any right to pray, if you are there querying the foundation, how can you build the superstructure? In a time of crisis one has no time to be thinking about these things, one must be able to presume or assume them, and go immediately to God. That is why Paul is so concerned about this. 'If you are right about this first matter,' he is saying in effect to these Philippians, 'then,

whatever may happen to you, all will be well between you
and God, and nothing can come between you. So make certain of where you stand.'

And I suggest to you that this is something which comes
with force to us also. It is not for me to prophesy – who can
prophesy in days like these? But are there not many signs in
the world at this time which seem to point to the fact that
you and I may have to face a period in which nothing will
matter but this and the one thing that will count is that we
know God? That is why I say that there is nothing more
important than that we should know exactly what it means
to be a Christian. So that with the Apostle Paul I make no
apology for calling your attention to this subject, so that you
may be very familiar with it, because for all of us 'it is safe'
that I should do so.

Now the Apostle puts his case, as I have reminded you,
in terms of the Judaisers. They went around teaching that it
was not enough to believe in Christ. 'You must be a Jew,'
they said; 'you must be circumcised.' And they went to the
new Gentile churches with that message. 'Ah, yes,' they
continued, 'you believe the gospel as preached by Paul, but
he did not go far enough. If you want to be a true Christian
you must be circumcised. You must know something about
temple worship. You cannot do away with all those sacrifices, they are still essential – it must be Christ-plus.' That
was their message and that is the message that Paul counters
in his three-fold reply.

Of course, you and I do not meet teaching in that precise
form but the principle which underlies it is still with us, and
as we proceed to study the Apostle's definition I think you
will see very clearly that we are not doing something that is
merely of academic interest. That may be the case in times
when the world is at ease, as, for example, in the days of the
Victorian era, but we are looking at things which are relevant today, and are as threatening to us as they were to the
Philippians. That is why we must be so careful truly to
understand Paul's three-fold definition of the Christian.

The first characteristic which Paul gives of Christian

people is that they 'worship God in the spirit'; or, to give an
alternative translation (it is impossible to decide which is
correct), 'We are the circumcision who worship by the Spirit
of God.' Either may be right, it does not matter, because
essentially both these translations are saying the same thing.
In other words, the first thing we have to face if we are anxious to know whether we are truly Christian or not, is the
whole question of worship. What is our idea or definition of
worship? What do we really mean when we say that we worship God? 'Surely,' says someone, 'you are not asking us to
consider something so elementary?' But I ask it because the
Apostle shows us very clearly that the mere fact that we
think we are worshipping does not prove that we really do
worship.

There is, then, a false way of worship which is opposite to
the true. The Apostle, you see, puts it in a form which con-
tradicts the false teaching of the Judaisers. 'They talk about
"the circumcision"', he says, in effect, to the Philippians,
'these other teachers, who are trying to impress upon you
that they are right. They are always telling you that you
must be circumcised and go back to the Jewish ceremonials
and rituals and temple worship, but I tell you that you cannot worship by doing things that way. We are the circumcision which worship God in the spirit.' What does that mean?
Well, in the first instance, the Christian is one who worships
God in the spirit and knows that these other things are no
longer necessary. There is a new way to God, another
method, which is now the right one; the other has been done
away with. It is not that it was wrong in itself, but when you
become a Christian it is not necessary, and to go back to it
is to deny Christ. That is Paul's message.

This is surely a subject that is still relevant at the present
time. There has been a great deal of talk in recent years
about worship, and there are sections of the Church that put
very great emphasis upon it. I once attended a conference at
which an excellent man, who happened to belong to the
Anglican Church, was speaking, and without any desire to
be offensive, he said: 'Of course, the real difference

between those of us who are Anglican, and others who are nonconformist is that we emphasise worship.' And it fell to my lot to suggest that he clearly was not able to differentiate between liturgy and true worship. He meant that they paid more attention to form and ceremony than to preaching and proclaiming the word, and he forgot that every part of the service is worship of God.

Now I use that merely as an illustration to show you what I mean. It is very interesting, as you look back across the history of the last fifty years or so, to see certain tendencies that are coming into the Church. I am concerned about these because of the state of the Church at the present time. We all, I am sure, bemoan the fact that the number of Christians in this country is so small. There are some who love to say that all is well, and that the country is almost full of Christians, but I imagine that most of us would not want to argue like that. We see that Christians do not count, that the Church does not count, and that the spiritual life of the nation is going down. So the question that arises is: Why? Well, to me it is not without significance that there has been an increasing tendency during past years to return to a more elaborate form of service, to the use of written prayers and of liturgy. There is a tendency to exalt buildings, especially ornate buildings, and a tendency to go back to mechanical forms of Christian life and of worship.

It seems to me that this has been a marked tendency recently in nonconformity as well as in Anglicanism, and it is something, therefore, which surely we ought to face together, because it is based upon a certain idea of worship. There is a tendency to exaggerate, and impress upon us the form and the dignity of worship, and to laugh at our forefathers who worshipped with greater liberty, and prayed so freely, and praised God so freely; there is a tendency to look down upon their worship and feel that it was somehow lacking in solemnity. Today, so-called worship has been reverting to a form, and people have believed that that is true worship. To me it has always been so pathetic to hear

a service in some great church, when they have merely
meant the effect upon them of a particular kind of building.
The way to test whether or not people are truly worshipping
is to observe their behaviour. Worship has nothing to do
with the effect of a particular kind of building. The pagan in
his pagan temple may have marvellous feelings, but is it true
worship?

It is, in other words, to mistake the appearance for the
reality, and that suggests an attitude of reverence, rather
than true reverence. A true worshipper is not the one who
goes devotedly to early morning celebration and then claims
a right to the rest of the day, but the one who worships with
the heart and with the spirit. There is always the danger of
assuming that we are clear about what worship means, while
in truth we are being misled. But apart from those obvious
dangers, I would ask a much more personal and direct question – what about our own individual and private worship?
We do not have liturgies for that, we do not have ceremonies and forms, but God forbid that we should therefore
assume that our worship is right and true. I ask the direct
question: Do you really worship God? The first characteristic of the Christian, says Paul, is that he worships by the
Spirit of God – that is real worship. What does he mean?
Let me suggest some questions that I should ask myself in
order to determine whether I am really worshipping in the
way that the Apostle here states.

Here is my first question: Do I worship as a matter of duty
or am I aware of a desire to worship? Do I find worship a
chore, or does it rise spontaneously from within? You see,
the Apostle defines Christians as those who worship as the
result of the operation of the Holy Spirit upon them, so that
worshipping God is no longer a matter of duty, it is a desire.
Secondly, to put it in a slightly different form, to worship
God by the Spirit means that we do not have to force ourselves to worship him, but are conscious of being moved,
and being led, to worship. Is that not the acid test? Most of
us know what it is to be forced to go to a place of worship.
That happened to us when we were children. And perhaps

when we were older, we were made to go to church, either
by our parents, or because we were told it was the thing to
do. We did not want to go, there was a sense of compulsion,
and we gave in to it. Is there not all the difference in the
world between that and being conscious of being moved, of
being led, of something within which urges and directs us.
There is all the difference between getting down mechanically on our knees at our bedside because it is the thing to
do, and that experience which comes perhaps when we are
reading our Bible, or walking along a road or meditating.
We are moved, we are disturbed, we feel there is a leading
of the Spirit. This consciousness of being moved inwardly
and being gripped and led is the characteristic of worship by
the Spirit.

To worship by the Spirit of God is not something cold and
formal, it is always warm and loving and free. You
remember how Paul puts it when writing to the church at
Rome; he says, 'The love of God is shed abroad in our
hearts by the Holy Ghost' (Rom. 5:5). If the Holy Spirit is
in us there must be something of the love of God in us, and
we must have this love for God so that our prayers are not
cold and formal or even just beautiful. No, that is not the
characteristic of worship by the Spirit; there should be
warmth; there should be feeling and some kindling of the
heart; there should be freedom; we should know something
about being lost in praise as we worship. It is the warmth of
the Spirit, not a cold formality.

But let me put it still more specifically. As men worship
God more and more by the Spirit, they become less and less
dependent upon means. By 'means' I mean buildings, liturgies, priests, or even other people. I suggest that if you read
the biographies of the saints, indeed, if you read the lives of
some people who have never left the Roman Catholic
Church, but who seem to me to have been thoroughly
evangelical in spite of that, without exception you will find
that as men really come to know God and worship him in an
evangelical sense, they begin to drop their written prayers
and their liturgy and their forms, and begin to pray from the

heart; their prayers become extempore. You find this in the account of the Methodist Revival of the eighteenth century. I think we all probably find that it is easier to worship God in a prayer meeting than in a formal church setting, but as we become more and more spiritual we shall be less dependent even upon our friends, and we shall know that same liberty and freedom when alone with God.

Let me go still further. True worship of God in the spirit can be tested in this way: the man who worships God in the spirit does not think of God as some distant abstraction, almost a philosophical concept, away in the distance. The man who worships in the spirit realises the presence of God; he knows that God is there at his side. If he is led by the Spirit he is aware of being in the presence of the Almighty. What a test that is of spiritual worship!

But let me suggest a last thing, and I think that this is perhaps the best of all. We can be quite sure that we worship God in the spirit when we have that perfect admixture of, on the one hand, a sense of reverence and godly fear, and on the other the spirit of adoption whereby we cry, 'Abba Father'. I want to emphasise that because there are those who may agree with everything I have said so far. They may say, 'You are perfectly right in what you say about liturgy and form and appearance, I believe in the freedom of worship about which you are speaking.' They regard free worship as something that means a lot of shouting, and perhaps the banging of a timbrel; they feel that that is real worship.

But the opposite of liturgy, and form and ceremony is not the flesh; and true spiritual worship is not in fleshly, carnal customs. Surely anyone who worships by the Spirit of God, or who worships God in the spirit, must be aware of what our Lord said to the woman of Samaria: 'God is a Spirit: and they that worship him must worship him in spirit and in truth' (John 4:24). Anyone who realises the presence of God realises something of his holiness and feels unworthy. I cannot rush into his presence. I cannot be easily familiar, I cannot shout, I cannot yield to the flesh – no, as the writer of the epistle to the Hebrews puts it, there must be 'reverence and godly fear' (Heb. 12:28). Yes, but at the same time we 'have not received the spirit of bondage again to fear; but ye have received the Spirit of adoption, whereby we cry, Abba, Father' (Rom. 8:15). That is the ultimate and true spiritual worship. I realise the holiness of God, so that I approach him with reverence and awe, and yet at the same time I know that he is my Father and I say to him, 'Abba Father.' I know that he is not just an abstraction. I know that he has loved me with a Father's love, he has even sent his Son to the cross to save me. He is concerned about me to the extent that the very hairs of my head are numbered, and nothing can happen to me apart from him.

Oh, let us test ourselves by these things! Is our worship like that? Are we worshipping God in the Spirit, or is it merely a matter of form and appearance? Do I pray and read my Bible occasionally, or do I know that the Holy Spirit is dealing with me? Am I aware of being led? They are the sons of God that are led by the Spirit of God (Rom. 8:14). He leads, he gives freedom, he kindles the love. Do we know God, do we love God, can we say 'Abba Father' to him? God forbid that we should be relying upon some wrong notion and conception of worship; God grant rather that we may be able to see that we are the circumcision because we worship him by the Spirit.

Chapter 3

All in Christ

We are the circumcision, which worship God in the spirit,
and rejoice in Christ Jesus, and have no confidence in the
flesh (Phil. 3:3).

As we continue with our consideration of this verse, let me
remind you that Paul gave this particular definition of the
Christian in order to counteract the false teaching which was
being offered to the Philippians by the so-called Judaisers.
It is important that we should bear that in mind because this
definition can, in a sense, only be fully understood when we
study it in its setting. It is definitely polemical. It is not only
a positive statement, it is at the same time a contradiction of
something else about which he is writing. It is an affirmation, but it is also a denial, and it is against that background
that we see the dual element in Paul's definition.

Now it is a remarkable thing that the Apostle, in such a
brief compass, is able to give us a perfect and complete
definition of the Christian. There is nothing lacking, and if
we honestly examine ourselves in the light of this statement
we should be clear and certain in our minds and hearts as to
whether we are Christians or not. The big things, the essential things, are each one of them mentioned in this one
verse. Let us look at them again.

The first, of course, is our attitude towards God. That
must always come first. In our attempt to discover whether
we are Christians or not, we must not start with our lives, or
with our sensations or experiences. We must not merely ask,
'Am I happy? Am I successful in life? Am I committing

32

certain sins?' Our answers may tell us something about the Christian, but if we start and stop at that, we are obviously in a very dangerous condition. All sorts of delusions could give people such experiences – false teachings can do that – so the definition must never begin there. It must start, obviously, with our relationship to God. This is what we were looking at in chapter 2 – we worship God 'by the Spirit'. The contrast between the letter and the spirit is frequently brought out in the New Testament. And in this verse we are at once held face to face with the doctrine of God the Father and the doctrine of the Holy Spirit. We are not Christians, says Paul, unless we worship God in this way. Such worship is the result of the operation of the Holy Spirit.

So, then, having considered that, let us come to the second statement which the Apostle makes. He has opened with the words: 'We are the circumcision which worship God the Spirit . . .' and now he follows with his second statement: '. . . and rejoice in Christ Jesus.' In other words, the second great test of our Christianity is our attitude towards the Lord Jesus Christ, that is, the place which the Lord Jesus Christ occupies in our lives. Here again we come to something that the Apostle is constantly repeating. We have already seen how the Apostle concentrates attention upon this;* indeed, as has so often been pointed out, Paul was a 'Christ-intoxicated man'. Paul cannot leave Christ out, he is always talking about him. This point is obvious. The very name, 'Christian', should itself be sufficient to make us see that Christ is absolutely central. We worship God in the spirit; yes, that is right, and the big characteristic of that worship is the place that the Lord Jesus Christ occupies in it.

Now the Apostle puts it in rather a striking manner, and here, I regret to say, we must slightly correct the translation of the Authorised Version, not because it is not true, and not because it is not right, but because it does not give the

---

*See Volume 1, *The Life of Joy*.

particular shade of meaning which the Apostle is anxious to convey. In the first verse of this chapter, Paul writes, 'Finally, my brethren, rejoice in the Lord.' And here again in the third verse we read '. . . which worship God in the spirit, and rejoice in Christ Jesus.' In the Authorised Version the same English word 'rejoice' is used in both verses, but it is not the same word in the original. The word Paul uses in verse 3 does mean rejoicing, but it is a particular form of rejoicing. I am concerned to stress this because of the polemical background of this statement. Paul is dealing with these other people, these Judaisers, who are guilty of teaching error, and that is why he uses a different word at this point.

So what, then, does he mean by 'rejoice in Christ Jesus'? Well, a better translation at this point would be the word 'boast': 'We are the circumcision which worship God by the Spirit and boast in Christ Jesus', or, if you prefer it, 'glory in Christ Jesus', or 'are proud of', or, perhaps still better, 'talk loudly about Christ Jesus'. Now that is actually the meaning of the word which the Apostle employed in this third verse. You may say, of course, that anyone who boasts in Christ Jesus is rejoicing in him, but you see the difference in the shade of meaning. The other people, the Judaisers, were boasting about something else. They were boasting about the fact that they were Jews and that they had been circumcised, and had kept the law. We who are Christians, said Paul, do not boast in these things but in Christ Jesus. They were boasting, it was their great characteristic, so the Apostle deliberately uses this particular word.

It is the same word that we see in 1 Corinthians 1. There Paul is pointing out that not many mighty, and not many noble are called, and the reason, he says, is 'that no flesh should glory [boast] in his presence' (v. 29). It is the word that is here translated 'rejoice'. And we find it again in the last verse of 1 Corinthians 1 where Paul says – 'According as it is written, he that glorieth, let him glory in the Lord.' Again the same word twice over, not translated 'rejoice', but 'glorieth', and rightly so, though I suggest that an even better translation would have been this word 'boast' – 'According as it is written, he that boasteth let him boast, let him glory, let him be proud of the Lord, let him speak loudly of the Lord.'

And that is what the Apostle means here by rejoicing in Christ Jesus. It is a very profound statement and we must try to realise something of its depth. It does not merely mean believing; it does mean that, but how much more than that! You can believe in a person, or in a dynasty, or in a country and yet not be proud of it. What a world of difference there is between that and boasting in it and rejoicing in it! Many people believe in one cause or another, and are prepared to give their general support, but others are on fire on behalf of their cause, they are zealous and keen and active, and are prepared to shed the last drop of blood in their veins for it. They are proud of it, they glory in it – that is the word.

That is the attitude of those who are Christians, that is one of the hallmarks of true believers, says Paul; they boast in Christ Jesus, they exult, they not only believe on him but their whole being is moved as they contemplate him. In other words, he is all and in all to them, and because of that, they desire to ascribe all honour and glory to him. Or perhaps we can put it like this: the characteristic, always, of the man who boasts is that, as the word suggests in the Greek, he talks loudly about himself – which is what I have suggested as an alternative translation. When you describe a man as a 'boaster' you mean that he wants everybody to know what a fine fellow he is and so he speaks loudly about himself. According to this translation, Christians are people who are always talking about Christ, they are always praising him and want everybody else to hear about him. They want other people to know how wonderful he is, so they are ever paying tribute to him, and ascribing glory and honour to him. All their talking is about him, they cannot stop doing it: it is always Christ.

Think of it also in contrast with the Judaisers who were for ever talking about their nationality and about all those things that Paul mentions later. Paul, of course, knew it all so well; I have no doubt but that in writing his epistle he was not only thinking of the Judaisers, he was thinking of himself before his conversion – what a proud man he had been. It is very interesting to go through all Paul's epistles with your eye on this Greek word that should be translated boasting – I commend this to those of you who are Bible scholars – you will find that it is one of Paul's great words. He goes on to say in the next verse, 'I might also have confidence in the flesh. If any other man thinketh that he hath whereof he might trust in the flesh, I more' (v. 4) – and how often he repeats that! It was his great characteristic. But now, he says, it is not like that any longer. He now boasts in the Lord Jesus Christ. He glories in him. Christ is the one Paul talks about. 'I determined,' he says to the Corinthians, 'not to know any thing among you, save Jesus Christ, and him crucified' (1 Cor. 2:2) – rejoice, glory, boast, exult in Christ Jesus.

Now if that is what is meant by glorying or rejoicing, let us ask this question in order to elucidate the matter still further. Why does the Christian thus boast in Christ? Why should he? Why is it the hallmark and the acid test of the Christian? I do not hesitate to use such expressions. To me, the great test that differentiates between those who are Christians and those who are not is the place of Christ in their lives. Is he central, is he essential, is he absolute? If that is not our position, then, according to the New Testament, we are not Christians. What would happen to us if we suddenly heard Christ had never existed? Would our lives be unaffected? If they would, we cannot be Christians according to this definition. But why is it, then, that the Christian thus boasts and glories in the Lord Jesus Christ. Well, of course, the answer to that is the whole gospel. I will simply mention here certain central things with which you may be perfectly familiar, but I make no apology for standing with the great Apostle when he says, 'To write the same things to you, to me indeed is not grievous . . .' Not only that, if you have ever found yourself becoming tired of hearing about the Lord Jesus Christ, then you had better examine the foundations again. The saints, God's people, are never tired of praising his virtues and telling forth his glory and wonder.

What is it, therefore, that should make us boast in him alone? In the first place, it is the very fact of his person; he stands out from all others. I should boast in him and glory in him, because he is indeed the only begotten Son of God. It is the miracle of the incarnation. It is everything that Paul was describing in those first verses of the second chapter, the whole amazing process that brought the Son of God from heaven to earth, and made him live here in the likeness of sinful flesh, and assume the form of a servant and do all that he did. As you look at him, and see it all, and realise its meaning, there is only one thing to do, and that is to boast in him, and to glory and exult in him.

So our first reason is his person, and that alone is enough. We have all got a good deal of the hero worshipper in us, and how often have we boasted in man, how often have we praised great men in the world, leaders and those in high places and positions? If we have been distantly related to them, how proud we have been, how we have always liked people to know of it! Well, multiply that by infinity, and there you have the Lord Jesus Christ, the very Son of God incarnate – in the flesh – here in this world, living life as a man. If you want to boast, boast of that, and boast of the fact that you know that by the operation of the Holy Spirit upon you, you belong to him and are related to him. Boast of the greatness and the wonder and the glory of the person of Christ.

But let me move on to something else, for it does not stop at that. The Christian glories in Christ because he realises that the whole point of the incarnation was that Christ might save us from our sins and reconcile us to God. The incarnation in itself, merely as a spectacle, is something big enough and great enough to absorb all our praise and all our boasting. But when we realise the meaning and the purpose of it, when we realise that he did all that for us, for our sakes, for our sins, and for our deliverance and emancipation in every sense, does not this desire to boast become infinitely greater? According to the New Testament, he came specifically to save us, and as we realise that, with this great Apostle, we shall feel that nothing matters but Christ alone.

Or let us put it still more personally, and this, of course, is essential because I really do want us to know what it is to boast in him. Certainly I must look at the truth objectively, but if my view is only objective, this element of boasting will not arise. The boasting comes in at the point when we realise that our personal salvation is entirely dependent upon him. That is why Paul put it like this in Galatians 2:20: '. . . the Son of God,' he says, 'who loved me, and gave himself for me.' It is an amazing thing to see the Son of God bearing the sins of mankind there in his own body on the tree. That, in itself, is enough to make me drop upon my knees and worship and praise him. But when I realise that he was doing that for me, even me, that I myself am involved, then at that point I am lost in wonder. Because he has done it all for me I boast and make my boast in him. When I realise that that is the way in which God saves me, and that there is no salvation for me apart from that, then I glory in him.

And what does all that mean for us? Well, the New Testament puts this in an almost endless variety of ways. First, it is only in Christ that I really come to see my trouble and my need. Before he really saw the Lord Jesus Christ, the Apostle Paul lived a life which satisfied him. However, fundamentally there was something wrong, and that is why, later, when he had come to the right view, he went on to say that all those things of which he had boasted had become refuse to him. Before he knew Christ he was in a kind of fool's paradise, feeling that he could justify himself, and that all was well with him. In effect, he says, 'I would have gone on living like that, had it not been for Christ; it was he who made me see myself and the wrong, and the danger of my whole position.' That is the first thing that Christ does; it is he who makes us see our sin and our need, and makes us know our desperate plight.

But thank God it does not stop at that, because the moment we see that, we then instinctively try to do something to put ourselves right, and to get rid of this sin and guilt. I know of nothing that is more depressing and discouraging, nothing that is so truly killing to the soul and spirit, than that continual fight to fit ourselves to stand in the presence of God; it cannot be done. Paul knew something about that, and it was after some such struggle, that he saw that Christ was, once more, the answer. He saw the whole meaning of the death upon the cross; he saw that Christ was there setting him right with God. He could not do it for himself, neither could anyone else do it. He saw that the whole meaning of the cross was that 'God was in Christ, reconciling the world unto himself,' that, 'God hath made him to be sin for us, who knew no sin' (2 Cor. 5:19–21). These are Paul's words. Again he writes, 'whom God hath set forth to be a propitiation' (Rom. 3:25), which means that there on Calvary God was doing something which enabled him to forgive. He had laid the sins of Paul upon Christ, and had punished them in Christ, so that Paul was forgiven and free – that is what it means. And Paul had come to see that, and he had found peace and rest and knew that he was reconciled to God.

And then the new life begins, the new strength, the new power, the new outlook, the new understanding, the new everything and – but I am attempting the impossible! You see, Paul himself seems to realise, at the end of 1 Corinthians 1, that this is something which he can never express, so he puts it like this: 'But of him are ye in Christ Jesus, who of God is made unto us wisdom, and righteousness, and sanctification, and redemption' (1 Cor. 1:30). Is there anything greater than that? He is everything. The Alpha and the Omega, the beginning and the end, the start and the finish, the All in all, and in him we are complete. Is there anything that you can conceive of or imagine that you need or want for your soul? It is all in him: 'in him dwelleth all the fulness of the Godhead bodily' (Col. 2:9). There is nothing that the soul of man can need in time or eternity but that it

is all in Christ. You need pardon? There it is. You need
reconciliation to God? The man Christ Jesus is the one and
only mediator between God and man. You need new life
and a new nature? You receive it from him. You need
strength and power? He sent the Holy Spirit that you might
have it. You need an Advocate with the Father? There he
is, seated at the right hand of God. You tremble at the
thought of death and of going to face God in the judgment?
You are assured that you will be clothed with his righteousness and he will present you spotless. What else do you
need? He is everything: Prophet, Priest and King, the All in
all,

> He's the lily of the valley
> The Bright and Morning Star,
> He's the fairest of ten thousand to my soul.

The man who believes that, must make his boast in Christ.
Christ is everything: wisdom, knowledge, understanding, a
view of life, a view of God, a view of the world. Paul found
all that in Christ. He had a very different view before; he
used to regard the Gentiles as dogs, but now he sees them
coming into the Church. He sees a whole plan unveiled and
continuing.

At this point let us ask ourselves a simple question. Is
Christ that to us? Do we make our boast in him? Do we
glory in him? Do we say honestly that Christ is everything
to us, that without him we are nothing? Do we say that we
cannot even begin the Christian life, we cannot approach it,
without him? He is the life, 'I am the way, the truth and the
life,' he says, 'no man cometh unto the Father, but by me'
(John 14:6). Is he vital to our whole outlook and all our con-
ceiving? Do we realise that our utter and entire dependence
is upon him? Do we realise that, in a sense, there is no such
thing as prayer except through him? Is he at the centre of
our life, on the throne of our heart?

So the second great characteristic of the Christian, says
the Apostle, is that he boasts in Christ Jesus. He says with

the Apostle, 'God forbid that I should glory' – this, again, is the same word 'boast' – 'God forbid that I should boast, save in the cross of our Lord Jesus Christ, by whom the world is crucified unto me, and I unto the world' (Gal. 6:14). God forbid that I should ever, for a second, boast in anything or anyone else but in him.

> In the Cross of Christ I glory
> Towering o'er the wrecks of time
> All the light of sacred story
> Gathers round his head sublime.
>
> J. Bowring

Does that strike a chord in you? If it does, you are a Christian, you are within the definition. You boast in Christ Jesus.

Let me just comment briefly on the last characteristic of the Christian – 'And have no confidence in the flesh.' I wonder why Paul went on to that, after his earlier glorious statement? I think he recognised the danger that was threatening these people at Philippi, and so he put before them what should be their attitude to God, and then at the end gave their attitude to themselves – 'no confidence in the flesh'. Let me give you some headings on this because I think that will be sufficient. Paul means, first, that he does not boast in his nationality. He used to – he was proud of being 'a Hebrew of the Hebrews' – but, now, he says in effect, 'I have no confidence in nationality any longer. My confidence is entirely in Christ.' To repose our confidence in nationality is a denial of the Christian gospel and we are emancipated from that. It is our birth in Christ which reconciles us to God, and we boast in that; not in family, not in the tribe of Benjamin, not in being Jewish, or British: birth does not count.

Other things make no difference either, as Paul shows in 1 Corinthians 1; not upbringing, nor training, for example. You may have had excellent training, it may have been one better than anybody else's, but that does not save you. You may have had the finest upbringing in the world, and yet not

know him. Nor are you saved by a love and zeal for politics
and economics. Paul was better than most other people:
'touching the righteousness which is in the law, blameless'
(Phil. 3:6); but he had no confidence in that kind of thing.
Nor did he trust in philosophy and the understanding and
wisdom of this world – what a subtle enemy! One of the last
things we let go of, because of our pride, is intellect – the
boasting of philosophy and understanding and thought. I
have no confidence in it any longer, says Paul, no confidence
in the flesh. If I have any confidence in these things and not
in Christ alone, I am in a dangerous position. Christ is the
end as he was the beginning, and I must have my confidence
in him from beginning to end. It is in him I am saved, in him
I have been sanctified, it is all in him: wisdom, righteousness, sanctification and redemption. I must be entirely
dependent upon him, with no confidence in the flesh in any
shape or form.

That, then, is the definition of the Christian. Let me
finally put it like this. The Apostle says here that we – the
people who worship God by the Spirit, and who rejoice in
Christ Jesus and have no confidence in the flesh – we are the
circumcision. This means that all those great promises of
God to the Children of Israel in the old dispensation, in the
Old Testament, the promises made to Abraham, the promises repeated through Isaac and Jacob and right down the
running centuries, all the extraordinary promises of God
that were given to that nation now apply to us. We, the
Christians in every nation, are the circumcision; we are
God's Israel who worship God in the spirit and have no confidence in the flesh. All the gracious promises of God originally made to the nation of Israel are now made to the
Church, to Christian people.

You and I, in other words, if we are Christians, are the
inheritors of all those promises, and no one else. The nation
of Israel has been put aside, as our Lord himself said,
because of their rejection of him and their unworthiness;
and the promises belong to the nation bringing forth the
fruit thereof: the Church. And Paul is saying the same thing:

'we are the circumcision'. Oh, the tragedy that the Jews should still be claiming it for themselves! We, Christian people, are the inheritors of those gracious and glorious promises; we are the citizens of the Kingdom and we are going to reign with him and enjoy the blessings of the everlasting Kingdom, world without end. What a privilege! We are the circumcision, the people of God, and we prove it by worshipping him by the Spirit, by glorying in Christ Jesus, and by having no confidence in the flesh in any form.

Chapter 4

The Christian life

Though I might also have confidence in the flesh. If any other man thinketh that he hath whereof he might trust in the flesh, I more: Circumcised the eighth day, of the stock of Israel, of the tribe of Benjamin, an Hebrew of the Hebrews; as touching the law, a Pharisee; concerning zeal, persecuting the church; touching the righteousness which is in the law, blameless. But what things were gain to me, those I counted loss for Christ. Yea doubtless, and I count all things but loss for the excellency of the knowledge of Christ Jesus my Lord: for whom I have suffered the loss of all things, and do count them but dung, that I may win Christ, and be found in him, not having mine own righteousness, which is of the law, but that which is through the faith of Christ, the righteousness which is of God by faith: That I may know him, and the power of his resurrection, and the fellowship of his sufferings, being made conformable unto his death; if by any means I might attain unto the resurrection of the dead. Not as though I had already attained, either were already perfect: but I follow after, if that I may apprehend that for which also I am apprehended of Christ Jesus. Brethren, I count not myself to have apprehended: but this one thing I do, forgetting those things which are behind, and reaching forth unto those things which are before, I press toward the mark for the prize of the high calling of God in Christ Jesus
(Phil. 3:4–14).

It seems to me that it is essential that we should consider this passage as a whole before we come to consider its various parts. It is an elaboration of what the Apostle has been saying in the first three verses of the chapter, especially the third verse, in which he has claimed, you remember, that 'we are the circumcision which worship God in the spirit [by the Spirit], and rejoice in Christ Jesus, and have no confidence in the flesh'. Now verses 4 to 14 are, in a way, an exposition of the theme as stated in verse 3, and it is worked out in a magnificent and truly glorious manner in these following verses. In other words, the Apostle is here finally demolishing the false teachings and arguments of the Judaisers, who would have these Gentile Christians believe that in addition to faith in Christ it is essential for them to become Jews, that is, to be circumcised and to follow certain Jewish practices, before they can truly claim to be Christian.

The argument is something like this. These men are making claims about the importance of the fact that they are Hebrews, Jews, and they are boasting about their good works and so on. Now, says Paul, if any man has a right to boast at all, surely I am the man; and then he gives a list of what he used to be and what he used to do; but he does that only in order once and for ever to contrast his old self with this new nature which he has obtained in the Lord Jesus Christ. So we have here, in effect, one of the guarantees, and certainly one of the most eloquent statements, of what it really means to be a Christian. The Apostle, in showing the contrast between the Christian life and that other life, has given us a wonderful, positive picture of the Christian life itself, and that is what we must look at together now.

But, before we do so, there is one caution which it is perhaps necessary to make, and I say this on the basis of experience. The caution is that we must bear in mind that the Apostle here is not only describing what was true for him, he is also stating what should be true for every Christian. I have often met men who, confronted by a passage like this, have said, 'Ah yes, that is all right, that was Paul, but we are not Paul.' They mistakenly think that the unique experience which Paul had on the road to Damascus is something which puts the whole of his Christian experience in a category apart.

It is vitally important, therefore, that we should be clear about this point. Of course, the experience which Paul had on the road to Damascus was unique. Paul, you remember, going down to Damascus to persecute and massacre the Christians in that city, was given a view of the risen Lord himself. It was not a vision, it was an ocular manifestation. He really did see the risen Lord, he says so. It is quite clear that that sight of the risen Lord was given to Paul in order that he might be counted as an Apostle, because one of the distinctive marks of an Apostle was that he must have seen the risen Lord with his naked eye. So that is the sight that was given to him in a very special and remarkable manner, as he tells us in 1 Corinthians 15:8, where he calls himself 'one born out of due time'. We as Christian people do not see, and must not expect to see the risen Lord in the way that Paul saw him on the road to Damascus. But after all, that is not vital to the Christian experience, that is not what makes someone a Christian; that was only essential to the calling of an Apostle.

But in this passage here, Paul is saying what is true of him as a Christian believer, and in this, therefore, the Apostle, of all men, would have been concerned to argue that he was not in a category apart. Does he not tell us, in 1 Timothy 1:15, that he is the greatest of all sinners the world has ever known? And he makes it patently plain that he is nothing but a sinner saved by the grace of God in Christ in exactly the same way as every other Christian. So we must not challenge this magnificent statement by trying to emphasise the difference between his experience on the road to Damascus and what is known to be true of us. No, what the Apostle says here about the normal Christian experience is to be true of each and every one of us. God forbid that we should perpetuate that false Roman Catholic division between Christians and call some spiritual and some ordinary, some exceptional and some mundane. There is no distinction in the New Testament: we are all in the same position, we are all to have the same experience of God's salvation, whatever form it may take, and we are all to strive after the same things.

So with that word of caution, which I give simply because I so often have to argue with people on that point, people who are avoiding the whole challenge because they put Paul into a separate compartment, let us consider something of what the Apostle says here. As I said, at this juncture we shall only deal with this magnificent description in a general manner. We shall have to go into the details again, but I think it is important that, sometimes at any rate, we should take a composite view of the Christian life, so that some of these big principles may stand out in our minds.

What, then, does Paul tell us here, in general, about the Christian life and experience? First, he tells us that it is something that takes hold of us and masters us and holds us. That is, of course, the statement of the twelfth verse. 'Not as though,' says Paul, 'I had already attained, either were already perfect: but I follow after, if that I may apprehend that for which also I am apprehended of Christ Jesus.' I start with that verse because I suggest that, to be logical, it really must come first. Now you may say, and I would agree with you, that at this point the Apostle is undoubtedly thinking of what happened to him on the road to Damascus. It is more or less inevitable that he should do so because that was how he became a Christian. He says, in effect, 'There was I, this proud, self-righteous, boastful Pharisee, going down to Damascus truly believing I was serving God, when suddenly this great light began to shine such as I have never seen before. I saw him, and what really happened to me was that he took hold of me, he grasped me, he held me and he has held me ever since.' And, says Paul, 'my position now is that I am trying to grasp that which grasped me.'

And we find a great principle there that is true not only of Paul but of every other Christian. We all tend to want that kind of climactic experience, like the one that Paul had on the way to Damascus, but it is not a part of the preaching of the gospel to say that one must be converted suddenly. What does matter is that we should know something of what the Apostle means when he says that he has been taken hold of by something or Somebody. Whether it happened suddenly or not, does not matter – that is irrelevant – it can come in a thousand ways and forms, but what is all important is this awareness of being taken hold of by something, of being held in the grip of something: that is what is so vital to the Christian position.

The Christian, in other words, is not a man who has taken up something as an interest, he is a man who has been taken up by the interest and he cannot escape it. The Christian, therefore, can never be half-hearted, because he is conscious of this vice-like grip which holds him. I am not going too far when I venture to put it like this, because I sometimes think it is perhaps one of the most delicate tests we can ever give ourselves: Do we know what it is to feel sometimes that we would like to get away from it, but it has got us in a grip, it has mastered us? This is expressed in that well-known hymn: 'O love that wilt not let me go' – that is it. There may be times in our folly and blindness and sin when we would like to be released, but he will not let us go, we are taken hold of, and grasped firmly.

That is the first thing that is true of this new life in which Paul finds himself. 'It is not,' he says in effect, 'that I have given up Judaism and taken up Christianity; it is not that having heard something about it, I find it rather interesting, and I like reading about it and discussing it in a casual, external, objective manner. Not at all! That is not the Christian position. The thing that is characteristic of the Christian in the first place is that he is suddenly aware that this thing has taken hold of him and he cannot get away from it; he is taken up, apprehended by it, and then he tries to apprehend.'

Now this is basic, it is something one finds very difficult to put into words, and yet, I repeat, I know of nothing that is a more thorough-going test of our whole position. Is your Christian faith something that you take up and, as it were, carry in your hand like a bag? Or are you rather in the position of the slave, mastered and grasped, possessed and taken up; sometimes aware of that foolish, sinful desire to get away, and yet knowing that you cannot? That is always the New Testament picture of Christian people. They know that God has been dealing with them, God has done something to them, God is moving in their direction, God has interfered in their lives. They do not quite understand it, but they know that it is the action of God. We are apprehended – that is the first thing.

The second thing, surely, about this new life – we are only dealing with the over-all principles now, we must go into this again in detail – is that it is something that leads to a complete change of outlook and values, and that, of course, is the great theme of verses 7 and 8. It was something Paul was never tired of saying. Having given this list of his perfections as a Jew, and a proud Pharisee, he then goes on to say, 'But what things were gain to me, those I counted loss for Christ. Yea doubtless, and I count all things but loss for the excellency of the knowledge of Christ Jesus my Lord: for whom I have suffered the loss of all things, and do count them but dung, that I may win Christ.'

Now here he is describing a complete transformation, a turning point. There he was climbing upwards when suddenly he found himself looking at an entirely different landscape. I would put it like this: Christianity is never an addition to our lives, it is never something that is added on to that which we have previously had: it is central or it is nowhere. If it is not controlling the whole of your life, then you are just not a Christian. Christians are not people of whom it can be said that their lives are identical with everybody else's, they have an extra something in addition, and in the end they are seen to be Christians. No, to be a Christian, says Paul, means that at the very centre, at the very core of your being and existence, this new something has come in and controls everything. A radical change takes place when you become a Christian, you are suddenly aware of it; it is a change of outlook upon all things. I do not hesitate to use the term which the Apostle uses in verse 8 – all things have become 'loss'.

This is something which Paul elaborates in his various epistles, and I think it follows of necessity. If to be a Chris-

tian means that I have been affected profoundly at the very
centre of my being, in what the New Testament calls the
heart (the heart does not mean the emotion or the seat of
emotions – it means the centre of the personality), if the
centre of my personality has been affected, well, then,
everything else must be changed. My thinking must be
changed, my feeling, my willing, must be changed; and that
is exactly what the Apostle claims for the Christian.

Paul says it again more explicitly in 2 Corinthians 5: 'if
any man be in Christ, he is a new creature: old things are
passed away; behold, all things are become new' (v. 17);
and that is literally true, nothing remains the same in the
heart. In verses 7–8, Paul puts it all in terms of profit and
loss – 'But what things were gain to me, those I counted loss
for Christ.' If you study these verses carefully for yourselves, you will notice how Paul repeats these words. He is
saying that far from being gain, those things have actually
become loss. He could not have expressed the entire transaction in stronger language than he does by using that particular analogy.

In what respects, then, is it right to say that life is entirely
changed? Well, Paul answers that question here in these
verses. He had a completely new view of himself – he who
had been so proud is now ashamed of himself; before, he
thought he was better than everybody else, now he sees
himself as the chief of sinners. What a transformation! And
that, again, is something that should be true of every Christian. The more we grow as Christians, the more we should
be aware of the corruption of our own hearts; and not to be
aware of that is a very serious symptom. Here is a man who
in terms of morality could stand face to face with any chal-
lenger, and yet once he has been enlightened, he is aware of
his corruption and sin, and can cry out in agony, 'O
wretched man that I am! who shall deliver me from the body
of this death?' (Rom. 7:24).

He also has a new view of God – he sees that his view of
God has been seriously and tragically defective. He has a
new view of religion. He was formerly content with an

external religion, but now he becomes aware of a spiritual nature. His whole idea of how God should be approached is different. Before, he approached him in terms of his own righteousness and merit, but now he humbles himself before the throne of mercy and whispers the words, 'Jesus Christ, my Lord.'

What else? Life itself, and his whole view of it, has become different. He has been a Pharisee, a great teacher, proud of his position and with great prospects of promotion. What is his view of life now? Well, he has already told us: 'to me to live is Christ' (1:21); he has lost those false motives, and his one desire is to know Christ better and to be able to serve him more truly. He now has an entirely different view of the purpose and meaning of life, and, as he has told us in the first chapter, he has an entirely new view of death. Death is now of no account to Paul because it means to be with Christ, which is far better. And he has a new view of the Gentiles. He once regarded them as dogs, outside the commonwealth of Israel, but now he rejoices in them as beloved brothers, inheritors of the everlasting Kingdom.

That is how Paul shows us his complete transformation. But we are not only dealing with Paul, we are dealing with ourselves. Christians by definition must have an entirely different view of everything from those who are not Christians: a new vision of themselves, a different view of God and of how God is to be approached, a different view of life. Now I think this is very important at this present time. Because we are governed by new principles, we should be viewing events in a different way – our whole attitude towards everything is essentially different from the non-Christian attitude. Our view of death should be different, and our view of all other people should be different as well.

As we have seen, Paul goes so far as to say that the things that were gain to him have actually become loss. Is he thereby condemning the law of God which was given to the Children of Israel? Is he condemning the Jewish religion which was given by God? No, Paul does not say that these things are wrong in and of themselves, but he does say: 'I was relying upon them, I had a false view of them, I thought they were gain; I see now they were loss, they were the things that stood between me and Christ, therefore I regard them as refuse.'

And the Christian knows exactly what Paul means when he says that. There are many good, innocent and harmless things in this world, but because of the new view which we now have we can see that these very things are robbing us of something which is still greater, and the things which we had thought were gain are actually loss.

The next principle is that this truth, which has mastered and grasped the Christian, is something for which he is clearly prepared to lose and to sacrifice everything else. Paul expresses this in his magnificent words: 'But what things were gain to me, those I counted loss for Christ. Yea doubtless, and I count all things but loss for the excellency of the knowledge of Christ Jesus my Lord: for whom I have suffered the loss of all things, and do count them but dung, that I may win Christ.' That is not hyperbolical. Paul is stating literal facts. Those things have no meaning at all for Paul because he is now a Christian. All his wonderful pride as a Pharisee has gone. He was a highly intellectual man, he had done better in the schools than anybody else, he had sat at the feet of Gamaliel, he was at the top of the list, he was one of the outstanding teachers of the law; and to become a Christian meant for Paul that he was regarded as a fool. He was denounced by his own people, all his prospects of position and greatness were gone, he lost it all, but he does not object, he is perfectly satisfied. If I may use his own language, he is pleased with the bargain. There he was in the old life keeping a list in the ledger, but now, he says, he has something on the other side which is infinitely greater.

And, of course, he suffered persecution. In 2 Corinthians 2 he describes all that he had suffered for Christ's sake and he suffered it all perfectly happily. I sometimes think that the greatest thing he had to lose was this: here was this highly intelligent man, this man who could meet with Jews at their best, as an equal, and even surpass them, and yet he had to spend most of his subsequent life amongst Gentiles and not only that, but ignorant Gentiles, many of them slaves and serfs who did not understand and did not appreciate his greatness, even as a natural man, so that he had to work with his own hands as a tent maker. It seems to me that the greatest test of all was to have to come down to such a level and spend his life with such people. But he gloried in it, he rejoiced in it, he suffered the loss of all things, and he tells us he did it gladly.

And why was that true of him? This is the last principle. All that we have been talking about is due to one thing, and that one thing is what Paul describes here as 'the excellency of the knowledge of Christ Jesus my Lord'. That is what explains everything else, that is the thing that has mastered him, that is the thing that has changed his outlook, and for which he is prepared to give up everything. What is it about this knowledge which is so wonderful, what is 'the excellency of the knowledge'? It is almost foolish to ask such a question – but let me just give you some brief suggestions.

The nature of the knowledge itself entitles it to that description. It is knowledge that brought Paul into an immediate, direct, personal contact with the most glorious person that this world has ever seen. Paul had met Gamaliel and had sat at his feet, he had met the great theologians, he was conversant with Greek philosophy, but now he had seen someone who is in a category apart. We, too, probably meet great people in this life, but here is knowledge that can enable us to meet God, that can enable us to meet the Lord Jesus Christ and to have fellowship and communion with him. The excellency of the knowledge is because of the greatness of the Person.

And then, it was knowledge that gave him understanding of God's marvellous way of salvation. You see, there is no need to detract from human knowledge. Philosophy is very good and wonderful, you can read your literature and enjoy your music and all these other interests, but when you take them at their best and highest, and contrast them with the scheme outlined in the Bible, they pale into insignificance. The excellency of the knowledge is because of God's plan of salvation.

What else? Undoubtedly Paul thought of it in terms of what it had done for him. It had saved him and delivered him from hell. He had been going there, and he saw that this knowledge had saved him from eternal damnation. What an excellent knowledge that could put a man right for eternity and save him from perdition, that could give him a knowledge of sins forgiven and reconciliation to God! Is there any knowledge comparable to knowing that your conscience is clear, that the book is put right, that your sins are erased, and that God in mercy has forgiven you? What excellent knowledge! This knowledge, then, brings peace and joy, a tranquil, quiet mind, a joy that is greater than the world can ever know or give or take away. New life, and power to live in a manner worthy of the name of man – that is what it had given him.

And then it told him about what was going to happen to him, it gave him promises with respect to his future. It told him that he had become a child of God and because of that, was an heir, and therefore a joint heir with Christ. It gave him an insight into glory and life beyond this world and death and the grave: it showed him the perfect life that he as a Christian would share with God to all eternity. When Paul saw that, everything else had become very small and insignificant, and he says, 'I count it as dung, refuse.' The excellency of the knowledge: it is excellent in itself, excellent in what it has already done for us, excellent in what it is going to do.

So, briefly and inadequately, we have taken a general view of this amazing Christian life. Let me end with a question. Have you been possessed by that kind of life? Do you know that God has dealt with you? Have you felt the hand of God upon you? Have you been taken hold of, do you feel that he is dealing with you, do you know something of the feeling that you cannot get away from it? Are you aware of being taken up rather than of taking up? Is your outlook on life entirely different from that of the non-Christians around you? Have you seen something which makes you feel you would sooner give up everything else, rather than lose this? As you think of the New Testament gospel, do you agree with Paul that there is only one way of describing it – the excellency of the knowledge of Christ Jesus, my Lord. Is he your Lord? That is the Christian position. He makes himself your Lord and mine, he has bought us, he has purchased us, he has taken hold of us and he holds us in his mighty grasp.

Chapter 5

The righteousness of God

And be found in him, not having mine own righteousness, which is of the law, but that which is through the faith of Christ, the righteousness which is of God by faith (Phil. 3:9).

In verses 4 to 14 of chapter 3, Paul has been telling the Philippians how he counts all the things of which he used to boast before he became a Christian, but loss, 'for the excellency of the knowledge' of Christ Jesus his Lord. And here, now, in this ninth verse, he proceeds to tell us of one more aspect of the excellency of that knowledge. It is something that thrills the Apostle, something that makes him feel that anything else which comes into competition with it must not be considered for a second – therefore we must now concentrate our attention on this. The knowledge of which Paul is now speaking concerns the whole question of righteousness – a word that all who are familiar with their Bibles know very well, for it is a word that you constantly find in the Scriptures.

What, then, does it mean? Now there is a sense in which the question of righteousness was always a problem to the Apostle. It is the whole question of how we can stand in the presence of God. It was the old question propounded by Job right back at the beginning of history: 'How should man be just with God?' (Job 9:2). That is the problem. How is any one of us, in this life and in this world, ultimately going to stand face to face with God in the judgment? That is the problem, and it is because he has discovered the gospel's answer to it that the Apostle tells us that nothing else is of any value at all. All that he had gloried in and boasted of, he now regards as refuse, it was loss because it had stood between him and this great answer.

Now this is, of course, the outstanding theme of the New Testament, and particularly of the New Testament epistles. It is perhaps more particularly the great theme of the Apostle Paul. It is his central doctrine, which you will find him illustrating almost everywhere in all his epistles.

Take, for example, Paul's statement at the end of 1 Corinthians 1: 'But of him are ye in Christ Jesus, who of God is made unto us wisdom, and righteousness, and sanctification, and redemption.' Again, you will find it in 2 Corinthians 5:21: 'For he hath made him to be sin for us, who knew no sin; that we might be made the righteousness of God in him' – it is the same thing again. Then take Galatians 3, which is nothing but another exposition of this self-same doctrine. But perhaps the classic passage on this theme is Romans 3. It is, indeed, the theme of the whole epistle to the Romans, until you come to the practical portions, but it is especially the theme of chapter 3, and the verses from verse 20 onwards stand out prominently in this respect.

There is nothing, therefore, that is so characteristic of Paul's whole outlook as his understanding of the question of righteousness. No subject so roused him as this; and there is nothing that made him so often burst forth in hymns of praise as his understanding of it. It is, indeed, the key of the whole doctrine of the Apostle, and if we are not clear about Paul's teaching on righteousness, we shall not understand any of his teaching; it is the first, it is the centre, it is the doctrine out of which, and from which, he derives every other doctrine in his teaching; it is indeed pivotal.

But we can go further and say that throughout the long history of the Christian Church no doctrine has produced such momentous results as this doctrine of man's righteousness in the presence of God through our Lord and Saviour Jesus Christ. It was, of course, the great doctrine which was propounded by St Augustine; it was when Augustine came to see this that his whole life was changed and entirely reversed. It was the doctrine that changed the course of Martin Luther's life. Martin Luther had been reared in that old religion, the Roman Catholic religion, which was nothing, in a sense, but a return of the Judaisers – an attempt to earn merit, an attempt to arrive at righteousness before God by one's own efforts. When Luther saw the doctrine that Paul announces in this ninth verse, his life was immediately changed and the Protestant Reformation came into being. It was this truth that made Luther defy, not only the powerful Catholic Church of his day, but all the tradition accumulated in the centuries which had gone before. This one man alone pitted himself against all that tradition, and it was all because of the certainty of the excellency of this knowledge; his constant challenges to that Church were in terms of this particular truth. Having seen it, he was prepared to risk everything, his life included, rather than give it up. It revolutionised everything, and that has been the effect it has always had when men and women have truly understood it. This doctrine is the whole explanation of most subsequent history, not only in the Church but even in secular history – it is a pivotal doctrine.

If you want another illustration of the same thing, you will find it in the life of John Wesley. It was when Wesley suddenly came to see this truth that his life, too, was reversed spiritually; his preaching became quite new and it was attended by the results with which we are so familiar.

Now I have given those illustrations in order that we may realise something of the background against which we should always consider this doctrine. Let me put it still more emphatically and bluntly: I wonder if we can say with the Apostle Paul that the doctrine of the righteousness of God in Christ Jesus is to us the most amazing and astounding and thrilling thing we have ever heard? That is what Paul says. This is wonderful! he declares. This excellent knowledge which I have received in Christ Jesus makes me say without hesitation that I count everything else but refuse, loss, and useless.

Perhaps the best way to approach this great doctrine is to try to define the word 'righteousness'. The best definition that I have encountered is this: 'Righteousness signifieth both justice and righteousness', that is to say, righteousness means conformity to law. Now, conformity to law can express itself in two ways. Firstly, justice means conformity to the law in carrying out the judgment, or sentence, imposed by the law; secondly, it means conformity to the law in obeying the precepts of the law. Paul uses the word 'righteousness' in both senses in that third chapter of Romans to which I have already referred.

Righteousness in the sense of enforcing the law comes in verses 25–26: 'Whom God hath set forth to be a propitiation through faith in his blood, to declare his righteousness for the remission of sins that are past, through the forbearance of God; to declare, I say, at this time his righteousness: that he might be just, and the justifier of him which believeth in Jesus.'

This use of the word righteousness really means 'justice'; the words, 'to declare, I say, at this time his righteousness', refers to his justice. Christ, by his death on the cross, says Paul, justifies God's forgiveness of sins.

Righteousness in the second sense of conformity to the law, of obeying its precepts, comes in verses 20–22: 'Therefore by the deeds of the law there shall no flesh be justified in his sight: for by the law is the knowledge of sin. But now the righteousness of God without the law is manifested, being witnessed by the law and the prophets; even the righteousness of God which is by faith of Jesus Christ unto all and upon all them that believe: for there is no difference.'

Our righteousness is conformity to the law in the matter of obedience; *God's* righteousness is conformity to the law in carrying out its sentence. God is the law-giver. When he forgives us he manifests his righteousness, or his justice. It has been necessary to work this out in detail because if we do not hold these two meanings clearly in our minds, we shall find that third chapter of Romans somewhat confusing. If we bear in mind that it refers to God's part and our part, in these two senses, then I think that it will become clear.

So, then, the question that arises for us is this: how can we conform to God's holy law? What can we do in order that we may conform to the demands of the law of God in all its fulness; for that is our position and the position of every person who is born in this world. Whether we like it or not, we are under God, and we are under God's law; whether we like it or not it is a fact. Everyone who is born in a particular country is born under the laws of that country; they may say they do not care for them, but they are under the law and can be challenged by that law. In the same way we are all born into this life under God's law. God has stated and revealed his law, and we are all under it. So the question confronting us is: What can we do in order to meet the demands of God's justice? What can we do about our life in this world so that when the law ultimately faces us and challenges us with the demands that it has made, we can answer it in such a way as to be free to enjoy happiness throughout the countless ages of eternity? That is the question.

And here Paul tells us that, in the last analysis, there are only two ways of doing that. There is, first of all, the old way that he had followed as a Jew. Now that old way is one with which we are all perfectly familiar. Our system is not that of the Jews, but it is the same in principle, so that what Paul says about the whole method of seeking righteousness under the Jewish law is true of everyone who has not seen the absolute necessity of believing on the Lord Jesus Christ. And I think we will all agree that this most common and fatal obstacle still stands between men and women and belief in the gospel. Ask the average person today what it means to be a Christian and, if I am not greatly mistaken, I think you will find that almost invariably you will be told what he or she does, or tries to do – the answer will be given in terms of personal human efforts. And that is the modern statement of this old Jewish position which Paul tells us he had forsaken.

Bearing that in mind, let us examine its characteristics and these are two-fold. The first is what Paul tells us here: in that old life, he had depended upon himself, upon his own efforts, on 'having my own righteousness, which is of the law' – that is it. It was an effort to produce his own righteousness; it was a righteousness dependent upon himself and his own excellencies; it was his own diligence with regard to the keeping of the law, especially the ceremonial law; it was his personal effort.

The second thing about it was that it consisted of an outlook which conformed to the ceremonial commands of the law. Paul tells us in verse 6 that, judged by the righteousness which is in the law, he was blameless. That was part of his boasting; he was 'circumcised the eighth day, of the stock of Israel, of the tribe of Benjamin, an Hebrew of the Hebrews; as touching the law, a Pharisee; concerning zeal, persecuting the church; touching the righteousness which is in the law blameless' (vv. 5–6). In what sense was he right to say that he was blameless? Well, this is what he came to see. He had thought that under the law he was absolutely blameless and that he could stand in the presence of God and claim that, but, he now tells us, he came to see that his blamelessness was merely in the matter of outward conformity to the ceremonial commands of the law.

In other words, the Jewish law commanded that the people were to bring burnt offerings and sacrifices, they were to do certain things, and Paul had equated the law of God with that outward, external, mechanical, ceremonial of the law. In that respect he was blameless. But it was only in that respect, for Paul had come to see that the righteousness of which he had boasted so much was, in deed and in truth, nothing but his own righteousness. He saw that instead of taking the law of God as it really was, he had substituted his own understanding and interpretation of it, and was thus conforming to his own little interpretation. Paul is very fond of saying that. In Romans 10 you will find he puts it very clearly: 'Brethren, my heart's desire and prayer to God for Israel is, that they might be saved. For I bear them record that they have a zeal of God, but not according to knowledge. For they being ignorant of God's righteousness, and going about to establish their own righteousness, have not submitted themselves unto the righteousness of God' (vv. 1–3). The tragedy of my countrymen, the Jews, says Paul, is that they think that they are pleasing God; they think that the righteousness they are working out is the righteousness God demands, but the trouble is that they are ignorant of God's righteousness, and are going about trying to establish their own.

And that was, of course, the whole trouble with the Pharisees. Our Lord constantly made the same point. Ah, he said, you authorities, you claim you are teachers on the subject of rejoicing in the law, and yet the whole time you are doing nothing but worshipping your own tradition, you have substituted the tradition and opinions of men for the law of God. Paul had done the same thing. He had fondly imagined that he was blameless. There he was, boasting that he was better than others. But suddenly he came to see that it was not God's law at all, he had simply been keeping his own little idea of God's law – it was his own righteousness.

Now this is a tragic attitude, but it is very common, as we have already seen. Men and women tell us that they do not see any need to believe in the death of Christ upon the cross, it seems to them almost immoral. 'Surely,' they say, 'if people live a good life and do all the good they can, that is what God demands.' The answer is, that it is not – and that is the only reply to make to such a statement. They are constructing a law, and then having made it, and having equated it with God's law, they say that they are keeping God's law. But the truth is that it is nothing but their own righteousness – they are going about to establish their own righteousness, and have not submitted themselves to the righteousness of God.

Now Paul came to see that the law was not just mechanical, external conformity to certain dictates; the law was this: 'Thou shalt love the Lord thy God with all thine heart, and with all thy soul, and with all thy might' (Deut. 6:5). He describes it all in Romans 7:7–9, and says that when he came to see the spiritual nature of the law and its demands, when he came to see that God demands man's total allegiance – his heart and the whole of his being – then Paul was utterly condemned and, he writes, 'I died.'

But not only that, he saw also that the law is something that pronounces judgment upon sin. The Lord said, 'The soul that sinneth, it shall die' (Ezek. 18:4); that is God's law and the punishment for sin is spiritual death and separation from God. The law first of all gives positive commandments and asks us to keep them, and then, on the other hand, it pronounces judgment. There are, therefore, these two sides to the law and Paul came to see clearly that he had failed in both respects.

So, in the light of that, what does he mean by the 'excellent knowledge'? This is the real message of the gospel, this is the wonderful thing that Christ came to proclaim, and its characteristics are these. The first is that it is God's righteousness. 'Not having mine own righteousness, which is of the law, but that which is through the faith of Christ, the righteousness which is of God by faith.' Let us be sure that we understand exactly what Paul means here. It is God's righteousness in the sense that it is God's way of dealing with the problem of righteousness; it is not the righteousness that God demands or requires, it is that which he provides. That is what makes Paul go into such ecstasies. Here are men and women who have sinned against God, trying to establish a righteousness that will please God, but they cannot, and the wonderful thing is that God, in his word, has shown us the righteousness that he himself has freely provided for fallen, helpless, sinful mankind.

Now we must be clear about that, because it is the essence of the doctrine of justification by faith. The gospel shows us how, at one and the same time, we can fulfil the demands of the law, and God can accept us without violating his own justice. The law, I would remind you again, demands that we live a life of obedience to it and honour it; it also denounces our failure to do so, and when we define 'law' we must include those two things. Something must happen that delivers me from the penalty, and something must come into

my possession which enables me to give that positive assent
to the law so that I may honour it by keeping it. That is my
problem, and the answer is that the gospel tells us of the
provision that God has made for us in that two-fold respect.
The righteousness which God provides is God's righteousness and not my own. That is the first thing.

The second characteristic is that this has become possible
in Jesus Christ – 'And be found in him, not having my own
righteousness . . . but that which is through the faith of
Christ . . .' This righteousness comes to me by my believing
that which has happened in Christ. It is all made possible for
me in Christ. Again, this is something of which Paul loves to
speak. For example, there is his great statement in
1 Corinthians 1:30. '[Christ] is made unto us wisdom, and
righteousness, and sanctification, and redemption' – it is all
in Christ. This is God's way of salvation, this is his way of
providing us with righteousness. Here we are in this life; we
have all sinned against God and his holy law, and there will
be that two-fold demand. Under the law, the condemnation
of sin is death and I have to meet that. I have also to face
the questions: Have I kept the law and have I honoured it?
But I have not.

So how does Christ help me with that problem? Here is
the answer. He came into this world, he was made of
woman, made under the law. Though he was the Son of
God, he was born into this world as a human being. He put
himself under the law, and in his life here on earth he
rendered a perfect, absolute obedience to that law of God.
He never forgot it in any respect or in any detail. He gave it
the maximum obedience, the maximum allegiance; he
worked out a perfect, full, positive righteousness. Then on
that first Palm Sunday he went deliberately to Jerusalem,
and afterwards he went deliberately to the cross.

Why did he do that? He went there because the law's
demands had to be fulfilled. He was innocent, pure and
absolutely righteous, the law could not point a finger against
him, it could not find a single blemish in him, but he deliberately took our sins upon himself, and God punished our sins

there in his body on the tree. God made him responsible for our penalty; God was there inflicting his penalty upon the Son, so that in Christ we see the demand and the penalty of the law satisfied, and we see the positive demand of the law in the matter of righteousness satisfied. Thus Christ is righteous in the full sense in that he has yielded obedience to the law both in its penalty and in its requirements, and the amazing, astounding message of the gospel is that God now takes that righteousness and gives it to us – 'Not having mine own righteousness, which is of the law, but that which is through the faith of Christ, the righteousness which is of God by faith.' We can put it like this. God turns to the sinner and says, 'There is perfect righteousness and I will give you that righteousness exactly as you are.' That is the offer of the gospel; that is what Paul came to see, and without doing anything at all, exactly as he was, he received and accepted it. He saw that it was his only hope, he submitted to it, and he was saved; God pardoned him and regarded him as justified – it is the righteousness of God by faith.

Let us be clear about this point. 'Through faith' does not mean that our faith is part of the righteousness. Righteousness is entirely in Christ, nothing that we can do can satisfy that law, we can never pay its penalty, we can never conform perfectly to its demands – righteousness is in Christ. He is our righteousness, it is all in him. My faith does not make me righteous; faith is simply the generator by which I receive that righteousness. Righteousness is of God, it is God who gives it to me and the way in which that happens, says Paul, is that I, by faith, am joined to Christ – 'that I may be found in him'. My faith in him makes me part of him. I enter into a mystical union with him, I belong to him, I am in him by faith, so that everything that is true of him becomes true of me – his righteousness is my righteousness.

And the results are that as believers we are being given all the great benefits of Christ. Is it surprising that Paul spoke in such a lyrical manner? Do you realise what it

means? It means that you and I are delivered from the
penalty of the law. It means more than that – it means we
receive the reward of obedience. Archbishop Leighton
once put it like this: 'The sinner stands guiltless of any
breach, yea, as having fulfilled the whole law' – that is
exactly what this doctrine means. If I am in Christ, God
regards me as guiltless; not only that, God regards me as
one who has kept the law fully. Christ has kept it and I am
in Christ. I receive all the benefits of his perfect life and
atoning death exactly as I am. That is the doctrine: 'Just as
I am without one plea' – with nothing, nothing at all,
indeed to start to do anything is a denial of the doctrine.
You can do nothing, Christ has done everything. God
offers his righteousness, he offers it as a gift. It is not our
righteousness he requires, it is the righteousness he gives,
so that we must no longer rely upon our own efforts and
endeavours and activities. We must realise that if we lived
to be a thousand years old we would be no more righteous
in the sight of God then than we are now. You may grow
in grace, but on your death bed your only hope will be the
righteousness of Christ. It is all in Christ and all you do is
believe on him and, to use the New Testament image, you
are covered, you are clothed by that.

In Revelation 3:18 the Lord tells the Laodiceans that
they must have white raiment that they may be clothed.
And you remember how we are told in Revelation 19:7–8
that the bride is clothed with a robe of perfect whiteness.
This symbolises the righteousness of Christ himself. That is
the gospel message, so do you not see how it came to Paul
as the most thrilling thing he had heard? There is that self-
righteous Pharisee trying to build up his righteousness, and
suddenly he sees that it has been given him. Look at
Luther praying in his cell, trying to bring about his own
righteousness, and then in a flash he sees that God gives it
all in Christ. Whatever I can do, I can never do that, it is
a gift. Christ is absolutely righteous and God gives me his
righteousness. By faith I am incorporated in him and all
that is true of him becomes true of me. God will reward

me for keeping the law though it was Christ who did it. The righteousness which is of God by faith – that is 'the excellency of the knowledge of Christ Jesus my Lord'.

Chapter 6

Paul's great ambition

That I may know him, and the power of his resurrection, and the fellowship of his sufferings, being made conformable unto his death; if by any means I might attain unto the resurrection of the dead (Phil. 3:10–11).

The Apostle Paul's object in this whole passage is, as we have seen, to denounce all types of religion which would add anything to the Christian faith beyond what has been accomplished by the Lord Jesus Christ himself. In our last study, we looked at verse 9 and saw that there the first and fundamental thing in 'the excellency of the knowledge' is the truth concerning the righteousness of God which is given to us in Christ. As Paul contemplates this, he scarcely knows how to restrain himself and he piles up epithet upon epithet as he thinks of the glory of this knowledge. But that, according to the Apostle, is only the first part of it. It is the first part, and it is a very vital one, but, thank God, it does not stop at that. Paul's position is that he has come to see that everything, all this 'excellent knowledge', is there in the person of the Lord Jesus Christ – his perfect life of obedience and his atoning death.

But as Paul contemplates these things he also sees something else, and he goes on to tell us in verses 10 and 11 of this further knowledge which he has found in Christ and which he desires to know still better. In verses 10–11 he states his ambition for which he counts everything else as loss. He is straining, as he tells us, like a dog at the leash. He wants to know it, he wants to apprehend it and he wants to be held by it.

And the first thing he tells us about this further knowledge is that he is anxious to know Christ himself better. 'That I may know him'. Now it is very important that we should be clear about this statement. Paul does not say that he is anxious to have a greater knowledge about Christ. Nor does he say that he is anxious to be still more aware of certain truths concerning Christ. There was a sense in which the Apostle desired this, but what he says is something that goes well beyond all that. He tells us that he longs for a greater and more intimate personal knowledge of the Lord himself.

Now the steps in his statement are perfectly clear. He has been looking at our Lord's earthly life, and at his death, and he sees that without them he would have nothing at all: he would have no hope, nothing on which to stand. 'Already,' says Paul, in effect, 'I see that in his life and death he has done all that for me, but, thank God, he did not remain in the grave. He rose again, he triumphed over death, he appeared to his disciples and he ascended into heaven.' This was something that Paul never forgot, for he himself had literally seen Christ that midday on his journey to Damascus; he had actually seen the face of the risen and glorified Lord and he had heard his voice. In a sense, he is asking here for a more intense and deepened experience of his initial experience on the road to Damascus.

If we consider some of Paul's experiences, which are recorded in Acts and in his epistles, we shall see perhaps still more clearly what he has in his mind. There, on the Damascus road, he had that amazing sight of the risen Lord, he had communion and fellowship with him, he heard a voice and the Lord spoke to him, he had contact with the person of Jesus. But we are also told that Paul subsequently had certain visions of the Lord. The Lord appeared to him in the temple and spoke to him; there was no question about it, Paul knew he was receiving a direct message from the risen, glorified Lord. Then, in Acts we are told that when he was in Corinth he was having a difficult time trying to preach the gospel because everything seemed to be against him. So he was rather dejected – Paul knew what it was to be dejected – and when he was feeling utterly hopeless, and the task seemed to be impossible, the Lord appeared to him in the night and said, 'Be not afraid, but speak . . . for I am with thee, and no man shall set on thee to hurt thee: for I have much people in this city' (Acts 18:9–10).

Again, he tells us in 2 Corinthians 12, that he once knew a man, some fourteen years before, who had been caught up into the third heaven and heard unspeakable words – and that man was Paul himself. He had been taken hold of and had actually been in that sensitive, ethereal atmosphere above the flesh, above the world, in a sense, having immediate communion with the Lord. That is not some general mysticism; it is Christian mysticism. It is not a man feeling that he is in tune with the Infinite; it is communion with the Lord of glory himself. And, says Paul, that is what I am longing for; '. . . that I may know him', that I may get to know him better.

An example from everyday life illustrates this perfectly. You are introduced to a man whom you have never met before, and immediately you are charmed, so afterwards you say to the friend who introduced you, 'I should like to meet that man again – I should like to see more of him and get to know him better.' That is what Paul is saying. He had met his Lord, and had communion with him, and now the one thing that matters to Paul in life, is to have more and more of that. He is always expecting, always anxious, to enter into more direct and personal communion and contact.

Now this is something that should not only be true of the Apostle Paul, it is something that is meant to be true of all of us. Let us be quite clear about this. We are not likely to have a view of the risen Lord such as Paul had, because, as we have seen, that was unique. Paul had been given that view on the way to Damascus because he was called to be an Apostle, and an Apostle by definition had to be a witness of the resurrection. In effect, he says in 1 Corinthians 15, 'I did not see him during the forty days as the others did, I saw him afterwards; that special view was given to me to make me an Apostle.' We are not to have that experience, because it is not meant for us, but we are meant to have a personal, living, real fellowship and communion with the risen Lord. If as a Christian all I can say is that I believe certain things about Christ, then I am but a very young and small babe in Christ. Of course, I am to believe things about him, and my faith is to rest upon him objectively, but the Christian position does not stop there. The one who is truly Christian is the one who has this fellowship and living communion with him.

Nor does it follow that you and I, of necessity, are to have visions. These are given to some Christian people, there is no question about that – you cannot read the lives of the saints without realising that from time to time visions are given to God's people. But we must not covet them; what we are to covet is this communion, this personal intercourse and fellowship with him, and, thank God, that is gloriously possible. In the absence of a direct view, without hearing a voice, without any ecstasy, quite apart from all that, it is possible for us to say with Henry Twells:

> What if Thy form we cannot see
> We know and feel that Thou art near.

Or we can say with the writer of another hymn –

> I need Thee every hour
> Stay Thou near by,
> Temptations lose their power
> When Thou art nigh.
>
> Annie Sherwood Hawkes

No, I have not seen him, I have not had a vision, I have not heard an audible voice addressing me, but thank God I can say those words. I know he is there, and I feel his presence. That is what Paul is speaking of, and that is the thing that we should covet, and long for.

'That I may know him.' Oh, not merely believing certain things about him, but really being aware of his presence. Sometimes when you are praying alone, sometimes when you are reading the Scriptures, sometimes when you are meditating upon these things, there comes the strange awareness that there is another, someone else, present, that you are not alone, and that he seems to be speaking to you. You do not hear, but you grasp the message. You understand what he is saying. He is there encouraging you about something you have done, or perhaps chastising or upbraiding you. He is showing himself in his glory and wonder, asking you to come nearer and to spend more time with him. These are the things, this is part of the fellowship about which the Apostle is speaking.

'That I may know him.' He is risen, he is alive, the Apostle actually saw him, but it is possible to have this communion by faith and Paul longed for more of it. And the question for us is, do we also long for more of it? To me it seems more and more the one thing that should be of concern to all of us who are Christians; indeed, I think it is the one thing that differentiates the true Christian from every other person in this world. Everybody desires something; everybody is anxious to have something; you and I may have ambitions of all kinds. Now the suggestion is that the Christian is someone who says, 'What I long for, above everything else, is that I may know him better, and when I think of that, everything else becomes relatively unimportant. If by selling all I have, or forsaking all I have been hitherto, if by doing that, I could have a deeper knowledge, a truer understanding, a closer communion, I would gladly do it all.' That is the test, that was Paul's experience and it should be the experience of each of us. 'The excellency of the knowledge of Christ Jesus' in this matter of knowing him still better, is something that transcends the whole world and all its wealth, its riches and possibilities.

So the first thing Paul wanted was to know Christ: 'That I may know him.' The next thing he wanted was to be more like him. Verse 10 continues: '. . . and the power of his resurrection, and the fellowship of his sufferings, being made conformable unto his death.' You see the inevitable logic? Whenever you meet someone whom you admire, you have an instinctive feeling within you that you want to be like that person. That is equally true of our relationship with the Lord. The man or woman who wants to know him better, is one who wants to be more like him, and that was Paul's constant experience.

And here he tells us three things that are necessary before we can become more like Christ. The first is that we must know 'the power of his resurrection'. The Apostle was very fond of this picture. As you read his epistles, notice the frequency with which he repeats the idea that he is presenting in these two verses. His favourite phrase is 'to be in Christ'; the Christian is 'in Christ' and Paul explains what he means by that. He makes the bold and, as he says himself, the incredible statement, that those of us who are Christ's and who are, therefore, 'in Christ', have died with Christ. When Christ died, I died with him; but, says Paul, not only did I die with him, when Christ rose again, I rose again with him. If I am in him, that must be true; if I am attached to him by faith, if I belong to him, if I am a member of his body, then whatever has happened to him has happened to me also – buried with him in baptism, rising also with him in newness of life.

Now if you want the best exposition of that which even Paul can give, turn to Romans 6. In the first five chapters of Romans Paul has been emphasising the great doctrine of justification by faith. We must not look to ourselves and our own merits at all; we are saved in Christ, by what he has done. Then Paul imagines some clever man in Rome saying, 'I see the doctrine, if we are justified by faith, it does not matter what we do, so shall we continue in sin that grace may abound? Surely,' says this person, 'the logic of your argument is this: if it is all in Christ, then I can do whatever I like, I am covered by the blood of Christ and I am forgiven and all is well.'

'Ah,' says Paul, in effect, 'the man who speaks like that has never understood the doctrine of righteousness; he has never understood the meaning of the death of Christ upon the cross, and he is being utterly ridiculous.' Then Paul goes on to explain it in the sixth chapter. 'Romans,' he says, 'understand this, that if you are in Christ and have died with him, you have received newness of life. Well, then, walk with him in this risen life that you share with him.' And that is exactly what he is saying here in this tenth verse of Philippians 3.

No, for those who understand this doctrine there is no real danger of what is called 'antinomianism'; the people who want to know Christ better are those who want to be more like him. But what about the man or woman who comes to me and says, 'Here am I in my weakness, conscious of sin within me, temptation always around and about me, the whole world organised on the side of sin and Satan and evil. It is difficult enough to keep straight and moral at all in a world like this, and you are asking me to live the kind of life that Jesus of Nazareth lived on this earth – it is impossible.' The answer to such a person is, 'the power of his resurrection'. He is risen, he has given a manifestation of his power, and that power is being offered to us. That is the power that can become ours, however weak we are; it can lift us and raise us up in newness of life, and enable us to walk with him.

Paul puts this most dramatically in Romans 7, in fact these verses in Philippians are but a very brief synopsis of the sixth, seventh and eighth chapters of that epistle. What can I do? Paul says. I want to be better, I want to live the Christian life, but I cannot do it. I do love the law of God, I know it is right and I want to live according to it, but, 'I see another law in my members, warring against the law of my mind, and bringing me into captivity to the law of sin which is in my members. O wretched man that I am! who shall deliver me from the body of this death?' And there is only one answer, 'I thank God through Jesus Christ my Lord' (vv. 23, 25). The one who conquered sin and Satan and death, and who rose triumphant will enable me. His power can become mine, I may experience the power of his resurrected life. And as I realise more and more that I am in him and get to know him better, I shall feel his mighty power flowing into me and raising me up above myself and out of sin – 'the power of his resurrection'.

What else? The second thing that is essential to becoming more like Christ is 'the fellowship of his sufferings'. What does this mean? Why does Paul go back to Christ's sufferings after talking about the resurrection? Well I think that, experimentally, it is perfect logic. I want, says Paul, to be in him before I can become more like him, and I realise that nothing but the power of his resurrection can make me more like him. And I want to be like him in this sense, that, because I am so much like him, I shall repeat some of his experiences in my own life in this world. It is a world of sin, so that when even the Son of God came into it, he suffered because he was holy and the world was sinful. Jesus Christ could not have suffered as he did if he had not been perfect. The sufferings of the Son of Man on earth were entirely the result of sin, and, Paul says, the more I become like him, the more I shall suffer as he suffered.

It is a tremendous and a terrifying thought. Paul, in writing to Timothy who was suffering and actually grumbling, says, Timothy, my friend, you have it the wrong way round. You ought to be glad about this, 'Yea, and all that will live godly in Christ Jesus shall suffer persecution' (2 Tim. 3:12). 'The disciple is not above his master, nor the servant above his lord,' said Christ himself, '. . . if they have called the master of the house Beelzebub, how much more shall they call them of his household?' (Matt. 10:24–25). 'My brethren, count it all joy,' says James, 'when ye fall into divers temptations' (Jas. 1:2).

> It is the way the Master went,
> Should not the servant tread it still?
>
> Horatius Bonar

That is what Paul means. He says, 'I can see clearly that the more holy I become – the more I become like Christ – the more his experiences will be re-enacted in my life.'

Our Lord was 'a man of sorrows and acquainted with grief' partly because his holy soul was troubled when he saw what sin had done to his Father's creation. When he saw the foulness and the ugliness of sin, it hurt and it grieved him. So the more we approximate to our Lord and his life, the more will the sin of this world grieve and hurt us. Does it wound us? I am not asking whether we are irritated by it; a person who is merely moral can be, and often is, irritated by sin, but that is not what our Lord felt. He was not irritated, he was hurt, it grieved him, it became a burden on him. And Paul says that he longs to enter into the fellowship of those sufferings. In addition, the more we are like him, the more we are likely to be persecuted by those who do not understand him, by those who cry out: 'Away with him, crucify him.' That is what Paul means by living the life our Lord lived, and I know I am living it as I experience, in a measure, what the world did to him.

Then Paul says next, '. . . being made conformable unto his death,' which means that I become so obedient to God that, like my Lord before me, I am ready, if necessary, even to lay down my life. If it is a question of loyalty to him and his holy commandments, I do not hesitate. My Lord was confronted by that very possibility and he gave his life willingly and readily so that God's holy will might be done. And I, too, says Paul, shall be so dead to sin, so dead to the world, so dead to everything that is not of him or is opposed to him, that, like my Lord before me, I will be able to give my very life, even, if necessary, unto death itself.

There, briefly, are the three steps in becoming more like Christ – knowing the power of his resurrection, sharing the experiences of his sufferings, even being made conformable unto his death. But, lastly, Paul's ultimate ambition was to be with Christ in glory. 'That I may know him, and the power of his resurrection and the fellowship of his sufferings, being made conformable unto his death; if by any means I might attain unto the resurrection of the dead.' You see the steps: more frequent communion with him, more like him, then ultimately with him for ever. Paul could never get away from those steps; let us make sure we understand them:

    verse 9, justification – his righteousness;

    verse 10, sanctification;

    verse 11, glorification.

These are the inevitable, indelible steps. Note, too, that you cannot be justified without being sanctified, and without being glorified. You remember how Paul put it in Romans 8: 'For whom he did foreknow, he also did predestinate to be conformed to the image of his Son, that he might be the firstborn among many brethren. Moreover whom he did predestinate, them he also called: and whom he called, them he also justified: and whom he justified, them he also glorified' (vv. 29–30). Those are the steps and it is all in Christ.

Now let us be quite clear as to what Paul means here when he says, 'If by any means I might attain unto the resurrection of the dead.' 'But I thought,' says someone, 'that every person who has lived on the face of this earth is ultimately going to rise at the last day?'

True, there will be a general resurrection of the dead. Every one of us is going to be raised one day, that is inevitable, that is the decree of God for all mankind, but that is not what Paul means here. He means this other truth to which we have just referred; he is looking forward, not to the resurrection that is going to lead to the second death, to damnation and to hell, but to the resurrection of the just, the resurrection of the righteous, the resurrection that leads to glory, to be for ever with the Lord.

Paul is looking forward to that state into which all Christian people shall finally enter, in which they will be entirely free from sin. It is incredible, but it is going to happen. You and I, if we are in Christ, shall rise, and no trace of sin will be left in us. There will be no such thing as an evil thought or imagination; we shall be blameless and faultless, without spot or blemish; the eye of God will detect nothing amiss in us and we shall be glorified, perfect, even as he is. Paul works that out in the last verse of this third chapter: we look at him 'who shall change our vile body, that it may be fashioned like unto his glorious body, according to the working whereby he is able even to subdue all things unto himself'. The day is coming when sin shall not only be taken out of my soul and spirit, but even out of my body. There will be nothing imperfect in it, I shall have a new glorified body, I shall be like him. This is how John puts it: '. . . it doth not yet appear what we shall be: but we know that, when he shall appear, we shall be like him; for we shall see him as he is' (1 John 3:2).

> Changed from glory into glory,
> Till in heaven we take our place,
> Till we cast our crowns before Thee,
> Lost in wonder, love, and praise.
>
> Charles Wesley

That is what Paul longed for above everything else – the day that was to come, the glorious day of the resurrection. Again he refers to it in that eighth chapter of Romans. He says the whole creation is looking forward to it, even the animals, the birds, the flowers, everything groaning as they wait for it. The whole world is to be renovated, there is to be a new heaven and a new earth, and everything is waiting for the manifestation of the signs of his glory – the final glorification.

Christ lived the perfect life, he died the atoning death, he was buried in a grave, he has risen and has entered into the glory, he is living the life of glory and all who are in Christ are certain of the same glory. The extent to which we realise something of this is the extent to which we shall know, with the Apostle Paul, what it is to long for it, and to say that in the light of this everything else is unimportant, it is rubbish. The world and its kingdoms and all its glories, what are they as I think of that other glory? And, therefore, my ambition is: 'If by any means I might attain unto the resurrection of the dead' – and an entry into that glory.

Chapter 7

The ultimate goal

> Not as though I had already attained, either were already
> perfect: but I follow after, if that I may apprehend that for
> which also I am apprehended of Christ Jesus. Brethren, I
> count not myself to have apprehended: but this one thing
> I do, forgetting those things which are behind, and reach-
> ing forth unto those things which are before, I press
> toward the mark for the prize of the high calling of God
> in Christ Jesus (Phil. 3:12–14).

On any showing, this is a most remarkable and important
passage. I suppose that in many ways it is one of the Apostle's most familiar statements, but it has also led to much
controversy and misunderstanding.

These three verses are part of the statement which the
Apostle is making with respect to his own faith and his own
position. You remember the background: he has set out to
contrast the position of the Judaisers with that of Christianity, and he puts it in terms of his own experience – as well
he might, for he himself had experienced the position of the
Jews, and he had given years of his life in an attempt to
make himself acceptable in the sight of God before being
given this understanding of the truth as it is in Christ Jesus.

And in what a glowing, moving and dramatic way he
finally contrasts these two positions! Once he had obtained
this excellent knowledge that is in Christ, all else seemed to
him not only trivial, but indeed a hindrance. And he goes on
to say that he would gladly sacrifice everything else that
remains to him – though he has sacrificed so much already –

if that were necessary in order to win Christ and be found in him, not having his own righteousness which is of the law, but that which is through the faith of Christ, the righteousness which is of God by faith. Paul's ambition is to 'know him, and the power of his resurrection, and the fellowship of his sufferings, being made conformable unto his death; if by any means I might attain unto the resurrection of the dead.' And then there follows the passage that we are going to consider now.

This is an important statement, if only from the standpoint of Paul himself. He is a subject well worthy of our consideration: one of the greatest men of all times, judged by any standard, one of the outstanding masterminds of history and the world. This passage is important simply because it helps us to understand him and his position more clearly and more truly. But, after all, we are not here to take merely a theoretical interest in the great Apostle, fascinating though that is from the standpoint of theology and psychology. We are concerned about this statement because it has a very definite relevance to us, because it has something to tell us about our own state and position.

While we recognise clearly that the Apostle is a man of gifts and that, as an Apostle, he stands in a category apart, we must nevertheless understand that what Paul says of himself as a Christian is to be true of every Christian. The Apostle himself makes that quite clear; he says, 'we are', and he constantly includes other Christians with himself. In this particular section he writes in the first person singular because he is dealing with his own experience, but what he says about himself should be true of all of us as Christian people and should therefore be a part of our experience, too. So it becomes urgently important for us to discover exactly what the Apostle is really saying about himself here.

Furthermore, our experience depends upon and follows from what we believe, so that if our belief as to what is possible to us and for us is wrong, then it is more than likely that our experience will be correspondingly wrong. There can be no doubt but that many, if not most, of the difficulties in the

Christian life and experience arise from a failure to understand the doctrine, from a failure to understand the possibilities that are laid open to us by this glorious gospel. So the vital question for us to consider is what, in reality, the Apostle is saying in these verses about himself and his experience.

What is he saying? People generally answer that question with one of two opposing answers – but I want to suggest that both answers are wrong. The first answer is that we are told here that Paul is saying he is uncertain of his salvation. If ever you have been engaged in a discussion on the question of assurance of salvation, or if you do become involved in such a discussion with people who have some knowledge of their Scriptures, I think you will find that those who lack assurance themselves go even further than that and say that no one should be certain of salvation; and they are very fond of quoting these verses. They say, 'How can a man be certain of his salvation when the great Apostle himself was not? "Brethren I count not myself to have apprehended" – does that not mean,' they say, 'that the Apostle was not certain? Does it not show that his whole position was that he hoped he would eventually be saved? Is he not there showing, and has he not been suggesting that, in the previous verses? "If by any means" – does that not denote uncertainty? Does not the language he uses at that point specifically show that the Apostle, great as he was, nevertheless was not sure that he was saved, was not certain that his sins were forgiven and was not confident that he was a child of God? He hoped he was going to be eventually, but he was uncertain about it.'

That, then, is the suggestion that has often been put forward. But an argument like that, it seems to me, at once brings us face to face with a vital principle. Whenever we are confronted by a difficult text, there is always the danger of basing our doctrine upon that alone instead of taking it in the light of the whole teaching of the Scriptures. Now I think I can show you that the language that the Apostle uses at this point in no way supports the suggestion that he is uncertain of his salvation. Indeed, if we say that he is, then

we are forced to the conclusion that the Apostle is contra-
dicting what he has stated so categorically and explicitly in
various other places in his writings: 'I know whom I have
believed, and am persuaded that he is able to keep that
which I have committed unto him against that day' – that is
the statement of the Apostle Paul in 2 Timothy 1:12; or
again, he says in Romans 8:38 and 39, '. . . I am persuaded,
that neither death, nor life, nor angels, nor principalities,
nor powers, nor things present, nor things to come, nor
height, nor depth, nor any other creature, shall be able to
separate us from the love of God, which is in Christ Jesus
our Lord.'

Then in this very epistle, you remember, in chapter 1:6,
he says, 'He which hath begun a good work in you will perform it until the day of Jesus Christ.'* Is that the language
of uncertainty? 'For to me to live is Christ, and to die is
gain,' he continues in verse 21, and in verse 23: 'For I am in
a strait betwixt two,' on the one hand, 'having a desire to
depart, and to be with Christ; which is far better.' I ask
again, is that the language of a man who is uncertain of his
position, the language of a man who is merely hoping that
he may eventually be saved or that somehow or other, in
spite of everything, he may find himself among the
redeemed? Surely the language of the Apostle is an utter
contradiction of that suggestion. If ever a man wrote out of
a full, abounding confidence in that which he knew concerning himself and his position in Christ, it was this man
– 'For whom he did foreknow, he also did predestinate to
be conformed to the image of his Son, that he might be the
firstborn among many brethren. Moreover whom he did
predestinate, them he also called: and whom he called,
them he also justified: and whom he justified, them he also
glorified' (Rom. 8:29–30). That is his language. 'Who shall
lay any thing to the charge of God's elect? Paul asks in
Romans 8:33. The thing is impossible. No, the Apostle is
certain of his salvation, he is assured; 'For we are the

---

* See Volume 1, *The Life of Joy*.

circumcision, which worship God in the spirit, and rejoice in Christ Jesus, and have no confidence in the flesh.' All his language everywhere, and even here in Philippians, makes it quite impossible for us to say that the interpretation of these verses is that Paul is uncertain of his salvation.

Then let me put to you the other suggestion that has been offered, which is the exact opposite of the one I have just been outlining. It is held by those who agree that Paul was certain of his salvation. These people feel that since the Apostle was absolutely certain of his salvation, the only way to explain these verses is to say that Paul means he has not yet finished his life's journey, he has not arrived at the ultimate resurrection of the dead. They solemnly put forward that as an explanation of these words. They say Paul's statement can only mean, 'If by any means I might arrive at the resurrection, but, brethren, I have not arrived yet.'

But this, surely, is yet another suggestion which is not only patently inadequate, but is, indeed, even ridiculous. It would mean in effect that the Apostle, actually writing or dictating a letter to the people at Philippi, tells them, 'I am still alive and in this world; I am still going forward in the journey.' But that is unnecessary, the fact that he is writing tells them all that there is no need for a man who writes a letter to say he is still alive!

So, then, if we cannot accept either of these two suggestions, what is our interpretation of what the Apostle says? Well, there seem to me to be three main statements in the section from verses 10 to 14. Here is the first: Paul tells us that Christ has laid hold of him, and still holds him, in order that he may arrive at a particular goal – 'Not as though I had already attained, either were already perfect: but I follow after, if that I may apprehend [lay hold of, grasp] that for which also I am apprehended of [laid hold of, held by] Christ Jesus.' That is the first great statement. In other words the Apostle is telling us here that as he went down to Damascus on that famous occasion, he was suddenly laid hold of by the Lord Jesus Christ. He was grasped – that is what 'apprehended' means. We still use the word in this sense, though not as frequently as in the days of the Authorised translation. However, we still talk about the police apprehending a man when they hold him in order that certain investigations may be made. Paul says he was apprehended by Christ; Christ had put his hand upon him, and was holding him still.

But, you notice, he says that this happened to him for a certain, specific reason: '. . . if that I may apprehend that for which also I am apprehended'. Paul was apprehended for this particular reason. Now that, it seems to me, is the key to understanding this particular statement. What was it that Paul was apprehended for? Why was he laid hold of on the road to Damascus? In a sense, he has already been telling us. He was grasped by Christ, not merely that he might know forgiveness, and not merely that he might give up the attempt to work out his own righteousness. He was laid hold of not merely that he might cease from persecuting the Christian Church, and not merely that he might be delivered and emancipated from that which was wrong.

Why, then, was he apprehended? Well, for this positive reason: he was saved, as is every other Christian, in order that he might eventually reach a particular goal, and he describes that goal in verse 10 – that he might know Christ fully and perfectly; and not only that, but that he might become like Christ, that he might know 'the power of his resurrection, and the fellowship of his sufferings, being made conformable unto his death'. The Apostle is very fond of teaching this particular truth. This is how he puts it in his letter to Titus: 'For the grace of God that bringeth salvation hath appeared to all men, teaching us that, denying ungodliness and worldly lusts, we should live soberly, righteously, and godly, in this present world; looking for that blessed hope, and the glorious appearing of the great God and our Saviour Jesus Christ; who gave himself for us, that he might redeem us from all iniquity, and purify unto himself a peculiar people, zealous of good works' (Tit. 2:11–14). That is the same idea exactly.

The goal, then, that Paul tells us has been set before him,

the thing for which he has been apprehended, is that he may come to that intimate knowledge of Christ, that perfect communion, and that he may be delivered, not only from the guilt of sin, about which he is perfectly certain, but also from the power and pollution of sin, and become like Christ in his life, in his death, in everything; that he may reproduce in his life the kind of life that was lived by the Lord Jesus Christ himself. I have been grasped for that, says Paul. So that is the first statement. Our Lord laid hold of him that afternoon on the road to Damascus in order that he might enter in along that path. And that is the Apostle's ambition – to arrive at that.

Then his second statement tells us that he has not arrived at that goal. Oh yes, he knows he is saved; he realises that his ultimate salvation is as certain as anything can be; he is in Christ and knows he is going to be with Christ – there is no question about that; he has left all these other things behind him and has given up any belief in any other righteousness. He now has that righteousness which is by faith in Christ Jesus and he knows his ultimate destiny. But what he is dissatisfied about is his failure to arrive at that goal for which he has been arrested – the experimental knowledge of Christ and his conformity to Christ in his whole life and living. 'Not as though I had already attained' – Paul is not referring to the resurrection nor, as I have shown, is it necessary for him to say that he is alive – no, it is, '. . . that I may know him, and the power of his resurrection.' I have not attained to that, says Paul, and that is what I am pressing after. He has not reached the goal for which he has been apprehended and so his third statement is that he longs to arrive at it and he strains every nerve in order that he may do so: '. . . reaching forth unto those things which are before, I press toward the mark . . .'

These are the three things which the Apostle says in these verses: he defines the goal, the ambition of the Christian; he confesses that he has not attained unto it; and he tells us that his whole concern in life is to arrive at it and that he is doing those things which are necessary to arrive there. So, having explained the Apostle's words, let us proceed to deduce the doctrine; in other words, let us apply what the Apostle says about himself to ourselves.

Now this is a matter about which there is a great deal of confusion and there is much loose talk on the one side and on the other. There are those who claim more than the Apostle claimed and there are those who do not claim as much. Those two dangers are always present. Some people say that you must not claim that you are sure of your salvation; you must just say that you are doing your best and are hoping to reach that goal at the end. Others maintain that Christians in this world are already perfect and should certainly claim that they have attained to such a state of perfection. We shall see, however, that the Apostle avoids both these statements and is saying something quite different here. The doctrine can be put like this.

First, there is no such thing as perfection in this life and world, it is impossible. The case of the great Apostle alone is, in and of itself, quite sufficient to satisfy us upon this matter once and for ever. 'Not as though I had already attained,' says this mighty man of God, 'either were already perfect.' Paul himself was not perfect.

'But,' says someone, 'does he not go on to say in verse 15, "Let us therefore, as many as be perfect"?'

But surely the Apostle would not contradict himself within a few verses! The word 'perfect' in verse 15 is one of those limiting terms that we find used by the Apostle in many places. For example, in 1 Corinthians 2, he says, 'Howbeit we speak wisdom among them that are perfect' (v. 6). He is contrasting those who are babes with those who are in a more advanced position; he says he cannot give the higher doctrine to the people at Corinth because they are still babes in Christ, they are 'yet carnal' (1 Cor. 3:3). 'Howbeit,' he says in effect, 'we speak wisdom to those who are more advanced and mature.' And in Philippians 3:15 he says the same thing: 'Let . . . as many as be perfect . . .' It is not absolute perfection, it is relative. But in verse 12 it does mean absolute perfection: I have not already been made perfect, he says, I have not arrived at that.

Thus, it is obvious that the great Apostle is not satisfied with the life that he is living; there are elements in his life which cause him a good deal of dissatisfaction. On the basis of this one instance, without going any further or quoting other Scriptures, which I could easily do, we can lay down the principle that perfection is not possible in this life. What right have we to claim that it has happened to us? The Apostle does not claim that it has happened to him.

'Then,' someone asks, 'why is it that God does not make perfection possible to us here?' To which the only ultimate answer is that we do not know. All we do know is that if it were God's will for us to be made perfect by the operation of the Holy Spirit upon us it would happen. 'But why does God not do that?' someone insists. However, there are certain questions that you and I should not ask; all we know is that he has chosen not to do so.

Certain answers can be put forward. It may well be that because of sin and its effect upon us, God leaves us just as we are in this life to keep us humble, lest we boast, lest we fail to realise our utter dependence upon him. It is our failures that drive us back to him, it is our consciousness of imperfection that keeps us in communion with him. God has chosen to do this even as he did in the lives of the Children of Israel; it seems that God works in that way. I do not understand it, but I simply recognise the fact that the great Apostle says he is not perfect, and from that I deduce that we are not meant to be perfect in this world.

Let me put it negatively: claims to perfection are based upon two errors, and the first is an incomplete self-examination. People who claim to have arrived at a state of perfection – and there have been such, you read of them in history – have generally done so because they have been guilty of not examining themselves completely. They have said that because they are not guilty of certain sins, they are perfect; they have not examined the heart or the imagination; they have not realised that in the matter of perfection our state is as important as our actions.

The second error is the error of setting up too low a standard. People see that they are better than they were before because they no longer commit certain sins. They also find themselves better than other people around them – and they think therefore that they have reached perfection. But their standard is too low. Let me remind you that the standard the Apostle sets for himself and all Christians is nothing less than this: to know Christ in a perfect state of communion and fellowship; to know the power of his resurrection delivering us not only from acts of sin, but from thoughts of sin, from the machinations of sin, and from this toying with sin, delivering us from the guilt and power and pollution of everything connected with sin; that is the standard and nothing less. It is the fellowship of his sufferings, being made conformable unto his death. And no one can honestly claim that he or she has attained unto such a standard.

Then my next proposition is that perfection and complete sanctification are not to be attained suddenly. I think that obviously follows as the next step. Those who teach a kind of perfectionism would have us believe that this is a state that one can achieve suddenly. They often tell us that it has happened in a Convention or in a meeting, that suddenly they have received this other blessing and have been made perfect. They say there was a sudden transition from one condition to another.

Now, surely, the language of the Apostle here denies any such doctrine. He speaks of 'following after': '. . . this one thing I do, forgetting those things which are behind, and reaching forth unto those things which are before, I press towards the mark.' There is nothing sudden about it; his whole picture is one of development and progress. He is like a man running along the road, going step by step and yet ever going forward. There is no sudden transition from a state of improvement to a state of perfection. Indeed, a good illustration, used by Paul and the other New Testament writers on the same subject, is that of the 'babe in Christ', where the whole idea suggests growth and development, with steps and stages. Or take again Paul's other example of the plants and the flowers. He talks about the husbandman planting seeds (for example, 2 Cor. 3:6–7), and in that illustration there is the same idea. Perfection and complete sanctification must never be conceived of as something that happens suddenly. In a meeting or a convention you may have a new view of the love of God, but that is very different from perfection and complete sanctification. The Apostle's method is 'pressing forward', striving and going forward, step by step and stage by stage.

That leads me to the next important principle. This progressive work means activity for us and not passivity. The teaching on perfection is almost always a teaching that is connected with passivity. We are told that people will persist in striving after holiness, in trying to sanctify themselves, but that the thing to do is to 'let go and let God'. The Apostle's language, on the other hand, is this: 'I follow after'; 'This one thing I do, forgetting those things which are behind . . . I press forward.' He talks in 1 Timothy 6:12 about fighting 'the good fight of faith.' All these expressions are indicative of great activity on the part of the Christian in the matter of salvation. In the matter of our righteousness and justification we can never say too often that we do nothing, we can do nothing, it is entirely the work of Christ. But once we are saved and given this new life, then the progressive work of sanctification does not call for passivity, and we are exhorted to activity.

The last principle in this doctrine is that our consciousness of imperfection, far from robbing us of assurance of salvation, is, in a sense, almost the ground of assurance of salvation. And that is so in this way: I suggest to you that the only people who speak like Paul are those who are saved, those who have life in them. The vast majority of men and women in the world do not say that their greatest ambition is to 'know him, and the power of his resurrection, and the fellowship of his sufferings, being made conformable unto his death'; they are not interested, that is not their ambition at all; they are interested in things that are almost the exact opposite. But, surely, the people who say, 'I am dissatisfied,

I am conscious of my imperfection, I am aware of sin, I am not what I ought to be, "O wretched man that I am! who shall deliver me from the body of this death?'" – they are the people who have spiritual life in them.

Do you, as you look at yourself in the light of the truth, feel, like Paul, that you have not attained, that you have not arrived, that you have not grasped, that you are much too far back along the road and wish you were further forward? If you do, then it is a proof that you have spiritual life. If this is your ambition, far from suggesting uncertainty about whether or not you are Christian, it is proof that you are.

Finally, let me apply what I have been trying to say by asking a few questions. Are we satisfied with our lives? The Apostle Paul was not. Look at him, look at the life he lived. Here was a man who had seen Christ, who had had visions, who had heard an audible voice. Here was a man who had been lifted up into the third heaven, a man who had preached the gospel day and night. But he was not satisfied. Are we complacent? Do we feel we are all right simply because we are better than the vast majority of people who do not darken the doors of a place of worship? Are we content with our lives? If we are, we are very different from this Apostle. Do we long to go forward? Paul, this mighty servant of God, longed to go still further forward along the road, he was straining to arrive at the goal. Can we say that we are advancing in that way? Are we striving with all our might to do so?

Well, there is this great and vital doctrine which is taught by the Apostle at this point. It is a picture of the Christian. Christians are assured of their salvation; they see clearly what they are meant to be and they know that they are not; but they long to be and they give all their energy in order to arrive. May God deliver us from a false doctrine of perfection, and implant within us and encourage the growth within us of this principle that was so plainly evidenced in Paul, this realisation of the ultimate standard, this longing for it and this determination to spare no effort in order to arrive at it.

Chapter 8

The one thing

Not as though I had already attained, either were already perfect: but I follow after, if that I may apprehend that for which also I am apprehended of Christ Jesus. Brethren, I count not myself to have apprehended: but this one thing I do, forgetting those things which are behind, and reaching forth unto those things which are before, I press toward the mark for the prize of the high calling of God in Christ Jesus (Phil. 3:12–14).

In our last study we considered these words mainly from the standpoint of what I may describe as their theological import. We have here, as you remember, a personal statement made by the Apostle – which was something he did but rarely. Paul only makes use of his own personal experience when it is essential for him to do so, for example, if he is to define his title as an Apostle or if his authority as a teacher is being queried. He calls upon his own experience here because it is clearly the best way of confuting the argument being put forward by the Judaisers who wrought such havoc in many of the early Christian churches.

So we have seen that Paul's description of the Christian's position in general terms is this – assurance with regard to the ultimate, dissatisfaction with present attainments. But having said that, we come now to a more practical consideration of the Christian position, for in these three verses the Apostle not only describes his state in theological terms, he also describes in detail what we may call the method of the Christian life. The Apostle gives us here a more intimate picture of his own spiritual life and the discipline of his Christian living than he does anywhere else in all his writings, and that is why these three verses are of supreme value. He gives us this one insight and glimpse into his own normal daily procedure; he tells us how he is dealing with this sense of dissatisfaction which he feels with his present attainments, and how he is pressing onwards and forwards to that ultimate goal towards which his face was set.

These verses, then, are of great practical importance to us, and we should thank God for them because I think that most of us must tend to think of this great Apostle in a way which is not altogether true. It is very easy to think of him as some person altogether apart whose life, therefore, is of no value and significance to us. There are so many things about Paul that mark him out as an exceptional man; he was exceptional by birth, exceptional in his ability, and exceptional in his training; and then his conversion took place in such an exceptional and unusual manner. He was given visions, and had such unique experiences that, unless we are careful, it is very easy, as we read the various references to him in the New Testament, just to think of him as some kind of miraculous person standing in a category quite on his own, and to think of his life as purely miraculous.

It is very difficult to think of Paul having the struggles and conflicts which we experience as Christian people. I suppose that most of us – some of us especially – tend to idealise the Apostle's life to such an extent that it almost becomes of no value to us as an example and illustration of Christian living. But here, in these few words, Paul disabuses our minds of any such ideas. Here, I think, he shows us very plainly that he finds it absolutely essential to work according to a given plan; that his life is not just a succession of miraculous events, but that he is the man he is because of his conformity to certain fundamental principles, and it is there that his case becomes of such value to us.

To put it in a directly practical form, we can ask ourselves a question: Are we anxious to have Paul's experience? Are we able to speak of life as this man spoke of it? Can we say that there is a sense in which what may happen to us in the future is a matter of supreme indifference to us? Can we say with Paul that whether it is going to be a life of imprisonment or whether it is going to be death, it is really immaterial, for, 'to me to live is Christ, and to die is gain'? Are we, as he was, in the position of being able to say, '. . . I have learned, in whatsoever state I am, therewith to be content' (4:11)? Can we say, 'I can do all things through Christ which strengtheneth me' (4:13)? That is Paul's experience; the question is: Have we longed to know that? How is that to be attained? How can we arrive at it?

Here, I suggest to you, the Apostle answers those questions. If we would have the experience of the Apostle, we must live the life of the Apostle. If we would share these amazing things that are recorded in the life of the saints of God, then we must conform to the pattern of their life. And it is of great interest to me to observe that all these people seem to conform to the same pattern. It does not matter whether you take the biographies of the saints who lived in the first century, or those of the twentieth, you will find that some essential things are always there they always live in a certain manner, and that manner is described perfectly in these three verses.

So then, as we come to consider the passage in detail, let me emphasise what I would call the two controlling principles in Paul's life. The first, which stands out very clearly, is that Paul did not live off his experiences. We read the story of his conversion, we read his account of the visions he was given, and of how, on one occasion, he was caught up into the third heaven and saw and heard things unspeakable, and yet nothing is so clear about the life of this man as that he did not live on those experiences. Indeed, in 2 Corinthians 12 he tells us quite explicitly that though he might boast about these things, he did not do so. He rather gloried in his infirmities and weakness and in the apparent perplexities of life, for he tells us that though he had these extraordinary experiences, he also knew what it was to have a thorn in the flesh and though he prayed that it should be removed the Lord did not take it away. Paul prayed that prayer three times, but the thorn did not go, and for a time he was bewildered by this. However, he came to understand the reason when the Lord said unto him, 'My grace is sufficient for thee' (2 Cor. 12:9) and then, Paul tells us, he arrived at his ultimate philosophy, '. . . when I am weak, then am I strong.'

That is the first great principle which we must always bear in mind. Many Christians are in trouble because they try to live off their past experiences. They remember their experiences and try to draw something from them; they are, as it were, drawing on some capital which was given to them in the past, and they are receiving nothing in the present. Paul denounces that; it is not his method at all. He does not grasp at the past, or live off his experiences; his method is active, pressing forward into the future.

This leads to the second principle underlying the Apostle's conception of holiness and spirituality: that the Christian life is not passive. I need not stay with that because I dealt with it in our last study, but I do think it is right that we should hold it in our minds as we come to consider Paul's spiritual method. We must not think of Paul as a man who spent most of his time in contemplation, either upon his knees or sitting waiting. There is nothing of the so-called 'spiritual method' of the Roman Catholic view of sanctity and holiness, with its 'dark night of the soul' and its passivity and abnegation. You cannot find it in the verses we are considering, or anywhere in the life of this Apostle – his life is, indeed, the very antithesis of that kind of passivity.

And so, bearing these two principles in mind, we come to Paul's method of living. In a sense, Paul here tells us that his life was nothing but an exemplification of what he has told the Philippians to do. In their case, you remember, his rule for them was given in verses 12 and 13 of the second chapter. 'Wherefore, my beloved, as ye have always obeyed, not as in my presence only, but now much more in my absence, work out your own salvation with fear and trembling. For it is God which worketh in you both to will and to do of his good pleasure.' That is the method. It is this apparent paradox in the Christian life. It is a working on our part and yet a realisation that we could not work unless we were being worked upon. It is a realisation that it is of God and yet that God has allowed to us, who have been given new life, our part and our portion – 'work out . . . for it is God that worketh in you.' That is what we see perfectly illustrated here in this practical method of the Apostle.

It is, of course, something he tells us everywhere. Take, for instance, the first chapter which we have already considered.* There he tells the Philippians that he is 'confident of this very thing, that he which hath begun a good work in you will perform it until the day of Jesus Christ' (v. 6). And yet, in spite of that confidence, he says in 1:9, 'And this I pray, that your love may abound yet more and more in knowledge and in all judgment' – and so on. The Apostle assures them of the ultimate, and of what God is doing, and then immediately follows that by an exhortation to activity and to work.

Those, therefore, are the principles behind the detailed method which we can now consider. So let us look at it like this. What is the character of the Christian life? According to the Apostle it is a striving, a struggle, an effort, an endeavour ever onwards and upwards in the direction of that goal in the distance, of which he has been given a view. Now let me introduce you to the terms – and all I am doing at this point is making one or two comments upon the words which Paul uses in these three verses. 'I follow after,' he says. It is not as though he had already grasped, or were already perfect, but, 'I follow after'. That is one of his terms, and then he has another in verse 14: 'I press toward . . .', and what is interesting is that in the original these two expressions are exactly the same word. And what is still more interesting is that it is precisely the same word which he has already used in the sixth verse. You remember how he gave an account of his life before his conversion –

---

* See Volume 1, *The Life of Joy*.

'Concerning zeal, persecuting the church . . .'? Now the word translated there as 'persecuting' is the word translated 'follow after' and 'pressing toward' in this passage.

And that gives us a perfect picture of the character or the nature of the Apostle's life. When we read the account of the Apostle's conversion in Acts 9 we see clearly his zeal and enthusiasm in persecuting the Church. He went to the rulers at Jerusalem and asked them for authority, for papers, to go down to Damascus to persecute the Christians. There never was a man keener on his job, there never was a man more zealous! He hated these Christians and spared no effort to wreak havoc amongst them. There he went down the road, breathing out threatenings and slaughter, persecuting the Church. And that is the way in which he is living the Christian life. Just as he once followed after the Christians and hounded them and sought them out in every nook and corner, so he is now following after this thing for which he has been apprehended: 'I follow after', 'I press toward', 'I persecute'. That is the description which he gives of his life as a Christian.

But Paul is not content even with that. In order to show us this zest, this keenness, this enthusiasm, he adds still another word: 'Brethren . . . forgetting those things which are behind, and reaching forth . . .' Now 'reaching forth' is even stronger than 'following after' or 'pressing toward'. Paul is using an illustration familiar from the Greek games. He is picturing a man running in a race and it is a wonderful pen-picture. You can almost see the man reaching forth, stretching forward with his hand. You know the anxiety of the man who is running a race – he stretches out his hand; it doesn't help him, but it does show his desire to win, to touch the finish before he gets there. His hand is stretched out, he is striving, pressing on, trying to grasp it – reaching forth.

That is the kind of Christian the Apostle Paul was. You see his keenness. He is a man who has seen something – a glorious possibility, the prize, and wants to get there. Paul is pressing on, he is running, he is stretching forth with all his power. In his unregenerate days Paul used that power to persecute, but now it has been harnessed and turned in the other direction. He is all out for this glorious, tremendous thing that lies there ahead of him in the future. That is the character, that is the nature of the Christian life. That, according to the Apostle, is the sort of person which the Christian is meant to be.

Now I should fail in my task as a preacher at this point if I merely painted the picture and then moved on, because there is surely a question which we all must ask ourselves: Is that a picture of us? We know what it is to be enthusiastic about something but is this keenness, which is in every one of us by nature, channelled in the direction of the ultimate goal of the Christian? That is the question. It is because it was true of him, that Paul could say with such confidence, 'To me to live is Christ, and to die is gain.' Christ is everything, and Paul is confident and assured.

Very well, if that is the nature or character of the Christian life in general, let me ask the next question, which is a still more practical one. How can we arrive at that goal? If we have seen it, and know about it, if our eye is fixed upon it; if we are in this race and if we are aiming at that goal, then how are we to get there? What are the Apostle's rules? How did he run in this race? What are the principles on which he operated? Let me just mention the terms – they are all here. The first is *self-examination*. 'Brethren,' says Paul, 'I count not myself to have apprehended,' or, 'I reckon not myself to have apprehended.' Now that denotes self-examination. Here is a man who examines himself. This is a great subject; every one of these four points I am going to note is worthy of not only one study to itself, but a whole series of studies. But as we are living in this twentieth century and not in the great days of the Puritans of the sixteenth century, we must just hurry on and note them in passing instead of spending two or three studies on each one of them!

Self-examination is a subject which can very easily be misunderstood. It does not mean that Paul was morbid, or

introspective; it does not mean that he was always feeling
his own spiritual pulse and taking his own spiritual temperature. No, but it does mean that he did not live on assumptions concerning himself. He was always looking at the standard and was constantly being measured by it. Perhaps one
of the greatest dangers confronting us as Christian people is
the danger of being content to go on assumptions, the
danger of thinking that because we are in a certain position
we are all right. I trust that I am not unjust in saying this,
but is not complacency perhaps one of our greatest dangers?
I feel that because I am not guilty of certain sins I am all
right, and I cease to examine myself. How easy it is to be
content with conversion and never to go any further. Paul
was always looking at himself and examining himself, in
order to make sure that he was still pressing forward
towards that goal. He was not satisfied with himself, and he
was not satisfied because of this self-examination, and he
exhorts others to do the same. Examine yourself, he says,
make sure that you are in the faith.

And this is something we constantly need to do. It is, of
course, one of the functions of preaching to encourage that.
Increasingly, I consider it the business of the preacher to ask
questions, and that is one of the first questions we must ask.
How often do we stop to examine ourselves? Do we dislike
self-examination? Do we face ourselves, or do we try to get
round it by doing good, by giving attention to this or that,
and in this way attempt to salve our own conscience? Now
this is the first essential. We should ask the Holy Spirit to
search us; we should meditate upon these things; we should
make notes, if necessary, of obvious weaknesses. We must
be honest and true with ourselves and face ourselves in the
mirror of the perfect law of liberty. Self-examination – 'I
count not myself,' says Paul.

Then let us hurry to the second word, which is *concentration*. 'One thing I do.' That is Paul's way of describing his
concentration. Let us look again at the man running in a
race. The man who runs in a race must not be interested in
the landscape. If he begins to look at the mountains and the

charm of the flowers in the hedgerows, he will not win the race; he must be intent on one thing only. There was a story I once read in a newspaper which struck me as a charming and perfect illustration of what I am saying. An agriculturist was describing how he was driving his car along a narrow road on his way to visit a farm, when suddenly he came upon a flock of sheep and a sheep dog. His problem was how to get past these sheep. Then he described the amazing way in which the sheep dog dealt with the situation, how he kept and had his eyes upon the flock and made his calculations, running backwards and forwards. But the interesting thing was that a little terrier belonging to a nearby house came out and tried to pick a quarrel with the sheep dog, coming at him and barking at him. The writer of the article pointed out the magnificence of that sheep dog who completely ignored the yapping terrier. He knew he had a great job to do – he had to get his sheep past the car – so he did not pay any attention to the terrier: 'One thing I do,' said the sheep dog.

That is the way in which Christians are to work. They do not look at these distractions – the world is full of distracting interests, some of them legitimate, some not. But those who want to be like the Apostle Paul do not look at them – only at one thing – concentration! They do not look around, they do not allow themselves to be interested in things that are going to distract them from their purpose; they keep their attention upon it. Furthermore, they are not fitful and spasmodic in their Christian life. God knows how we find ourselves searched by a word like this. Is it not the case with most of us that we constantly make resolutions about what we are going to do, but we are always going to do something; we make a start and then we stop. We start running, but those who know us know that before midday we will probably be lying down. This spasmodic, fitful Christian living! The Apostle says, 'One thing I do'; it is regular and it is constant. The Christian life is impossible without discipline. We must control ourselves, we must divide up our time, we must realise, in a world that is so set against us, that if we do not discipline our spiritual life we shall certainly find ourselves in trouble.

And then the third great principle is 'forgetting those things which are behind'. And here again the most important point, of course, is that we must be quite clear what Paul means. He does not mean that the Christian should deliberately forget the past experiences, nor does he say that he himself forgot about his conversion, he never forgot it. He does not say that he had forgotten all the things that had happened to him. No, he does not mean that. What, then, does he mean? He means that we must not rest upon our past experiences, we must not be for ever looking back upon them in a self-satisfied way in order to pride and preen ourselves upon them. It is like the man in the race. His business is not so much to consider how far he has arrived along the track as to discover how near he is to the goal that is ahead of him. What a temptation it is always to be looking back!

Of course, there is a sense in which that is perfectly legitimate. If you have ever climbed a mountain, you are probably acquainted with this very thing. If you look at the summit as you are climbing you feel discouraged, but when you look back, you feel better. That is all right as long as you do not stop to admire your achievement. That is what the Apostle is warning us against. Those who are always looking back are those who are not likely to be going forward very rapidly or securely. That is why I have felt that when people are repeatedly called upon in meetings to tell the experience of their conversion, though it may be good for those who are listening, it is probably very bad for those who give the experience. Anything which tends to cultivate this tendency to look back and to talk about past experiences or past achievements comes into conflict with the Apostle's great principle here. No, 'forgetting those things which are behind'. I would even put it as bluntly as this: do not look back in a spirit of self-satisfaction even upon your orthodoxy. You may have made great sacrifices for Christ's sake – forget it, and think of the things still awaiting you! That is what Paul means. Anything which makes us look back with a desire for self-admiration threatens our spiritual progress.

But lastly, of course, and, indeed, supremely, there is the importance of keeping our eye on the goal and on the prize, for is it not obvious that if we do that, the other things follow of necessity? And that was Paul's greatest secret: 'That I may apprehend that for which also I am apprehended.' The Apostle always looked at that; he saw that goal, and, of course, seeing the goal he did not want to look back on his past achievements. They were good and wonderful, yes, but now, looking at the goal, how poor they were, how small! And that, it seems to me, is the secret of the Christian life. Those who have their eye on the goal do not want to compare themselves favourably with other people; no, they see their own imperfections. That does away, too, with jealousy and envy. They do not want to look back, what they do want is to get to the goal. The Apostle kept his eye, his gaze, fixed upon that.

What, then, is that goal? We have already described it – 'That I may know him, and the power of his resurrection, and the fellowship of his sufferings, being made conformable unto his death . . .' That I might attain unto that final resurrection of the just and enter into glory – that is it, that is the one thing that counts with Paul. I rather like the one word which puts together all that we are considering in these verses: 'I press toward the mark for the prize of the high calling . . .' In the margin of some Bibles you will find another phrase – 'the upward calling'. It does not matter which you use, the idea is just this: it is a call that comes to us from on high, or, if you prefer it, it is a call to us to go upwards. The call raises us and summons us to ultimate glory in the presence of God himself.

That is the final secret. We must not compare ourselves with the sinful world around and about us; we must not compare ourselves with Christians who are obviously further back than we are in the race. No, we have been called, grasped, apprehended by Christ, to know him, to be like him, to be for ever with him. Christians are people who see that, and never lose sight of it. Nothing matters with them but attaining unto that, so they press onwards, they stretch forward, they are always reaching up, and they do so by watching themselves and their achievements, by this utter concentration upon the goal and by being forgetful of everything that has happened hitherto.

That, it seems to me, is the Apostle's method, the discipline of Christian living. So the effect of it should be something like this. Not a day should pass in our lives but that we should deliberately and solemnly remind ourselves of these things. I am destined for that glory. I am in Christ, I am going to be perfected in Christ – that is the goal. Do I know him? Am I like him? Am I being made conformable unto his death? I have been apprehended by Christ for that and that should be the centre of my life, the object of my every ambition.

God grant that we all may so see the goal, that we may be so charmed and attracted by it, that we shall have an eye for nothing but that – the prize, the mark of the high calling of God in Christ Jesus.

Chapter 9

Belief and conduct

Let us therefore, as many as be perfect, be thus minded:
and if in anything ye be otherwise minded, God shall
reveal even this unto you. Nevertheless, whereto we have
already attained, let us walk by the same rule, let us mind
the same thing. Brethren, be followers together of me,
and mark them which walk so as ye have us for an ensample. (For many walk, of whom I have told you often, and
now tell you even weeping, that they are the enemies of
the cross of Christ: whose end is destruction, whose God
is their belly, and whose glory is in their shame, who mind
earthly things) (Phil. 3:15–19).

Here in these verses, and, indeed, in the two following verses also, the Apostle Paul is applying what he has just been
saying about himself to the situation of the members of the
church at Philippi. In verses 4 to 14 we have seen, how, in
order to deal with the difficult subject of the Judaisers, he
gave an account of himself and of his experiences. He
described how he had been brought out of Judaism into the
Christian position, and he elaborated that statement in the
way that we have been considering together for a number of
studies.

But it is not Paul's intention simply to write about himself; his concern is to help the members of the church at
Philippi. It is possible that he might be put to death at any
moment and he is naturally anxious to safeguard their whole
future position. He has introduced himself merely by way of

an illustration; his purpose is to apply all he has said, in order that his readers might put into practice in their lives the governing principles of his own life and conduct. Here, then, he sums up the whole of the experience he has just been relating, and he sums it up to enforce it and apply it to the Philippians.

If we would know, therefore, how to live a full, successful and happy Christian life, the kind of life which the Apostle lived, if we would enjoy the experiences in the Christian life that he so singularly enjoyed, then Paul tells us here exactly what we have to do. Perhaps the best way to consider this is first of all just to indicate the various points and principles which Paul enunciates in these verses, and then, having commented upon them one by one, to look at the philosophy at the back of it all. The great theme is the inter-relationship of faith and practice, belief and conduct, but before we come to work out the teaching in terms of a principle like that, it might be good for us to note the separate items as the Apostle enumerates them.

The first thing Paul tells us is that we must have the right belief. 'Let us therefore, as many as be perfect, be thus minded . . .' Now the Apostle Paul is very fond of this word 'mind'. You notice how in this very section he keeps on repeating it. In the sixteenth verse he says, 'Nevertheless, whereto we have already attained, let us walk by the same rule, let us mind the same thing'; and in verse 19 he ends the description of those unworthy believers by adding 'who mind earthly things'. Again, back in the second chapter, he uses exactly the same word. In exhorting these Philippians to consider one another and to help one another, he says, 'Let this mind be in you.' In Romans 8, also, he points out that the difference between the natural and the spiritual person is that those who are of the flesh 'do mind the things of the flesh', whereas those who are spiritual 'do mind the things of the spirit' (Rom. 8:5). It is an expressive term and it generally means that these are the things which not only interest, but greatly concern people; they are the things with which people spend a lot of time, the things about which they form strong conclusions. That is why I put it in the form of a principle.

So we must make certain, first of all, that we have the right belief: 'Let us therefore, as many as be perfect . . .,' says Paul. I need not point out again the meaning of the word 'perfect', because I referred to it when we were dealing with it in verse 12 where Paul says, 'Not as though I had already attained, either were already perfect.' In that verse it is an absolute term, here in this fifteenth verse it is relative. It means those who are matured and have reached the adult state, those who have advanced so far in the Christian life. But what is it that we have to be clear about? Well, surely, this third chapter, which is pre-eminently the theological chapter of the four, itself answers that question.

Paul is warning the Philippians that there are two main errors which they must avoid at all costs. The first is the one dealt with at such length, the error of the Judaiser. 'If,' says the Apostle in effect, 'you are still prepared to listen to these people who teach and believe that unless you are circumcised you are not truly Christian, if you are going to put that into practice, then your whole Christian position is undone. It is no use exhorting you to live the Christian life so long as you have the wrong mind about the Christian faith.' In other words, Paul is, as it were, coming back to verse 3 where he says, 'For we are the circumcision, which worship God in the spirit, and rejoice in Christ Jesus, and have no confidence in the flesh.' We have to be absolutely certain about that, we must not be in any state of hesitation in our minds as to what it is that makes a person a Christian. Beware of the error of Judaism!

But there is also a second danger to which he has been referring in outlining his own experience. The Philippians must be equally clear about the error of perfectionism. Both these things must be avoided: Judaism and perfectionism. Judaism generally presents itself as a belief in the power of man to save himself by his own works, or in man's reliance upon his birth, upbringing or nationality, these purely carnal and natural things which the Apostle tells us he has left

behind once and for ever. We must avoid all that and realise
that as Christians we are in a spiritual realm and we must
not 'mind' – or set our minds upon – earthly things, but
heavenly things.

That is one danger, and the other is this equally dangerous error of perfectionism which, almost invariably, has
been accompanied by what is commonly known as
antinomianism. In other words, it is quite clear from this
passage that there were people in the church at Philippi who
were threatening the life and the peace and the welfare of
that church. There were people in the early Church (and
they have appeared in the Church from time to time ever
since) who believed that they had arrived at a state of perfection and who then, on being shown that they were guilty
of certain things, did not hesitate either to try to explain
those sins or defects away, or to say they did not matter. It
was, they said, the flesh, but they themselves were all right.
And that is the essence of antinomianism: it says that as long
as I am in Christ, it does not matter what I do; as long as I
am truly Christian, my practices are quite irrelevant.

Now the Apostle says that we must be perfectly clear
about these two things – 'Let us therefore, as many as be
perfect, be thus minded', and by being 'thus minded' he
means that we must be perfectly clear about the whole basis
of our position. You must, says Paul, agree with what I have
just been saying – that we must press on, that we do not rest
upon our oars, that we do not say we have arrived, or that
we have done all we have to do to maintain this state of perfection to which we have attained. It is not that, Paul says,
but rather, our lives in this world must be ever pressing forward towards the mark and the prize and the goal. We must
not congratulate ourselves on our achievements but be ever
'stretching forth'. We must be 'thus minded' – we must get
rid, once and for ever, of the dangers presented by the
Judaisers and by the perfectionists.

Now this is as true today as it was when the Apostle wrote
this letter to the church at Philippi. We must always start
with doctrine and with belief. There is no hope at all in the

Christian life if we are wrong at the very basis and foundation of our whole position. Therefore we agree with the Apostle and realise that the first thing is to have a right mind about these matters, so that if we are asked what it means to be a Christian we know exactly; we realise that we have a foundation which is solid because it is based upon the teaching of Scripture itself. That is the first principle.

But then Paul hurries on to the second point, which is equally important, and it is this: that we must practise that belief and walk in a manner that is consistent with it. 'Nevertheless, whereto we have already attained, let us walk by the same rule, let us mind the same thing.' Now, 'walking by the same rule' just means that we should put into practice that which we have already agreed about as being the right and correct belief. The Apostle is particularly insistent about this. Everywhere in his epistles you find him saying that there is no purpose in having the right belief unless we put that belief into operation. 'Let us therefore, as many as be perfect, be thus minded: and if in any thing ye be otherwise minded, God shall reveal even this unto you.' There are certain things, says Paul, which are absolutely central and vital. There must be no argument and no discussion about them, we must all be clear about them. But, he says, there may be other things about which you are not quite clear – 'if in anything ye be otherwise minded'. If there are certain aspects of the Christian life or of the Christian faith about which you are not clear in your minds, do not lose hold of your Christian faith and practice because of them.

This is surely a very healthy principle. The Apostle's way of dealing with those difficulties and with some intellectual perplexities is this: practice! Put into operation the central things about which you are certain and if you do that, God will then reveal unto you the truth concerning those other things. Do not spend the rest of your life arguing about the things which are not clear to you. There are certain matters in connection with the Christian faith about which Christian people have never been unanimous. I need not mention them now in detail, but Christians differ about Church gov-

ernment, for example. We are familiar with that in this
country. No man can say that one view is the truth and no
other. No, but about justification by faith you can and must
say that, and that is the distinction which the Apostle is trying to bring out. About justification by faith, about the
uselessness of works in the matter of saving one's own soul,
there is to be no question at all, we must all be thus minded,
it is dogmatic and definite.

But there are other matters about which we may not be
clear: a particular form of baptism, for instance, or a particular interpretation of prophetic teaching – pre-millennial,
post-millennial and a- or non-millennial. Now those are in
the realm where no one can say, 'This is the truth and there
is no other.' There is room for legitimate difference of opinion, and the saints of God have differed about these matters
throughout the ages. Very well, says Paul, get hold of the
essential things, put them into practice, and if you do that
honestly, then you can be perfectly sure in your mind that
God will reveal to you those other matters about which you
are not clear and certain at the moment. He does not say
when this is going to happen, but he does say that eventually
we shall be given clear teaching.

That, then, is the distinction. We must always maintain in
our minds that there are some things that are absolutely
essential to salvation, and there are other matters which are
not, though they may be important. So the essence of wisdom in the Christian life is to draw a sharp distinction
between these two things; never to regard the essential
matters with indifference and never to regard matters which
belong to the realm of indifference as if they were essential.
We must never mix matters about which there can be no
certainty in this life with matters which are central and all-
important in Christian living.

Anyone who is familiar with Church history, will realise
what an important principle this is. Have we not all known
Christian people who have made their Christian life
unhappy simply because they would take things which we
cannot arrive at with any certainty and make them tests of

orthodoxy, and insisted that we should agree with them absolutely before we could have fellowship with them? How much harm has been done in the Church because of that, because men and women would not implement the teaching of the Apostle at that point. 'Let us therefore . . . be thus minded: and if in anything ye be otherwise minded, God shall reveal even this unto you' – that is it. Out with Judaism! Out with perfectionism! 'Let us walk by the same rule, let us mind the same thing'; practise what you are certain of, put into operation that which is beyond a doubt, be careful and diligent always to implement these central matters about which there can be no discussion. I hope that all who are following me in this argument will join me in admiration of the balance and the sanity of Christian teaching, and I trust that we can see that most of the heresies of the Church, and also most of the unhappy divisions in the Church – for I would differentiate between happy and legitimate differences and unhappy divisions – have been due to the fact that men and women have failed to grasp this teaching and to draw these vital distinctions between central and peripheral, between absolute and doubtful.

The next piece of advice which Paul gives us is an exhortation to follow good examples – 'Brethren,' he says, 'be followers together of me.' Here again we cannot but be amazed at the magnificence of the Apostle's teaching and especially at his condescension. He is concerned about doctrine, and in order to help the members of the church at Philippi he says, in effect, 'I have given you the teaching in that bald, unvarnished, theoretical manner, but if you really want to know what I mean, let me put it like this: follow my example, and not only my example, but follow the example of those who are your teachers.' Now there is very little doubt but that he is referring partly to the two men of whom we read in the second chapter, Epaphroditus and Timothy. These men had helped in the teaching and the building up of the church at Philippi, he has already made reference to them, and Paul is exhorting the Philippians to look at them – people they have known.

Notice, too, the way in which the Apostle turns from himself and includes the others: 'Be followers together of me, and mark them which walk so as ye have us for an ensample.' I am not quite sure that I agree with those people who think this is said by the Apostle merely out of modesty. What he means is that he does not hesitate to ask them to follow him – that is not egotism on the part of the Apostle, it is simply stating a literal truth. This man who had been saved by the Lord Jesus Christ, and had given his whole life to pleasing his Lord, was the man who had a right to ask others to imitate and follow him. He does so frequently in his letters, and yet no man who has a spiritual mind at all would feel like charging the Apostle with pride. There was never a more humble man than Paul; his life was such that he could turn to these people and say, I am presenting you with an example and illustration, and this is the illustration: 'Not that I have already attained or were already perfect, but I follow after.' That is what he tells them to follow. 'I am exhorting you,' he says in effect, 'to do the very thing that I am doing myself. I am not satisfied with my life and achievements, so I am pressing on towards the mark and the goal. Be followers of me, do the same thing I am doing. But it is not only true of me, it is true also of Epaphroditus, and of Timothy.' And he thus exhorts these members of the church at Philippi to follow their great and glorious example.

Once again, is there anything that can be of greater practical value to the Christian who is anxious to live a truly Christian life than to follow such good examples? Is there anything that so helps us in our endeavour to attain unto that ultimate goal than to read the lives of God's saints, the biographies of good, godly men and women? Speaking for myself, I can certainly testify that I have found nothing of greater value and encouragement. You see the truth in practice; you see it translated from the realm of pure teaching and put into operation. To me it is one of the saddest features of the life of the Church today that so often people are ignorant of the great saints of the past. Our fathers were familiar with them and spent a lot of time reading about them and these great biographies are still available. Surely nothing can do us greater good than to read and study them, that we may follow their example even as the Apostle exhorts us at this point.

The last piece of advice which Paul gives is that we should take warning from bad examples: 'Many walk, of whom I have told you often, and now tell you even weeping, that they are the enemies of the cross of Christ . . . who mind earthly things.' It is not only right to follow good examples, it is equally important that we should observe these illustrations of bad Christian living. We are provided with many of them in the Bible itself, and there is no doubt that this is why the cases of these men and women are recorded there; they are set up as great warnings to God's people. We find the story of Cain, of the people of Sodom and Gomorrah, and we have the example of the Children of Israel; these various illustrations have surely been recorded for our benefit – we are told of people who have not lived the godly life and we behold what has happened to them.

And can we not find the same thing in subsequent Church history? Nothing is more valuable and useful than familiarising ourselves with the great history of the Church in the past, keeping our eye on the positive and the negative, as the Apostle exhorts us at this point. Here is the Apostle's prescription for a happy, successful and full Christian life; be absolutely certain in your mind about the things that are vital, and the moment you are certain of them, put them into practice.

But Paul is inculcating here a doctrine on the whole question of the relationship between faith and practice. Let me note what I regard as his essential teaching in this matter. The first thing, surely, is that our belief will always determine our conduct. The Apostle and his friends lived the life they lived because they were 'thus minded'. Paul lived the life he lived because he had seen the error of Judaism and has been delivered out of it; he had seen the positive truth concerning Christ and he had also seen the error of perfectionism. Thus the Apostle's conduct as he ran the Christian race was determined by the belief that he held.

In exactly the same way, he tells us, the conduct of people who are living unworthy lives and 'whose end is destruction' is also the outcome of their belief. The trouble with them is that they 'mind earthly things'; their real interest is in the world and in life as it is lived in this world. Their mind, their concern, their interest, their thoughts are earthbound, and Paul says that they are the people of whom we can say, 'their god is their belly', and 'their glory is in their shame'. Why? because 'they mind earthly things'. A man's conduct is finally determined by his belief and by his faith.

Is that not being painfully proved and manifested in this modern world of ours at this present time? Look at the conduct of the vast majority of people. What explains it? Well, surely, the simple answer is that they hold a wrong belief. That is why education, culture and all these things cannot save the situation. The trouble with the world for the last fifty years or so has been this: it has said, 'Yes, Christianity is all right, but we need not be bothered about Christian dogma and doctrine.' The world would like to hold on to Christian ethics, that is why it is so fond of praising the Sermon on the Mount, but it does not want all this talk about Jesus of Nazareth being the Son of God, and about his incarnation, and his death upon the cross. So the world has brushed aside Christian doctrine and has fondly believed that it can hold on to that which it thinks is good in Christian ethics. But that is impossible in the light of what the Bible says about belief and Christian teaching. It is useless for a man to say he believes in God, but does not see any need to keep the Ten Commandments; and it is equally idle to expect people to believe in the Ten Commandments without believing in God – which is the first commandment. Faith determines conduct and the modern world is nothing but an eloquent exhibition of the soundness of this fact. We must start with the belief and faith principle, for a man's conduct always expresses what he ultimately believes.

Let me put that in a slightly different form in a second

principle. Conduct is the best index to the nature and the value of our belief. In other words, show me a man's conduct and I can tell you his belief. That is the reason why the Apostle here so constantly exhorts these Christians to make certain that their conduct is in accordance with their belief. In Titus 2:3, Paul uses the expression 'as becometh holiness' – that is his argument for holy living. 'Can you not see,' he says in effect, 'that it is truly inconsistent to say you believe one thing, if you are doing the exact opposite?' That is the New Testament argument for sanctity and holiness. If we believe that Christ died for our sins in order to deliver us out of that realm, how can we continue in sin? It is utterly inconsistent and the Apostle does not hesitate to say that there is no value at all in the supposed faith and belief of a man who constantly lives the other life – 'Be not deceived; God is not mocked' (Gal. 6:7). It is possible for a man to make a whole series of intellectual assertions, but if he lives his life altogether in the other direction, it is proof positive that his faith is not of the slightest value and is indeed not real faith at all. There is no difference in this between James and Paul; they are saying exactly the same thing in different ways. A man's conduct is the final proof and testimony of the reality or the value of his profession and belief.

And then, lastly, the ultimate test of a man's belief and conduct is the cross. 'Many walk, of whom I have told you often . . . that they are the enemies of the cross of Christ . . .' Notice here that Paul says these people are the enemies of the cross of Christ. What really proves the ultimate error of the Judaisers is that they are doing away with the cross. Those who tell me that they can put themselves right with God by living a good life, are enemies of the cross of Christ because, in effect, they are saying that the cross of Christ will not save them. The friend of the cross says, 'Nothing but that cross can save me.' Any one who in any way adds to or detracts from it is an enemy of that cross – that is the final condemnation of the Judaiser and of the moraliser. All people who say that by their own efforts they can fit themselves to stand in the presence of God, are the enemies of the cross, they are detracting from its glory.

But you can do exactly the same thing in your conduct, says the Apostle. He is talking about people who are living the wrong kind of life, whose gods are their lusts, their passions, their carnal nature, who live for these things, who 'mind earthly things'. Paul says equally of them that they are enemies of the cross of Christ. Is there any class of person who brings the cross into greater disrepute than that? Have you seen people who talk about the cross and say that Christ died for them, and yet they are living an immoral life? I have seen a man in a drunken condition proclaiming that he believed that Christ died for him – preaching the cross as it were – and yet his very conduct not only denied it, but proved that he was an enemy of that cross. He brought it to shame and into disrepute.

If we believe what we claim about this cross, how careful we must be. By our behaviour, by our conduct, we can show we are the enemies of the cross, we can cause men to ridicule, blaspheme and laugh at it. Not only that, we are really denying its purpose and its function. Let me remind you of how Paul put it to Titus. He says Christ died, in order that he might 'purify unto himself a peculiar people, zealous of good works' (Tit. 2:14). Why did our Lord die that death on the cross? Why did he go to Calvary? There is the answer: that he might separate these people from sin, from iniquity, from shame, and make of them 'a people zealous of good works'. So if I am not zealous of good works, if I am living a sinful, worldly, carnal life, I am obviously the enemy of the cross of Christ.

The cross, therefore, is the ultimate test both of my faith and belief, and of my conduct and practice. What a tremendous responsibility there rests upon those of us who are Christians! How careful we must always be to see that these two things are intimately related, for as long as we keep the cross in front of us as the touchstone of our lives, we can never go far astray. Is the cross vital and everything to me? Does my life proclaim that I believe that he died there for me, not only that my sins might be forgiven, but that I might be delivered from the whole realm of sin and might become a child of God, being prepared by God for the glory that yet awaits me with him?

My faith determines my conduct; my conduct is a proclamation and statement with regard to my faith; and both of them together are always tested ultimately by what they say about the cross. God grant that we may all be people whose whole life, faith and conduct are centred there.

Chapter 10

Citizens of heaven

> For our conversation is in heaven; from whence also we
> look for the Saviour, the Lord Jesus Christ: who shall
> change our vile body, that it may be fashioned like
> unto his glorious body, according to the working
> whereby he is able even to subdue all things unto him-
> self (Phil. 3:20–21).

An alternative translation of these verses – which is more or
less that of the Revised Version – would be this: 'For our
citizenship is in heaven; from whence also we look for the
Saviour, the Lord Jesus Christ: who shall change this body
of our humiliation, that it may be fashioned [or made con-
formable] unto the body of his glorification, according to the
energy of his power whereby he is able to subdue all things
unto himself.'

We must all agree, I am sure, that these verses are a grand
climax to a great chapter. We have worked through this
third chapter of Paul's epistle to the Philippians in several
studies and we have seen that, from time to time, individual
statements in it stand out prominently and are some of the
most magnificent statements ever made by this great Apostle. It is a chapter full of great and noble and wonderful
things. It is a unique description of the Apostle's own
experience; his clear and unmistakable definition, several
times over, of the Christian; and we have seen the seriousness with which he rejects the false teaching of the Judaisers and the Antinomians and various other people. But
above all, running through it all, there is an exalted and

magnificent conception of the Christian life and the individual Christian position. And here in these two verses Paul winds it all up and brings it to a glorious and magnificent climax.

That is the way in which we approach these two verses. They must be regarded as the summary of everything that Paul has been saying in the great argument in this chapter. It is, therefore, perfectly true to describe these two verses as another reminder of just what it means to be a Christian. They express the essence of the position of the New Testament gospel as the Apostle puts it here. As we have seen, he has exhorted the members of the church at Philippi to follow his example: Be followers of me, he says, and of all who walk in the way I walk. And he has reinforced it by a negative; there are those, he says, 'of whom I have told you often, and now tell you even weeping, that they are the enemies of the cross of Christ: whose end is' not this glory to which we are moving but – destruction. Their God is not the Lord Jesus Christ, but their carnal lusts and passions; their glory is not the glorification that awaits us, but their shame, and they mind earthly things. That is their ultimate trouble. But, Paul concludes, 'our conversation [our citizenship] is in heaven.' In other words, he gives this particularly glorious definition here of the whole Christian position because he is anxious to make a final appeal to them for holy living and for running along this road of sanctification.

But before we come to look at these two verses in detail, it is, I think, important that we should bear in mind that one great principle: our citizenship is in heaven. This is typical of the New Testament appeal for holiness, which is always expressed in terms of what we are. That is where New Testament holiness is – I do not hesitate to say it – essentially different from morality. Morality is always interested in actions per se, that is why it has to produce particular arguments, whether in the matter of drink or of anything else. The whole business of morality is to show defects; but while the gospel does not deny all that, it is never the basis of its appeal. The New Testament never tells a man to avoid drunkenness because of the effect upon his body; the Christian teaching is that a man is not to be guilty of drunkenness because he is a citizen of heaven, a child of God. The argument is on a higher plane and, as I said, this is something we must always bear in mind.

I emphasise this because I believe much harm has been done to the Christian cause and the Christian Church because of that sad confusion between morality and New Testament holiness; because of a concern about details at the expense of principle; because of the failure to see that there is a different setting altogether to the New Testament concern about life and living and about holiness and conduct. It is the difference between Judaism and Christianity; between that concern about detail and the law, and this other grand and glorious conception of a state and position.

So, having reminded ourselves that we must never lose sight of this great principle, let us consider how Paul describes the Christian at this point. We can best divide our subject into two headings which suggest themselves at once. The Christian is to live this type of life, he is to follow Paul and all others who are partakers of the Christian life, and he is to do that first and foremost because he is what he is, and secondly, he is to do it because of what he hopes to be. Now let us take the first reason. What is a Christian? The Apostle's answer is that in the first place the Christian is a citizen of heaven; the Authorised Version has, 'Our conversation is in heaven', others have said that it should be translated: 'we are a colony of heaven' – they all mean the same. To me, the important thing to emphasise is the word *is* – our citizenship *is* in heaven. I put that emphasis in order to show that the Apostle is not saying, 'our citizenship will be in heaven', but it is so now!

In other words the authorities have agreed that the word 'is', that is used here by Paul, is the word which means 'being already in existence and manifesting itself'; or, as Dr Lightfoot puts it, 'our citizenship is even now in heaven'. It is even now already a fact – not that we are going to be, but that we are. And here again we are confronted by one of the primary, fundamental, New Testament doctrines. This is just another way of stating the doctrine of regeneration and of the rebirth. As we look at a great description like this of the Christian, does it not make us feel that the little definitions of the Christian that are so often current at the present time, are not only inadequate but almost insulting? Think of describing the Christian simply as one who lives a morally decent life! Perhaps I should not speak like this of morality, I do not do it in any controversial spirit, but because I am jealous of this glorious life we have in Christ and with the Apostle, and it makes me weep to think of the Christian life as just a good life, a life which is just a little better than that of the average person. Christians are people who are already citizens of heaven, people who have been translated and elevated.

Let me give you some of Paul's other statements which put this whole matter so perfectly. For example, in writing to the Ephesians, he says, 'But God, who is rich in mercy, for his great love wherewith he loved us, even when we were dead in sins, hath quickened us together with Christ, (by grace ye are saved;) and hath raised us up together, and made us sit together in heavenly places in Christ Jesus' (Eph. 2:4–6). The Christian is already sitting together with Christ Jesus in the heavenly places – we are there in a spiritual sense, we are citizens of heaven. Or take the way in which Paul puts it in his letter to the Colossians, where he says exactly the same things again: our Lord, 'hath delivered us from the power of darkness, and hath translated us into the kingdom of his dear Son' (Col. 1:13).

Now this is a conception which is so magnificent that it tends to elude us. It was difficult for the members of the church at Philippi, suffering as they were, to realise that they were already seated in the heavenly places in Christ. It is equally difficult for us today, and yet this is the first thing we must lay hold of. We are not citizens of that heavenly kingdom because we have taken up naturalisation papers; you can be a citizen of any other country by going through a legal procedure, but you remain the same person that you were before. That is not the New Testament conception. We are citizens of heaven because we have been born again, we are citizens by birth. We have not paid any price in order to obtain our citizenship; it is not a question of a legal transaction; we have been made, we are new beings, we are partakers of the divine nature, we are sons of God. We are in the kingdom and have our citizenship by birth and blood, and by nothing less. So the claim that Paul makes for the Christian is that the Christian is essentially different from all those who are not Christians.

The Apostle has, of course, got in his mind the contrast he has drawn of those people who are living an unworthy life, those people he has been calling the enemies of Christ – 'You should not for a moment even contemplate living like that,' he says in effect, 'you do not belong to the same realm. They belong to the kingdom of this world, you are citizens of heaven' – that is the New Testament position. As Christian people, if we are at all worthy of the name, we are at this moment essentially different from those who are not Christians, not just a little bit better, not merely different on the surface, but different in our being as the result of the rebirth. We have a new citizenship, we are in Christ, and because we are in Christ, we are seated in the heavenly places with him. Certain things will happen to us before we finally arrive in heaven, but our citizenship is as definite now as it will be then. There will be a physical translation when we die, but spiritually we are there already, we belong there. This point will become clearer as we move on to a further elaboration of the Christian.

What, then, does this citizenship mean? Why does the Apostle put it in this way? Perhaps the best way of explaining it, is to elaborate that contrast at which I have already hinted. Every living person, according to New Testament teaching, is in one of two kingdoms – there are only two, the kingdom of heaven and the kingdom of this world; the kingdom of God and the kingdom of Satan. The Apostle and the other New Testament writers talk about the kingdom of Satan, the dominion of Satan and the god of this world.

They talk about the prince of the power of the air who controls the lives of those who do not believe, and about the kingdom of darkness – these are the terms they use. And over and against all these is this other kingdom, the kingdom of God, the kingdom of heaven, the kingdom of his dear Son, the kingdom of light, and so on. There is no mean between these two opposites, there is no neutral ground; if we are not in the kingdom of God, we are in the kingdom of Satan, it is one or the other. So here, as he emphasises the fact that our citizenship is in heaven, Paul is saying that we are in a different kingdom and we claim a different allegiance.

The first characteristic of a kingdom is the king, the head of the state, the one to whom you give allegiance. Paul is drawing a contrast here. Of those other people, he says their 'god is their belly' and by that he means that they live to their instincts, their lusts, their passions; these are the things that govern and control them, and that is where their allegiance is. You can test where a man's allegiance is by the way he spends his time and money and energy. A man's treasure is where his heart is, and his heart is where his treasure is, as our Lord puts it in the Sermon on the Mount. A man very soon shows what and who his god is. But the position of Christian men and women is that their King is the Lord Jesus Christ, their King is God, he is supreme in their life, and they give their allegiance to him, and to nothing and to no one else. Christians are entirely different in that respect from non-Christians. The thing that must always be true of them is that they are conscious that their lives are dominated by God, that their first concern is the will of God, and his good pleasure.

You see, again, how different that is from morality. You can be perfectly moral without thinking of God, you can be doing a lot of good and living a decent life but God never enters into your thoughts. No, says Paul, that is not the way of the Christian. If you are a Christian you are in a relationship with God, God is your King and your thoughts, therefore, are about him.

The second characteristic is that the Christian lives under a different law, he lives a different type of life, under a different system. Take, for instance, the great argument worked out by Paul in Romans 6. He says, Before you became a Christian you were under the dominion of sin and of Satan but now you are under that dominion no longer. There is nothing, in other words, that is quite so ridiculous as to talk about men and women having a free will: that is not true, we are born in sin, and are under the dominion of sin and of Satan. And that is why people go further and further into sin; they are slaves of the things they do. In Luke 11:21 our Lord talks about the strong man armed who 'keepeth his palace, his goods are in peace' – that is Satan controlling the lives of men and women, while, of course, persuading them that they are at liberty.

This is something that can be easily understood in the international and in the political world at the present time. There is a form of tyranny which persuades you that you are free. And that is what Satan does – he persuades men that they are free, though they are bound in his dominion. But Christians are not in that position. They have been taken out, they are in the kingdom of God, they have a different law, they are subject to different rules and regulations. The whole ordering of their life is different, they have literally been taken right out of one kingdom and translated into another. As citizens of this new kingdom, they are aware of a new code altogether. As there are different customs and rules in the different countries, so there is an essential difference between the kingdom of God and the kingdom of Satan, and the people who are now citizens in the kingdom of God, are aware of altogether new ideas about life. They see things in a different way because they are aware of a new law: this perfect law of liberty.

And the third important thing that is true about citizenship is that it entitles us to different rights and privileges. As citizens of a country, we are entitled to do certain things which people who are not citizens are not entitled to do. In the Christian life this is something of vital importance. As citizens of heaven we have a right of audience with the King, a right of access to the throne, a right of taking our petitions to him and of making our requests to him. The Bible is full of these things. It tells us that God is particularly interested in his people. Speaking to the people through Amos, he says, 'You only have I known . . .' (Amos 3:2). He knew all the other nations, in a sense, but here it means to know in an intimate way. God is particularly concerned and interested in his people, he is in a unique relationship to them. And that is something that you find elaborated in the New Testament. Our Lord himself said to Christian people 'The very hairs of your head are all numbered' (Matt. 10:30). Nothing can happen to you without your Father knowing it. God our Father is interested in us in this intimate sense.

Is this not something upon which we should ponder and meditate at a time like this? Wherever you may find yourself, and in whatever position you may be; you may be at the end of the earth and surrounded by enemies, you may be in the most impossible position – you always have this right of access to your King. As the Psalmist puts it, 'From the end of the earth will I cry unto thee' (Ps. 61:2). These are privileges and rights which belong, inherently, to the citizens of the kingdom.

But let us move on now to something which is, in a sense, of more practical importance and something which we need to emphasise in these days. What are the implications of this citizenship? Now, of course, when Paul tells us that our citizenship is in heaven, he is not teaching that the Christian should not take any interest in this world and the affairs of this life. It is a spiritual relationship, and he is anxious to emphasise that. If I do take an interest, as I should, in this life and world, I must do it in a different way from the man or woman of the world who is not a citizen of the kingdom of heaven. In other words, the Christian, though he is in the world, is not of it. How trite and yet how profound this is; we are in this world like everybody else, but as Christians we are not of it. Many hymns have this kind of teaching, and they often express it by saying that this world is not our home; if we are Christians we are away from home.

> I am a stranger here,
> Heaven is my home

says the old writer, and every Christian should say that.

During the last hundred years people have rather scoffed at that kind of teaching, but as Christians we must come to see that we are but a colony here; our citizenship, our home, is there in heaven. We must be unworldly in that sense and our interest in this world should arise solely from the fact that we believe that it is God's world and we bemoan the havoc that men and women are making of it. It is not that we think that it is the only world and the only life, and that we may as well settle down in it and enjoy ourselves. Not at all! But we believe in restraining the evil, because this world belongs to God. At the same time, if I say I am not of this world, then I must realise the dangers of life in the world, the iniquity, the sin, the arrogance, the foulness that is in it. I am increasingly coming to the conclusion that there is no sounder test of whether people are truly Christians or not, than their view of life in this world. The criterion is not only whether we say we believe certain articles of the faith. Christians who are new men and women and who have a new nature must of necessity take a different view of life in this world from those who are not Christians – it is a thorough and absolute test. The Christian sees the danger of life in this world, and is constantly aware of it; or, to use the Apostle Paul's language, Christians 'mind' other things; their interest is in something else.

Now whether we like it or not, and strange as it may sound to ears which have become so accustomed to a worldly emphasis, New Testament Christians, as is true of Christians in every great period of revival and reawakening, had their minds and their affections set on things above, not on things of the earth. As I said, that does not mean that Christians retire out of life and take no interest in the affairs of this world – but heaven is the place on which their minds are set. They are looking at the things that are not seen, or, to go still further, their pride is in that heavenly citizenship. We all know how citizenship always leads to pride. Some of the deepest thinkers today are telling us that the main cause of our trouble is the pride that people take in national sovereignty, and there is undoubtedly a great truth in that, it can be very dangerous. But pride in citizenship is inevitable, and a true citizen is proud of the fact that he is a citizen. That comes first, that is the thing he boasts of, that is the thing for which he is prepared to sacrifice his life and everything.

Christian people, are we as ready to die for the citizenship which we have in heaven, as we are for our earthly kingdom? I am not setting these two up as opposites; it is just my way of reminding us all that our pride in our heavenly citizenship should be infinitely greater than the pride we have in any earthly position. We should desire the pride of the kingdom of heaven, and, above everything else, it should be our greatest ambition to be worthy of it. 'England expects every man this day will do his duty' – yes, and God and the kingdom of heaven expect it! Though you are away from home, remember that the honour and the dignity of the great kingdom to which you belong is in your hands. There are those other people around and about you who do not belong to your kingdom; they are watching you and they will judge your country by you. Therefore, says the Apostle, remember what you are and live a life that is worthy of this high calling of the heavenly citizen.

But finally, let us briefly consider the Christian's hope. Christians are people who live this kind of life because of the hope that is set before them. This is, perhaps, the greatest and most glorious consolation and encouragement that a Christian can ever have. Our position in the world is exactly as Paul described the position of the Philippians. We are in a world that is utterly hostile to us. It is controlled by Satan and sin, and all these evil forces are arrayed against us. Not only that, we ourselves are not perfect – 'Not as though I

had already attained . . . brethren, I count not myself to
have apprehended' – there are weaknesses and defects in us,
the very body itself gives us trouble, it is weak and subject
to disease and finally to death. That is our position in this
world, surrounded by enemies and weaknesses, troubles
within and without. How can we go on? What is the use of
telling us that we are citizens of heaven? It seems almost a
mockery.

No, says Paul, 'For our conversation is in heaven; from
whence also we look for the Saviour, the Lord Jesus Christ:
who shall change this body of our humiliation, that it may be
fashioned according to the body of his glorification, according to the working of his mighty power whereby he is able
to subdue all things unto himself.' You see what he means?
This is the ultimate consolation. We are looking forward to
something, and that something is the return of the Lord
Jesus Christ. He is going to return and when he returns he
will conquer hell; he will vanquish every foe – Satan, sin,
evil and iniquity. Everything that belongs to the kingdom of
darkness he will finally rout and utterly consume. We look
for the Saviour, the Lord Jesus Christ. Life can be hard, and
it may be worse; we may have to suffer persecution, we may
have to face some of the things that other Christians are facing at the present time. All this may come to us. This is our
answer: Let hell rage, let the kingdoms of this world arise in
their fury, whatever they may do we know that the day is
coming when the Saviour will return, our Lord Jesus Christ.
He will come from his throne in heaven back to this world
as King. He will have the ultimate victory over all and will
reign supreme.

But it does not stop at that. When he comes he is going to
do something else that, in a sense, is even more wonderful
for us. I read in the New Testament of that glory, of my
standing in the presence of God and seeing the holy angels
and seeing my Saviour as he is. I think of this renovated
earth and heaven where everything has been made anew
and I ask: How can I dwell in such a realm or live under
such conditions knowing myself to be what I am? Here is the

answer: Paul says that the Lord is even going to change my vile body – that is, the body of my humiliation – the word 'vile' in the Authorised Version is an unfortunate translation. What he is saying is that the difference between the body of infirmity (Paul was subject to such infirmities and we know, too, that with some people sin is associated with the body) and the glorious future that awaits me is this; he is going to deliver me from everything that is humiliating, it is all going to be taken away and I shall be given a new body. On the road to Damascus Paul saw the risen Lord in all his glory. The brightness was such that it struck him to the ground, and, Paul says, I am to have a body like that. It will be like the glory which came to our Lord on the Mount of Transfiguration, a glorification which will fit us and enable us to spend our eternity in the presence of God. That is what we have to look forward to. You may be weak, you may be tired, you may be conscious of imperfection, but, says the Apostle, go on pressing on down the road, you are not doing it on your own, the Saviour is coming.

That, then, is the final appeal which he makes to all of us – press on, but as you are pressing on, keep your eye on the distance, look forward to the glory, wait for him: 'Whence also we look for the Saviour.' What a word the word 'look' is! It means that we do not look at other things. It is a very powerful word and it means patient waiting, eagerly expecting and anticipating.

That, then, is how the Apostle appeals to men and women for holy living and for the sanctified life. We as Christian people are citizens of heaven. We belong to that realm and the day is coming when the King will return. Then we shall enter into our inheritance and we shall be completely changed. Sin will be entirely removed with all its effects and influences, and, perfect and glorified, we shall dwell with God in the glory for ever and ever. That is our birthright, that is our position. Is it necessary even to appeal to all of us to be worthy of our high calling and to glory in Christ and in his cross, and live for him?

Chapter 11

The life and work of the Church

> Therefore, my brethren dearly beloved and longed for,
> my joy and crown, so stand fast in the Lord, my dearly
> beloved. I beseech Euodias, and beseech Syntyche, that
> they be of the same mind in the Lord. And I intreat thee
> also, true yoke-fellow, help those women which laboured
> with me in the gospel, with Clement also, and with other
> my fellow-labourers, whose names are in the book of life
> (Phil. 4:1–3).

We come now to these first three verses of the fourth chapter, and the very word 'therefore' at the beginning of the
first verse reminds us that there is a close connection
between what the Apostle is now beginning to say and what
he has just been saying at the end of the third chapter.
There we looked at that glorious doctrine of the coming
again of our Lord, conquering his enemies, ridding the
world of evil and indeed even changing this, the body of our
humiliation, and fashioning it, that it might be made conformable to the body of his glorification according to the
energy of that great power of his, whereby he is able even
to subdue all things unto himself. It is a mighty doctrine, no
greater is to be found anywhere. 'Therefore . . .' says the
Apostle; and once more he does something that is characteristic of him. He never states a doctrine for the sake of
stating it, he always applies it, and here he begins to apply
what he has just been saying.

I always find these transitions in the thought of the Apostle Paul particularly fascinating. I can never quite decide for

myself whether he is greatest when he declares his doctrine or when he applies it; I try to discuss this question with myself, and frankly, I cannot arrive at any conclusion. I find him equally fascinating, equally moving, whichever he does. For the truth about the Apostle is that whether he is stating doctrine, or whether he is applying it, he is always doctrinal. He is incapable of handling a problem except in terms of doctrine, so it really makes very little difference whether he is asking us to look at the great declarations objectively, or whether he is putting them in a practical, and immediate and subjective, manner.

So, here, we are dealing with the application, but, as I hope to show you, we shall find that it is full of doctrine, full of teaching, and we shall see that once more Paul proves himself incapable of even handling the problem of quarrelling within the church without putting it in the great context of the whole truth. This 'therefore' is the connecting link and all Paul is going to say about this problem must be considered in the light of what he has been saying about the coming again of our Lord, 'from whence' – from heaven – 'we look for the Saviour'. In addition, we must remember the emphasis he has laid upon the fact that as Christian people we are already citizens of heaven; not 'going to be', we are. And if all that is true of us – 'therefore' that brings us to this particular question.

The Apostle here is still dealing with what we may call the doctrine of the Christian Church. He is doing this because of the particular problem that has arisen in the church at Philippi, but he cannot deal even with that minor problem without the whole character of the Church coming in. So we have here what we can describe as Paul's amazing picture of the nature of the Christian Church, and of the character of her life; and in doing that the Apostle does something else. I suggest it is quite unconscious, but he also gives us a wonderful picture of himself. I confess that it was a real temptation to me, in thinking about these three verses, and meditating upon them, to divide this matter into two, because we have here two pictures, one of Paul the pastor, and the other of the church in which he ministered. I have decided, however, that we cannot go into detail here with the picture of Paul himself, except perhaps, as it appears when we deal with the other doctrine; but I cannot refrain from pointing out the way in which Paul addresses this church: 'My brethren, dearly beloved and longed for, my joy and crown, so stand fast,' again it comes – 'my dearly beloved.' That is to be the relationship between a minister and the members of his church, and any minister who reads words like these must feel humbled and almost humiliated. That is the relationship between pastor and people, this burning, blazing love. Most of the Philippian church had entered into the kingdom as the result of Paul's preaching, so he calls them his joy and crown. They constitute a kind of garland which he will wear on the great day, a crown of victory. He loves them dearly, and here he gives us an extraordinary picture of this intimate, loving relationship.

Consider also the remarkable humility displayed by the Apostle. Notice how he addresses Euodias and Syntyche – he does not command, he beseeches them. This supreme evangelist and teacher, this great Apostle, asks these two women to come together. Please, says the Apostle, will you . . .? He might have commanded them, but he does not, he comes right down to their level and he begs them. It is a wonderful insight, in passing, into the character of this noble man of God.

But we must give our attention now to what these three verses tell us about the doctrine of the nature and character of the Christian Church. The problem with which the Apostle has to deal is the trouble in the church at Philippi between these two women, Euodias and Syntyche. These two, for some reason or other, are quarrelling and causing trouble in the church, and Paul, loving the church as he does, and anxious as he is for her perfection, has to deal with that trouble. And his way of doing so is to put the dispute in the setting of the whole doctrine of the Church. Oh, if the Christian Church had always remembered that, how many troubles would have been avoided! Every problem, it does not matter how small and insignificant, must always be put into its larger context. In a church there is no such thing as an isolated problem. You cannot consider such a problem without considering it in the light of the nature of the Church, and this is how Paul does it here.

He has three main things to say about the Church. The first concerns the task of the Church, which, according to the Apostle, is to 'labour in the gospel'. He speaks of Euodias and Syntyche as 'those women which laboured with me in the gospel'. Paul has already introduced us to this same thought at the beginning of the epistle; in chapter 1:5 he thanks the Philippians for their 'fellowship in the gospel from the first day until now'; they had been working or labouring with him – it was their fellowship, their partnership in the gospel. Then in the eighth verse he says, 'For God is my record, how greatly I long after you all in the bowels of Jesus Christ'; and also in the seventh verse, 'Even as it is meet for me to think this of you all, because I have you in my heart; inasmuch as both in my bonds, and in the defence and confirmation of the gospel, ye all are partakers of my grace'; and again in 1:27; it is the same thing in all these verses.

Clearly, therefore, that is the primary task of the Christian Church. It is a missionary task; that is always Paul's conception of the Church, and that is the New Testament picture of it. The Church is a body of people set in a world that is under the control of sin and Satan, a world opposed to God, a world that is rushing unconsciously to perdition. So what, in view of that, is the business of the Church? It is to hold forth the gospel, it is to speak to that world and to tell it about its sin and its desperate condition, to tell it about the Saviour and the only way of salvation – that is the business of the Church. Paul himself travelled over that ancient world doing just that, and wherever he got a body of people together he formed them into a church and told them to go out and do the same thing. He thanks God for the members of the church at Philippi because they are doing that work with him; they have helped him; they are all partakers in this ministry.

The Book of Acts is full of this. We read not only of the Apostles themselves but of the most ordinary Christians, who were all scattered abroad as the result of persecution, and wherever they went they preached the word. The record of the early Church in the first century bears abundant and eloquent testimony to the fact that the gospel was spread, in the first place, by the ordinary Christians. By telling people about it and living it in their daily lives, they spread it abroad.

But apart from that, this very section which we are considering together here impresses this upon our minds. This 'true yoke-fellow' was doing the same work, together with these women who had laboured with Paul in the gospel, and Clement also and those other fellow labourers. The missionary task of the Church is a task for every single individual Christian. We are all meant to be involved in it. The Church was in danger of losing sight of this particular truth many years ago, when the churches and chapels were full and when it was the fashionable and popular thing to be a Christian, and, surely, there is a very real danger of our forgetting it at this present time. For never was there a time, perhaps, when the individual Christian should realise his or her importance in this matter so much as today; in our daily life and living, we are to spread abroad this Good News.

It is to be done in many ways; we are not all to do it by preaching from pulpits. In a sense, we can all preach it, we are all to be engaged in prayer, prayer for the preaching and the propagation of the gospel and prayer for the souls of men and women. Then we can all do it by witnessing in our lives, and by the way in which we conduct our business, or practise our profession. People will see that there is something different about us, and then we can give the explanation. We can also bring others to listen to the word of God and we ourselves can attend meetings where the word of God is preached. Now every one of these people in Philippi, Paul tells us, was a helper; they were all taking part in the work and it is quite clear that they were taking part in some of those ways.

Do you know that you take part in the preaching of the gospel by being present? It is an encouragement to the preacher. I frankly confess that I never quite understand those who feel that it is sufficient for them, in desperate times like this, to attend the house of God but infrequently. When people who may not have been to church for years come into the house of God, they are impressed by the fact that large numbers of people still believe in listening to the gospel. So, my Christian friend, if you feel you have no gift, let me assure you here and now that you are one of those people whose name is written in the Book of Life, and your presence in a service of worship is a great help.

In addition, the Apostle makes it very plain in all his epistles that there were those who helped in the propagation of the gospel by just ministering to his own personal need. Take, for instance, the man called Onesiphorus. In 2 Timothy 1:16 Paul thanks God for that man because when he was a prisoner in Rome, Onesiphorus went and visited him. Now Paul was an outstanding mighty man, and you would have thought he would have been quite above any need like that, but he thanks God for this man who visited him in his bonds, and cheered up the great Apostle who was feeling a certain amount of depression. There is an endless number of ways in which we can all preach the gospel, and become labourers together in it, and spread it abroad.

But, above all, we do it by making the gospel attractive to others and awakening an interest in it as we live the Christian life. We can be such people that those who come into contact with us will know that there is something different about us and want to know the explanation.

But let me go on to something still more important. If labouring in the gospel is the great task of the Church, let us consider certain essentials to the performance of that task, and this is the burden of these three verses. Certain things are essential, and the first is that we should realise the lordship of Christ. Notice what the Apostle longs for:

'I beseech Euodias, and beseech Syntyche, that they be of the same mind in the Lord.' Now we have always got to start there – the lordship of Christ. All the Apostle's appeals were made in these terms. When dealing here with this little trouble that has arisen in the church at Philippi, Paul does not appeal to these women to put it right for his sake. He does not say, 'You are spoiling my church.' He does not beg them to put this thing right for the sake of his reputation. Not at all! He says, 'in the Lord', for the Lord's sake. Neither does he appeal to them to put this right for their own sake, or for the reputation of the church at Philippi. The New Testament never does that, it always makes its appeal in the name of the Lord. Perhaps the New Testament Christians were not as interested in the local church as we are. We are so fond of talking about our church or our denomination and it is always in this personal sense. But the Apostle says, 'in the Lord', and for this good reason: it is the Lord's work.

You remember that mighty statement in chapter 1:6? It is the Lord's work. He began it, and it is he, says the Apostle in the second chapter, who is keeping it going: God is working in you 'both to will and to do of his good pleasure'. And it is he who is going to bring it to its final consummation. Once more it must strike us, that if only the Church had been careful to observe this, how different its history would have been. It is the Lord's work; we would never have been in the Church but for the grace of the Lord. It is not our Church, it is the Church of God. The glory, therefore, must be his, the honour must be his, he must be in control and our every decision must be taken in his presence, for he is supreme. The Lord himself bought the Church with his own blood; it belongs to him and everything in the Church must always be put in that relationship. If only we were careful to start at that point, most of our difficulties would immediately and automatically disappear.

The second thing we are exhorted to do, the second essential principle for the Christian Church, is to 'stand fast in the Lord'. This, again, is one of Paul's great phrases. He says the same thing to the church at Corinth: 'Watch ye, stand fast in the faith, quit you like men, be strong' (1 Cor. 16:13). He has already told the Philippians to do this: 'Only let your conversation be as it becometh the gospel of Christ: that whether I come and see you, or else be absent, I may hear of your affairs, that ye stand fast in one spirit . . .' (Phil. 1:27) – stand firm, if you like, it means the same thing. Stand fast in the Lord. What does Paul mean when he uses this expression? We can put it like this: we must stand fast in the faith. You see the sequence? The task of the Church is a missionary task, she is to preach the gospel, she is to tell forth this good news, to bring salvation to men and women, but she cannot do that unless she is sure of her faith. Paul does not say stand fast together, but stand fast in the Lord, stand fast in the faith.

I am not anxious to be controversial at this point, but these days we hear a good deal of talk about ecumenicity, and with the general spirit of such talk we are all in agreement. But I am here to assert that, even before that, comes this truth: stand fast in the Lord. How can I stand fast and firm with the man who denies the deity of my Lord? How can I stand shoulder to shoulder, and in rank, with a man who does not believe in miracles and in the supernatural? How can I keep in line with a man who denies the substitutionary aspects of the atonement? No, we are not merely exhorted by the Apostle to stand together and present a common front against the enemy, not at all! That is not my standard, that is not what brings us together. It is the truth, the truth concerning the Lord himself. Stand fast, says Paul, do not compromise. Stand fast in the truth and hold on to what you know to be right. Put the Lord first, because if you are true to him, and stand fast in him, you can do mightier things than a great army that is uncertain about its truth and doctrine.

Furthermore, if you do not stand fast in the Lord, then you do not have a gospel to preach. If the Church is uncertain of her own message, how can she evangelise? The strength of the Church lies in her message and the power of the Holy Spirit. Alas, how often has she forgotten this! What a temptation it is to concentrate on being highly organised and to think that if we can present a great crowd it will have an impact upon the people. History denies that. Churches were filled a hundred or so years ago, but in spite of that we are faced with the present position. Numbers never convince. It is the truth that convinces, and the great thing for us is to put this first. We must stand firm in the truth, in the message, for without it we have no power. We may be very nice and kind to one another, but that will not convince the world of sin, and bring them to Jesus. The truth alone can do that. That is the second thing.

Then the next principle is that we must also be 'of the same mind'. 'I beseech Euodias, and beseech Syntyche, that they be of the same mind in the Lord.' Once more you see what a perfect picture this is of the Church. Here is the Church, her task is to be a missionary Church, she must be careful that she is doing everything for the Lord, and that she has the right message. She must not play with it or compromise with it in any sense. That is the danger of the heresy with which Paul has been dealing in the third chapter; it is one of the dangers that arises from within. And another danger was arising within the church at Philippi. These two women are clearly quarrelling with each other, they are trying to form rival factions and the Apostle beseeches them to stop, because such a thing will spoil the record, it will upset the whole testimony of the church and will overthrow everything he is trying to do.

We must be careful, therefore, not only to guard against heresies that come from without, but against our own spirits too, against the subtle temptations that arise from within ourselves which can spoil the work. That is the way in which the Apostle puts it negatively. We must not be like Euodias and Syntyche who were forming factions. They were not speaking to each other, they were trying to corrupt the people around them; there was a whispering, and they were refusing to work with each other. If only you realised, says the Apostle, that you are all under the Lord and that none of you would be in the Church but for his grace, you would not do this thing – stop doing it!

But let me show you how he puts it positively; I will just note the interesting words which Paul uses. 'I intreat thee also, true yokefellow, help those women which laboured with me in the gospel.' Now there has been much dispute about who is meant by 'yokefellow', but what the Apostle is saying is, 'You dear helper, help these women to come together.' And I am particularly entranced by the description which the Apostle gives here of this helper of his. He calls him 'true yokefellow'. You see the picture, do you not? Think of that long pole with the cross bar and a bit of leather at each end and an ox on each side of it. The oxen are yoked together and the secret of successful ploughing is that the two go forward together. And here was a man whom the Apostle describes as a true yokefellow. He was always doing the right thing, he was pulling together with Paul; that is the spirit which is needed in the Church.

Then Paul tells us that these women had once been doing the right thing: 'I intreat thee also, true yokefellow, help those women which laboured with me in the gospel.' That was the tragedy of Euodias and Syntyche; there was a time when they had been glad to help, when they had laboured with the Apostle in the gospel. Now it is a pity that the Authorised Version here uses this word 'laboured' because in this verse Paul refers to other people as 'fellow-labourers', and in the Greek it is not the same word. What Paul is actually saying is this: Help these women who were fellow athletes with me in the past. It is a picture of a group of athletes in a team – the Olympic games or something like that – and the whole secret was that you put loyalty to your team first. You did not run in the race to gain honour for yourself, you were working in a team; you were fellow athletes. Paul is saying that in the past Euodias and Syntyche had sacrificed everything in the interests of the Church and of the Lord. Help them to come back to that, says Paul.

That should be the spirit of a team: we should be working

together; or, as Paul puts it later on: we must be fellow workers, fellow labourers. Or perhaps, to put it at its very highest, our ambition should always be to become like the Apostle Paul himself. You notice the spirit of love that encompassed him and the way he loved the members of this church. You notice the humility. As we have seen, instead of commanding these women, he beseeches them, he is almost in tears as he comes down to their level. 'I beg you,' says Paul. 'Please put this right.'

Notice, too, Paul's wisdom and his discrimination. He does not command the two women, he *pleads* with them, he beseeches them; but when he has a man like this, whom he describes as his true yokefellow, he intreats him.* That is the thing needed in the Christian Church – discrimination in the way in which we deal with people. Why is this spirit so important? It is because, if the Church is not right in this respect, she grieves the Holy Spirit, and if she grieves the Holy Spirit, she loses her power and she cannot be a missionary Church. Moreover, if the Church fails in her spirit, it is a denial of the message she preaches, and above and beyond it all, it is dishonouring to the Lord himself and, after all, the Church is his.

So, then, those are the things that are essential – the lordship of Christ, standing fast and firm in the truth and guarding our spirits against every kind of subtle temptation. But let us finish with Paul's last great point – the encouragements to the performance of this task. How glorious they are! Paul says, 'I intreat thee also . . . help those women . . . with Clement also, and with other my fellow-labourers whose names are in the book of life.' Am I going too far when I suggest that what the Apostle was really saying was this: 'Not only these women and Clement, and all those other people – I have forgotten their names, it does not matter, these names are written in the book of life.' I know of

---

* In the Greek two different words are used and the second word is not as emphatic. The New International Version here uses the words 'plead' and 'ask', which perhaps makes Dr Martyn Lloyd-Jones' point even more clear. (Ed.)

no greater encouragement than that. Do you remember what our Lord said to his disciples who went out to preach? They were full of pride and elation; they said, 'Lord, even the devils are subject unto us through thy name,' but our Lord said to them, 'Rejoice not, that the spirits are subject unto you; but rather rejoice, because your names are written in heaven' (Luke 10:17, 20).

Beloved Christian people, that is the greatest ambition and the highest privilege we can ever have – that our names are written in the book of life. Here is your encouragement. All is known to God. The world may never know, the Church herself may never know what you have been doing. It may have been some quiet work behind the scenes and the devil may tempt you and say, 'Why go on with it? Why bother with it? Everybody talks about the man in the pulpit and certain obvious officials, but is your work worth going on with? Stay at home and do nothing!' But let me remind you of this, your name is written in the book of life. The minister may know nothing of what you are doing and neither may anyone else, but God knows it. Nothing you do goes unrecorded and your Father who sees in secret shall himself reward you openly. Remember also that he is the Judge; the books will be open to him and he is absolutely just. Do not feel that somebody else is having greater credit than you. That may be true on earth, but when you come before him it will not be true. You will have justice, all your humblest actions are recorded and known. He is absolutely fair, you need never fear. Do not worry what man may do unto you, the Lord is our judge and he is our keeper.

Furthermore, let me remind you that your reward is certain and glorious. If your name is written in that book, you are going to the glory and ultimately it does not matter very much what man may do to you. As Paul puts it once and for ever at the end of that mighty fifteenth chapter of the first epistle to the Corinthians, 'Forasmuch as ye know that your labour is not in vain in the Lord.' And so:

> Go labour on, spend and be spent
> Thy joy to do the Father's will.

H. Bonar

Your names are written in the book of life. Seeing that privilege, and holding on to it, go on with your work to the glory of the Lord.

Chapter 12

Rejoice always*

Rejoice in the Lord alway: and again I say, Rejoice (Phil. 4:4).

As we come now to consider this well-known exhortation of the Apostle Paul, it is important for us to remember that the whole history of the early Church, and indeed all the New Testament epistles, can only be understood in the light of the pouring forth of the Holy Spirit upon that infant Church in Jerusalem. It is one of those historical events that is in series with the great crucial events recorded in Scripture, with the story of the Children of Israel in the Old Testament, the call of Abraham, the calling out of Egypt, the crossing of the Red Sea and the crossing of Jordan. It is in a series with events like the incarnation, the birth of Christ, his death, his resurrection, and ascension.

Pentecost is an event which we must always hold firmly in our minds, because apart from that we cannot hope to understand either the Book of Acts itself, or any one of the New Testament epistles. Someone has said that the Acts of the Apostles might well be named the 'Acts of the Holy Ghost', and whether that is so or not, it is clear that the Holy Spirit did dominate the life of the early Church. You notice the constant repetition in Acts of phrases like, 'the Spirit hath not said', or 'the Spirit said' or 'the Spirit indicated' – the life of the Church was dominated by the power

---

*This sermon was preached on Whit Sunday, 1948.

141

of the Holy Spirit.

And the same thing is to be seen in the New Testament epistles. The kind of life that is depicted in them and in Acts is the kind of life that is produced by the working and operation of the Holy Spirit. The Christian life is the fruit, to use Paul's term in Galatians 5, of the Spirit and of his working and operation. In the New Testament itself that is sometimes stated explicitly – we have an instance of it in Galatians 5, where Paul specifically says, 'The fruit of the Spirit is love, joy, peace, longsuffering, gentleness, goodness, faith, meekness, temperance' (vv. 22–23). That is the kind of personality, or the kind of life which the Holy Spirit produces. But even where it is not stated explicitly, that doctrine is implied everywhere in the epistles. The life that they depict, and the appeals that they make for the Christian life, are almost all made in terms of the doctrine of the Holy Spirit – if you like, they take the doctrine of the Holy Spirit for granted.

Let me give you a perfect illustration of what I am saying. Take this fourth chapter of Philippians which we are now studying. Here in this section the Holy Spirit is not mentioned by name at all, so that if you read it superficially you might say that here is a passage which has nothing to do with the doctrine of the Holy Spirit. But wait a minute! What is Paul talking about in this section? In the first three verses he mentions love – 'Therefore, my brethren, dearly beloved'; and you remember that verses 2 and 3 are nothing but a great appeal to Euodias and Syntyche to love one another and to co-operate together. Furthermore, Paul appeals to all the other members of the Church to help them. The first three verses are a great exposition of love.

Then here we come to verse 4, 'Rejoice in the Lord' – joy. Then the next verse says, 'Let your moderation be known unto all men' – longsuffering. Then you go on – 'be careful for nothing'; and 'the peace of God' – love, joy, peace, longsuffering. That is a perfect illustration of the point I am making. Sometimes Paul states this doctrine of the life of the Holy Spirit explicitly, but implicitly it is everywhere.

This is something which is fundamental to our understanding of the whole New Testament doctrine of the Christian life. This chapter is nothing but another exposition by Paul of the fruit of the Spirit – love, joy, peace and so on. That is the essential background, therefore, to understanding these particular words in the fourth verse. Here Paul puts his emphasis upon one of these fruits of the Spirit – joy. 'Rejoice in the Lord alway: and again I say, Rejoice.'

Now there is nothing, perhaps, that is more typical of New Testament doctrine than just that injunction. It is something you find running right through the New Testament from the beginning to the end. Nothing was more characteristic of the life of the first Christians than this element of joy. Our Lord himself, you remember, had promised his followers that he would give them joy which the world could not take away. He said, 'You are going to be disappointed when you see me arrested and crucified, but your joy will be restored to you' (John 15:11; 16:22).

You cannot read the Book of Acts without being impressed by the amazing way in which these people were actually able to rejoice in the most untoward and difficult circumstances. In Acts we read how some of them were arrested, put into prison, and beaten, and when they came out they praised God that they had been accounted worthy to suffer for his name – they rejoiced in tribulation. When you go through the whole story you will find that in spite of the malignity of their enemies, in spite of the contradiction of the world around them, they continued to rejoice.

Then as you read the epistles you will find this great, dominating quality of joy everywhere in the life of the people. Read how Paul puts it in Romans 14:17: 'For the kingdom of God is not meat and drink; but righteousness, and peace, and joy in the Holy Ghost.' Peter, writing to similar people about the Lord Jesus Christ, says, 'Whom having not seen, ye love; in whom, though now ye see him not, yet believing, ye rejoice with joy unspeakable and full of glory' (1 Pet. 1:8). And even in the Book of Revelation, if we look at its general message instead of losing ourselves in the details, we see that it is a book which is intended to do one thing: to teach people at such a time, and in subsequent periods of the history of the Church, to rejoice in spite of adversity and difficulties, trials and troubles.

So it is everywhere, but as I have already pointed out, it is particularly the theme of this epistle to the Philippians. Paul's real reason for writing the letter was to teach these people how to rejoice in every kind of circumstance; and we have seen, therefore, how he has taken up various things that tend to rob Christian people of their joy, and how he has dealt with them one after another. To begin with, the Philippians were worrying about him; that is in the first chapter. Then various troubles within the Church tended to create discord, so he has to put that right, and he does so by giving us a great illustration of Christ in his humiliation and incarnation – 'Let this mind be in you, which was also in Christ Jesus.' Then they were troubled about the illness of Epaphroditus; Paul tells us that in the second chapter. Next, we have seen in the third chapter that he moves on to the great question of heresy and of wrong living and of how wrong belief can always rob people of their joy. And then comes this dispute between Euodias and Syntyche.

So this is Paul's great theme, and back he goes to it again. You can compare this letter to a kind of symphony. The theme is the question of joy; Paul plays his variations on it, and then he goes back to it. He has already told us at the beginning of the third chapter that this is his theme: 'Finally my brethren, rejoice in the Lord . . .' But he has not finished yet: 'Rejoice in the Lord alway: and again I say, Rejoice,' he says in 4:4. So he goes on repeating it. But why? Is it not clear that it was the thing that Paul desired for these people above everything else? It was their heritage as Christian people, and to Paul it was a tragedy that any Christian should be unhappy. Unhappiness was a denial of their profession of faith. They were missing something, they were being robbed of what is the most glorious thing about the faith, and so the Apostle could not leave it alone. He did not know whether he was to live much longer – he said that it was very doubtful, and he did not know whether he preferred to go or to stay. But, he said in effect, 'Whichever I do, the thing that I am concerned about is that you should be right, and that no one should rob you of this joy in the Holy Spirit that is possible for you and all who are true believers in the Lord Jesus Christ.'

So now as we approach it, let me ask a question. Do we know this joy? Do we have it in our lives? Is it a living fact in our experience? Are we rejoicing in the Lord? Let us, then, look at this together, bearing in mind the whole doctrine of the Holy Spirit and of his coming upon the Church on that day of Pentecost. Let me suggest the first principle: the nature of the joy. What is the character of this joy? Here let us note two points. The first is that it is something positive. That needs emphasis because we must always differentiate between this Christian quality of joy and mere negative resignation. Like the Apostle, I go on repeating this point because I think that, in a day and time like this, one of our grievous dangers is to mistake the stoical spirit of negative resignation for Christian courage, fortitude and joy. But Paul is not advocating that they should adopt a negative attitude to the things that are happening to them. No, it is essentially positive: 'Rejoice . . . and again I say, Rejoice.' You can hear him tapping it out like a bugle call. Christian joy is stimulating and stirring; never must we think of it as just something negative and passive.

Or, to put it another way, it is not merely a state of indifference. This, again, must constantly be repeated because the whole subject is so subtle. I suppose the more scientific mankind becomes, the more he becomes prone to the subtle temptation to mistake psychological solutions to problems for spiritual solutions. Let me explain. The child shows his feelings, whether pleasure or displeasure, satisfaction or dissatisfaction, and the more primitive people do exactly the same thing. But as we get older, and as the whole world gets older, there is a tendency to hide our feelings. Up to a point, that is perfectly right, but it can be a very real danger and it becomes a danger when it would have us feel and think that the Christian attitude towards problems is an attitude of indifference, as though people should say to themselves, 'Well, the only way to go through this life without being hurt is to put on a protective mechanism of indifference which says, "I don't care what anybody says, or what may happen to me."' The idea is that if you put up a screen of indifference around yourself, you will not react violently to the things that are happening to you.

But that is not what the Apostle has in mind here. People who hide themselves behind a screen of indifference do not have any joy; nor do stoics with their negative resignation. Paul is talking about a joy that is positive; it is active and there is an emotional element in it. It does not curb us, there is power and life in it – it is a spirit of exultation. 'Rejoice' – that is surely active and positive!

The second characteristic which I must note is that it is a specific joy. It is a joy in the Lord – 'Rejoice in the Lord alway; and again I say, Rejoice.' The New Testament never just exhorts people to be happy or tells them to cheer up while it gives out psychological sympathy. That is something it never does, and that is why I again suggest that there is perhaps no greater travesty of the gospel of Jesus Christ than psychological teaching which presents itself in Christian terms. A presentation of the gospel which will have us cheer up, or do something to make ourselves feel happier for the time being, is a denial of the gospel of Christ. We are to rejoice in the Lord. There is no need for a stoical mechanism here, it is something direct and immediate, and it is in terms of the Lord.

In other words, the joy that the Christian is to experience is a joy that is based solidly upon Christian truth and doctrine. You notice that it is only after Paul has told them to, 'Stand fast in the Lord,' that he tells them to, 'Rejoice in the Lord,' and anything which is not based on the doctrine concerning the Lord Jesus Christ is not joy. Many agencies can make us happy. Indeed, you can take alcohol and you may feel happy and full of joy – but it has nothing to do with the joy of the Lord. Paul is not talking about joy in a general sense, but about specific joy. He is not merely concerned with whether or not we are happy; his concern is that, because we are Christians, we should rejoice.

And so, having thus outlined the nature of Christian joy, let me say something about the hindrances to this joy. There are many, and I obviously cannot deal with them all in one study, so I shall simply try to pick out the more obvious ones mentioned in this context.

First of all, there is a hindrance to some people over the whole question of the mechanism of this joy, over the way in which it comes to us, of how it becomes available. Some people have an initial intellectual difficulty about this because here in this verse the Apostle confronts us, and tells us to, 'Rejoice in the Lord.' 'And yet,' says someone, 'in Galatians 5 Paul says that the "fruit of the Spirit is love, joy, peace . . .". How can this be something that I do and yet be the fruit and operation of the Spirit?' We are all familiar with the argument, it has gone on in the Church from the very beginning, the apparent conflict between the two types of Christian life, the life of activity and the life of passivity, of meditation; the contrast between those who believe that the thing to do in the Christian life is to be always engaged in activity, and those who believe in contemplation and in the mystical, monastic conception of the Christian life.

But when you examine the Scriptures more closely you will see that there is no contradiction. Take Galatians 5: before Paul tells us that 'the fruit of the Spirit is love, joy . . .', he has already said, 'Walk in the Spirit, and ye shall not fulfil the lust of the flesh' (5:16). The two things are there together in the same chapter. Thus we reconcile the apparent contradiction in this way – it is as we practise these things that the fruit of the Spirit will be manifested in our life. It is perfectly true that I cannot create or produce joy myself, but if I listen to and obey the dictates and leading of the Holy Spirit within me, if I practise the Christian life, if I work out the doctrine of the Holy Spirit, then the Holy Spirit will plant this fruit of joy within my life. We cannot find joy merely by rushing into activity or merely by sitting in contemplation. To try one or other of these two possibilities alone, is certain to lead to disaster. We must do both: we must meditate upon the truth and we must practise it, and as we do so the Holy Spirit will flood our lives with joy. That is not a theory only, and it is not only the teaching of the New Testament. If you read the lives of the saints, you will find it confirmed in abundance. We can also confirm it ourselves, thank God; it is literal, actual, present-day experience in the Christian life.

The second cause of failure to have this joy which is in Christ is the failure to be in the right relationship to him; that is why I emphasise 'in the Lord'. Many people do not know the joy of the Lord today for the one and only reason that they have never truly realised their own poverty, emptiness and deadness. Most people who have never experienced the joy of salvation are people who have never seen their full need of salvation. This may sound paradoxical, but how true it is! Our Lord put it perfectly in the Sermon on the Mount: 'Blessed are the poor in spirit: for theirs is the kingdom of heaven . . . Blessed are they which do hunger and thirst after righteousness: for they shall be filled.' You see, the only people who are going to be filled are those who hunger and thirst; the people who are going to have endless spiritual wealth and riches are the paupers in the realm of the spirit. There are many people who never know the joy of the Lord because they have failed to see themselves as miserable sinners. The only way to be happy in Christ is to be desperately unhappy without him.

In other words, there are people who have never known the joy of salvation because they are relying upon themselves and their own works. They still feel they can live the Christian life in their own power, and that they can put themselves right with God. But if you want to be filled with the joy of the Lord, you have to be absolutely empty, you have to see yourselves as wretched, hopeless sinners, you have to know that nothing you can do will avail you anything, but in utter poverty and helplessness you have to come to him. Then you are likely to know the joy of the

Lord, and not until then. Or to put it another way: such
people have never cast themselves utterly upon him. Those
are the two essentials to receiving this joy – experiencing the
utter misery of conviction of sin, as the New Testament
reveals us to ourselves in all our hopelessness and woe; and
then, empty handed, coming to Christ and casting ourselves
upon his mercy and his bounty, his love and compassion,
and saying to him –

> Nothing in my hand I bring
> Simply to Thy Cross I cling.
>
> Augustus Toplady

If you have anything in your hand, you will never get it filled
from him; you have to come with nothing at all and then you
will receive his joy.

And that is confirmed abundantly by the subsequent history of the Christian Church. It is the people who have said
the most terrible things about themselves, as they are by
nature, who have rejoiced most in Christ Jesus. It is those
who have said, 'Vile and full of sin I am,' who have been
able to say, 'Plenteous grace in Thee is found.' And the
people who have never quite admitted that they are vile sinners are the people who have never rejoiced in Christ Jesus
and have never known the abundance of Christian living.
We must be right about this, we must be in the right
relationship to Christ or we will never know the joy and
happiness, the peace and love, that he can give.

And that leads me to the next hindrance. There are many
who lack the joy of the Lord because they fail to maintain
that right relationship with him. You must not only enter
into it, you must maintain it, and you do this in your spirit
and in your attitude towards one another. These two women
who were quarrelling in the church had certainly lost their
joy; you cannot have the joy of the Lord if your spirit is not
wholesome and clean. It grieves the Spirit and he goes
away. Therefore, if we want to have the joy of the Lord we
must maintain the right spirit.

Furthermore, we must also maintain the right practice – we must live and walk in the right way. This is obvious from what Paul said to the Galatians. If we are guilty of certain practices and sins, we cannot know the joy of the Lord; as our Lord said, 'Ye cannot serve God and mammon' (Matt. 6:24). If you want the joy of the Lord, you must forsake other things. Walk in the Spirit, be led by the Spirit, and you will experience the joy of the Spirit.

And the next thing which Paul mentions here – 'Let your moderation be known unto all men' – he has already dealt with earlier so he goes on to the following injunction: we must maintain contact with Christ by prayer and communion. 'In everything by prayer and supplication with thanksgiving let your requests be made known unto God.' So I have not only to watch my spirit, I must spend a certain amount of time in talking to him. That is the source of joy; he alone can make me truly happy. What fools we are in this Christian life! We depend on so many other things, but the secret of the saints has always been the time they spend in conversation and communion with the Lord and in meditation upon him. We must maintain that contact; we must go to the source and fount of joy and go there readily and frequently.

And then, too, we must maintain this contact with him by never allowing ourselves to be tyrannised by circumstances. That is the most common cause of a loss of joy – the tyranny of events and circumstances. So many things come between us and him, and rob us of his presence and joy. Oh, these things that tend to worry us and cause us to be pulled down by anxiety! We think about them, they always seem to be coming up, and we go on worrying about them, and as we do so we become miserable, breakdowns occur and all such troubles.

Those, then, are some of the things that rob us of the joy. Now let us come to the positive side. If these are the things that rob us of joy, how can we maintain it? And the answer is quite simple: we must avoid all those things that prevent us concentrating upon him – 'Rejoice in the Lord alway . . .' Look on him, consider him, meditate upon him, his person, his work, all he has done, his death, his resurrection, his sending forth of the Holy Spirit. Consider, too, the things he is going to do, the whole of the New Testament scheme and plan for life, and the ultimate, that glorious hope that nothing can ever rob us of. These are the things; meditate upon him, on his person, and upon all the glory of his work.

And lastly, let me ask a question. Is this state of joy something that can continue? Is it always possible to know it? And Paul's answer is, Yes, always! 'Rejoice in the Lord alway: and again I say Rejoice.' You can say that of nothing else; every other source of joy and happiness must, of necessity, sooner or later fail us. Some people are foolish enough to find their joy in their work. As far as it goes that is all right, and apart from the gospel, it is not a bad thing. But, my friend, a day is coming when you will lose your work – you will become old or ill. What a tragic thing it is to see such people. They were so happy when they were working, but when they are laid aside they do not know what to do with themselves. They have been dependent for joy and happiness upon their own efforts and exertions.

Then think of the men and women who are only happy when they are successful. Our reply to them is, 'Uneasy lies the head that wears crown' – there are always others seeking that crown. You may be successful but look at that other person who is coming up fast, and who will soon beat and excel you. You will become tired, your powers will fail and somebody else will take your place. It is a tragedy that one sees in the lives of professional men and women. They have been happy in the days of their success and achievement, they are joyful as they reach the summit of their profession, but then they begin to come down the other side, and it is much more difficult to come down, than to go up. The pathos of such people! How foolish it is to let our joy depend upon our circumstances, because we live in a world where it is true to say, 'Change and decay in all around I see.' Circumstances are bound to let you down sooner or later. Do not depend upon them.

No, there is only one thing that never fails: it is to rejoice in the Lord. And this does not fail, because it is always concerned about the soul and its destiny; it is concerned about something which is safe and sure, something which the world can never affect because it is in Christ. This joy is beyond the reach of all those other powers, and you work it out like this: you say, 'Circumstances may certainly vary and may fail me, but nothing can affect my relationship to Christ. It does not matter what the world may do to me, my relationship to him cannot be affected by it.' You remember Paul's argument? 'For I am persuaded, that neither death, nor life, nor angels, nor principalities, nor powers, nor things present, nor things to come, nor height, nor depth, nor any other creature, shall be able to separate us from the love of God, which is in Christ Jesus our Lord' (Rom. 8:38–39).

In other words, you may be in prison, but there you may still find Christ. You may be stripped and rid of everything, but not of your soul or your eternal destiny, nor of the glory that awaits you in Christ – these things are beyond circumstances. To go even further, let me show you how you can rejoice in the Lord even in failure, even in sin. Is that a daring statement? No, 'Rejoice in the Lord alway' – even when I have failed or sinned? Yes, in this way – if as a Christian I fall into sin, the Holy Spirit will convict me, and that will make me miserable. But if I am truly led of the Spirit I will not stop at that. I will go back to Christ, I will go back to Calvary's hill, to the blood that was shed, the blood that still cleanses me, and as I go back I know I am washed and cleansed, and so I rejoice. If I am truly a Christian, if the Holy Spirit dwells within me, he must minister to my joy, and as I go back in contrition and shame, penitent and conscious of my unworthiness, his love is great enough to cover my sin and my failure. So I go back and I find it is greater than I thought it was. I have made a fresh discovery of his love and his mercy and compassion, and in my sin and failure I am made to rejoice all the same. Rejoice in the Lord always, in life, in death, in sins or failure, whatever may be happening to you, whatever your circumstances, 'Rejoice in the Lord alway: and again I say, Rejoice.'

Chapter 13

Moderation

Let your moderation be known unto all men. The Lord is
at hand (Phil. 4:5).

As one reads the various letters of the Apostle Paul, nothing
is more instructive and interesting than to observe the way
in which statements and remarks, which are apparently
casual, are nevertheless parts of a very definite logical system, and have a logical sequence of ideas which clearly gripped the Apostle's mind as he was writing them. As you read
the first few verses of this fourth chapter, you might at first
sight come to the conclusion that what you have here is a
series of outstanding injunctions, given one after another
without any definite order, which the Apostle worked out as
they came into his mind. But on closer examination, we find
that each one of these specific and particular injunctions is
related to the others, and that they all go together to form a
composite and complete whole.

In other words, the injunction we are considering
together now follows, I think you will see, directly from the
one we were considering in our last study on the fourth
verse, where Paul says, 'Rejoice in the Lord alway: and
again I say, Rejoice.' Now this injunction here follows
directly from that one because, as I think we all must agree,
nothing is so likely to rob us of our joy as trouble in our own
spirits or trouble in our relationships with other people. Let
me emphasise again that Paul's mastering idea in this epistle
is the whole question of joy, that is what he is really

concerned about, and so he talks about the various things that tend to rob us of the joy, and this happens to be one of them. We must pay attention, negatively, to our own spirit and condition and do so especially in relationship to other people.

But we must also look at this from another standpoint. The Apostle was not only concerned about the happiness and joy of the members of the church at Philippi, he was equally concerned that they should be displaying and portraying the Christian character in all its fulness. We have seen something of his love for these people; he speaks of them as his brethren, 'dearly beloved and longed for, my joy and crown'. Yes, but however great his love was for them, his love for his Lord was still greater, and it always urged and compelled him to write these various letters and exhortations to the early Christians in order that they might lead the Christian life in all its fulness, and all its glory. He wanted them to show, if one might use such an expression, the handiwork of God in salvation. In the last study we made the point in passing that miserable or unhappy Christians are not only a very poor advertisement for the gospel of Jesus Christ but they also detract from the glory of the Lord, if they are not showing the possibility of the Christian life in its fulness. And if that was true about the injunction to rejoice in the Lord, it is equally true with respect to this injunction that we are now considering, because it is an essential part of the Christian character, that we should let our moderation be known unto all men. It is as vital to the Christian character that we should exercise and display moderation, as it is that we should rejoice always and glory and exult in the Lord under all conditions.

So, then, these injunctions are very closely connected and interrelated. You cannot have true joy in the Lord if you are wrong on this point, and your Christian character is not complete unless this further aspect is also present.

Now it seems to me that a very interesting question for discussion, in a church fellowship meeting, or in any gathering of Christian people who are concerned about the Chris-

tian life, would be this: Which is the more difficult, the
injunction in verse 4, or this one in verse 5? Which is harder,
to rejoice in the Lord always, or to let our moderation be
known unto all men? I commend to you a meditation upon
that theme. May I suggest certain ideas to you as you
embark upon that process. As far as I am concerned, this
injunction in the fifth verse is altogether the more difficult of
the two. I find it easier to rejoice in the Lord always, than
to let my moderation be always known unto all men. Why is
that? I would suggest these reasons. In verse 4 the Apostle
is exhorting us to a certain state, and condition. He is concerned there about what we ought to be, but here he is concerned with the application of that state, and I think you will
agree that to apply a truth is generally much more difficult
than holding or possessing the truth itself.

Let me explain what I mean. I am sure we all know something of this – I am alone in my room, reading my Bible, and
I come across this injunction to rejoice in the Lord. So I
think of all the arguments that the Apostle provides me with
to rejoice in the Lord, and there, all alone, I can rejoice.
But it is very much more difficult to continue doing that
when I meet my fellow men and women, and when I come
face to face with trouble and difficulty. To accept theory is
generally easier than to practise it, and in this verse we are
in the realm of application. Or let me put it like this. I feel
that to rejoice in the Lord is easier than to let my 'moderation be known unto all men,' because when I am exhorted
to rejoice in the Lord always, I am exhorted to express
something, whereas in this exhortation I am exhorted to
practise restraint; and I would not hesitate to say that to
restrain oneself is always more difficult than to express oneself. There is something essentially positive about rejoicing
in the Lord; you want to sing and to praise God; the whole
of your being is involved. Yes, but when you are told, 'let
your moderation be known unto all men,' the element of
restraint comes in. It is not that it is negative (I shall show
that it is positive) but there is a negative element in it.

Or let me put it like this. The injunction in verse 4 is

easier than that in verse 5 because in verse 4 I am being
exhorted to look at my Lord, whereas in verse 5 I am
exhorted to be like my Lord. It is easy to rejoice in the Lord
while you look and meditate upon him, while you think of
his work, and as you are looking at him objectively in his
work. Yes, but here I am asked to do something more
difficult, I am asked to reproduce him. I am asked to conduct and comport myself exactly as he did when he was here
on earth, and facing the trials and contradictions in life that
I myself have to face. So, then, here in many ways we are
face to face with one of the highest demands of the Christian
gospel. I think we can safely say that the gospel, in a sense,
never calls us to a greater height than it does here with
regard to our life, our conduct and practice. Indeed, I would
say that it is much easier to rejoice, even in tribulations,
than it is to let my moderation be known unto all men.

That is why I thank God that the Apostle, true to his
method, as he is always and without exception, not only
gives me the injunction but also couples it with doctrine.
There is no Christian for whom I feel more sorry than the
one who has not yet realised the all-importance of doctrine.
We have already noticed that the Apostle never gives an
injunction without giving doctrine at the same time. In verse
4 he was not simply saying 'rejoice', but 'rejoice in the
Lord', that is the doctrine: it is 'in the Lord'. And here
again, the Apostle does not just say, 'Let your moderation
be known unto all men,' he adds, 'the Lord is at hand'. That
is mighty doctrine, and I thank God for it, because only a
full understanding and realisation of what Paul means by
that doctrine can ever truly enable me to carry out the
injunction. This is something so characteristic of this Apostle. He never asks us to do something without at the same
time showing us how it can be done. He never shows us the
height we have to climb without pointing us to the source of
power that will enable us to climb; never one without the
other. The New Testament is not interested in the fact that
we should just live a certain type of life for the sake of doing
so, the doctrine is fundamental and absolute.

Bearing all this in mind, then, let us look at the injunction directly. What does Paul mean by moderation? Let us first deal with two negatives before we come to the positive. By moderation, Paul does not mean just good nature, something which is animal. He is not talking about psychology or temperament. Nor, secondly, is he referring to what we may call a looseness, a flabbiness and lack of definition. That cannot be what the Apostle means by moderation, because he has already been saying to us, 'Stand fast in the Lord.' Never forget that these commands must all be taken together; this is one in a series of injunctions. The people who are to be moderate in all things are the people who are to stand fast in the Lord at all costs. They are not compromisers; they are not men and women who, because they believe nothing in particular themselves, can be indulgent with respect to everybody else. Nor are they people who, because they lack purpose, believe in a kind of coalition with every other person. No, they are to stand fast in the Lord. So we must get rid, once and for ever, of the idea that moderation means a kind of indifference, a vagueness, a nebulous attitude towards truth and life and everything else; the kind of person who is 'all things to all men' in a wrong and unworthy sense; a man who is always ready to compromise at all costs, 'peace at any price'. Not at all! Nothing is further removed from the grand and magnificent character of the Apostle. No, it is much more difficult than that. There are people, let us grant, who seem to be born like that, but you see that the Apostle is obviously not concerned about that, because he is writing to many different kinds of people. There were all sorts of people in the church at Philippi, as there are all types in the Church today, so Paul's injunction is not just to be worked out like that.

So we can put it positively like this: this word 'moderation' means control of oneself and one's spirit, and is shown by self-control, self-mastery, possession of one's spirit and of one's activity. It means not urging one's own right to the uttermost – that is the first idea inherent in these words. I must be free from that spirit that insists upon the last ounce in every single situation. It means the capacity to differentiate between what is really of vital importance and what is not, to stand like a rock by the things that are vital, but to be reasonable about the things that are not. It means not pressing my bargain to the very last drop of blood, it means being prepared, at times, and if necessary, to have less than is due to me for the sake of the Church and for the sake of others, but above all, for the Lord's sake. 'Let your moderation be known unto all men': not grasping, not so carried away that your whole spirit is involved. In other words, it is not so much what you are doing as the way in which you do it.

Let me put it another way. This word 'moderation' undoubtedly conveys the idea of forbearance, that is, a condition in which one is not easily offended. Here you are, says the Apostle, you are members together of the Church of Christ, and I am exhorting you to be so in control of your spirits, your mind and your whole selves that you cannot be easily put off and offended. We have already looked at that, you remember, in the case of Euodias and Syntyche – touchy, sensitive people, always ready to be offended. We all know something about this, the Lord have mercy upon us! It is a great and wonderful and noble quality of the Christian character, this quality of not being easily offended. Some people have a control and mastery over themselves, so that though darts are thrown, they do not find a sensitive place. Let me make it clear again that I am not advocating a kind of stoic indifference, or a negative, passive condition. No, this quality is essentially active. If you have it, it means that you have Christian grace in your personality, so that when these darts come, you can somehow receive them, and not worry about them – longsuffering, able to bear and forbear, not easily offended.

But it goes even further than that. It means that you have an active consideration for others. You see the steps in the definition of this word? First, in and of yourself you are prepared to have less than is your due. Second, when you come into contact with people who are irritating and difficult, you have some kind of shock absorber as far as they are concerned. Ah, yes, but you must go further if you want your moderation to be known unto all men: you must actively and positively consider them; you must try to find excuses for them and seek an explanation for their way of behaviour. You might say, 'Well, after all, they are having a difficult time,' or, 'I believe that person was born with a difficult temperament.' You are all the time trying to explain them to yourself, trying to take the edge off harsh and difficult behaviour. You go out of your way to meet people and to make up for any deficiency there may be in them – consideration for others, trying to understand them, and indeed to help them, and to make things easier for them. That is an essential part of this word 'moderation'.

Let me go still further. Notice the kind of person the Apostle is, notice the quality of his personality – a personality that never reacts violently to anything. Let your moderation be known unto all men, in all times and circumstances and under all conditions. Let me work it out like this. The Christian is never to react violently in any realm, not even with respect to joy. Your moderation is to be known unto all men, even in times of happiness. I need not stay with this. Is there anything more obvious and sad in the modern world than the lack of moderation in men and women who are enjoying themselves? They are carried away, right out of control, intoxicated by joy. But the Christian is never to be like that, there is to be an element of control even in his joy, and still more, perhaps, in his sorrow. At times of grief and sorrow the Christian is never to react too violently. Do not misunderstand me, I am not saying he is not to be natural. The Christian was never meant to be unnatural and God forbid we should ever think that. Christians are not only people who know joy, they know grief and sorrow – perhaps more than anybody else – yes, but it does not master them. This is the trouble: so often we are either overjoyed, on the mountain top, or we are down in the depths of despair. But Christians should not be like that, they must never react violently – there is always to be this control, in joy and in sorrow. They are never to be over-animated or over-depressed, but must always maintain a kind of balance and pose; they are to be controlled.

Yet I must make this important addition: they do all this in a spirit of cheerfulness; they are never to be morose, or sullen. Once more we must differentiate between the self-control of the Christian and the control of the Stoic. The Stoic accepts things, but the Christian's moderation is cheerful. There is a great deal of stoicism in the modern world; the world shows amazing self-control, but what a cold thing it is! There is no cheerfulness in it. That sort of control is not what Paul is talking about. You are to be controlled and happy at the same time, and you are also to have even this joy in moderation. Let me give you a perfect illustration of it. Paul, in writing to the church at Corinth, said, 'Now I Paul myself beseech you by the meekness and gentleness of Christ . . .' (2 Cor. 10:1) – the meekness and gentleness of Christ! And that is the Apostle's exhortation here to these Philippian Christians.

Again, I want to emphasise the fact that we are all called upon to show this moderation; Paul is not merely writing to certain people who may be balanced by temperament. No, even though you may be naturally impulsive, it does not matter, you are exhorted to let your moderation be known unto all men. Someone may ask whether this is possible for every type of personality; is it not asking for the impossible? I reply that it is possible to all. Let me give you a proof of that. I was reminded of it forcibly when attention was being called to the fact that it was the anniversary of the death of that great Christian statesman, William Gladstone. I remember once reading of something that Mrs Gladstone said to John Morgan about her husband. She said, 'You must remember that he had two sides, the one impetuous, impatient and unrestrainable, the other all self-control, able to dismiss everything but the great central subject, able to put aside what was weakening or disturbing. He achieved this self-mastery and sanity in the struggle from the age of twenty-three or twenty-four, first by the natural power of his character, and secondly by much wrestling in prayer to reach this injunction, "Let your moderation be known unto all men."' And Gladstone achieved it, this wonderful grace of the Christian character.

But of course, the supreme example of all is the example of our Lord himself. The Apostle Peter puts this very clearly when he says, 'Christ also suffered for us, leaving us an example, that ye should follow his steps: who did no sin, neither was guile found in his mouth: who, when he was reviled, reviled not again; when he suffered, he threatened not; but committed himself to him that judgeth righteously' (1 Pet. 2:21–23). Peter has already said: 'Servants, be subject to your masters . . . not only to the good and gentle, but also to the froward . . . For what glory is it, if, when ye be buffeted for your faults, ye shall take it patiently? but if, when ye do well, and suffer for it, ye take it patiently, this is acceptable with God' (1 Pet. 2:18–20). That is it – our Lord himself was like that; follow in his steps, be like him; 'Let your moderation be known unto all men.'

So, then, let me ask a second question. How is this to be manifested and to whom? And the answer is that we manifest it in practice, we reveal it in our lives and dealings with others. Yes, let me emphasise once more that we are to show this moderation to all men – to everyone, whether they are nice or not, whether they are loving and gentle, or cruel and harsh; whether they are tyrants or whether they are our greatest friends.

Not only that, we are to show moderation in every sphere and in every department of life. We are to show it when we are contending for the faith and standing fast in the Lord. In other words, we are to stand for the truth, yes, and we are to do it in this way. We must watch our spirits, there must be no harshness and no kind of petty-fogging legalism. We must learn to differentiate between what is vital and what is comparatively unimportant. We are to express and show this moderation in our business or in our profession. We are to let people see, by the way we transact our business, that we are Christians. This does not mean that we are to suffer wrong in a legal sense. No, the Apostle Paul himself appealed to Caesar and objected when he was thrown into prison without a trial. It does not mean that, but it does mean that we are always certain that we are not fighting only for ourselves, we are fighting for the truth – and how difficult it is at times to do that! How difficult it is to differentiate between holy zeal or righteous indignation, and the mere expression of a harsh, critical, judgmental spirit. We are told to behave with moderation to all men and at all times, and I would say that there is no greater testimony for the power and the grace of the gospel, than men and women who are showing their moderation in this way.

Let me finish with a word of encouragement which the Apostle provides to enable us to do this. How can we ever reach such a state? What is there that can help us? Here is the answer: 'The Lord is at hand.' This is the Apostle's way of telling us that we must learn increasingly to be indifferent to this world and its ways. As Christian people we have an entirely new view of life, we see things always in the light of the Lord, we see everything in the light of the salvation that he brought, by his life, by his birth, his death, his resurrection and ascension. We see it all in the light of the fact that he is going to return again to the earth, to conquer all his enemies and to bring in an entirely new order. The Lord is at hand.

There are those who try to argue that by these words Paul meant that the Lord is always near, but the whole context is surely against that. It is true, he is always near, but in many ways this is a greater truth. In all we do we must always remember that the Lord may return at any time. His coming is always at hand, yes, but we do not know when, and so we must always live in the realisation that he is coming. And that works out like this. If we always remember that the Lord is coming, we shall always remember that this world and life are nothing but a kind of preparatory school; we are but pilgrims and strangers here, we are here today and gone tomorrow. Very well then, if we always bear that in mind, we have already gone more than half way to displaying this moderation. It is because people think that this is the only life and world that they fight for the last ounce; but what are sixty, seventy or eighty years compared with eternity? 'The Lord is at hand' – remember that.

These words also remind us that he is the Judge, and not we ourselves. How ready we are to judge, but he is the Judge. The Lord is at hand. I am not the judge, and when I am reminded of that it solves many of my problems for me. Not only that, I am reminded of the truth that we ourselves shall be judged, and we shall have to render up an account for our lives and our deeds; therefore be careful in your judgments. You remember how Christ put it, 'Judge not, that ye be not judged. For with what judgment ye judge, ye shall be judged: and with what measure ye mete, it shall be measured to you again' (Matt. 7:1, 2). Do not forget, then, when you feel like condemning, that you yourself are going to be judged. The Lord is at hand, and when you realise that, you are prepared to overlook a great many things in this life and world.

But further, we must not be anxious to obtain the retribution or justice to which we feel we are entitled. The Lord himself will judge evildoers, or anybody who may have wronged us here, because everyone will have to stand before Christ. Do not worry, do not feel you must have immediate revenge. Paul says, 'Dearly beloved, avenge not yourselves, but rather give place unto wrath: for it is written, Vengeance is mine; I will repay, saith the Lord' (Rom. 12:19). If you believe that, you will be sorry for the people who have wronged you, you will tremble as you think of them having to stand before God, and your moderation will already be in active operation.

Or, finally, let me put it like this. You may be having a hard and difficult time – Paul does not minimise it – people may be very cruel and unkind, your position may be really grievous. You may be having to bear something terrible, people may be constantly nagging at you, day after day, night after night. But whatever you may have to suffer or endure in this life, the Lord is at hand and he is preparing an amazing reward for you. When he comes, and when the reign of glory begins, you will be with him, you will be reigning with him, and you will be sharing in his joy and all his glory. My friend, if your name is written in heaven, if you belong to him, your reward is absolutely certain. There is joy in glory awaiting you that you cannot imagine or conceive. So, then, remember that he is coming, the Lord is at hand – keep looking at that.

In other words, once more, you are just exhorted to do what our Lord did. This is what the epistle to the Hebrews says about him: 'who for the joy that was set before him endured the cross, despising the shame' (Heb. 12:2). Or consider how James puts it, 'Be patient therefore, brethren, unto the coming of the Lord. Behold the husbandman waiteth for the precious fruit of the earth, and hath long patience for it, until he receive the early and latter rain. Be ye also patient; stablish your hearts: for the coming of the Lord draweth nigh. Grudge not one against another, brethren, lest ye be condemned: behold, the judge standeth before the door' (Jas. 5:7–9).

Need I say any more? That is not a bit of psychology. Be moderate in all things. 'The Lord is at hand.' Your whole life is in that setting. As you realise that he is the judge and not yourself, as you realise the vengeance that he will manifest on sin and evil, and on all who have been wrong, and have harmed him and his people, pray for those who are going to suffer. But above all, contemplate being with him, spending eternity in his glorious presence, and sharing in that joy that is set before him. 'Let your moderation be known unto all men.'

Chapter 14

The peace of God

> Be careful for nothing; but in every thing by prayer and supplication with thanksgiving let your requests be made known unto God. And the peace of God, which passeth all understanding, shall keep your hearts and minds through Christ Jesus (Phil. 4:6, 7).

This is undoubtedly one of the noblest, greatest and most comforting statements which is to be found anywhere in any extant literature. One is tempted to say that about many passages in the Scriptures, and yet from the standpoint of our personal lives in this world, and from the standpoint of practical experience, nothing has greater comfort for God's people than these two verses. We saw in our last study how an unquiet spirit, a grasping desire to have our own way, so frequently robs us of our joy; and here in these verses Paul goes on to consider another factor that is perhaps more problematical than any of the others which tend to rob us of the joy of the Lord, and that is what we may well describe as the tyranny of circumstances, or the things that happen to us. How many they are, and how often they come! Here the Apostle deals with this question in a final manner. It is remarkable, as you read through the Bible, to notice how often this particular subject is dealt with. A very good case can be made out for saying that all the New Testament epistles face this particular problem, and were designed to help the first Christians deal with it. They lived in a very difficult world and had to suffer and endure a great deal; and these men, called of God, wrote their letters in order to show them how to overcome these things. It is the great theme of the New Testament; but you find it also in the Old Testament. Take the third and fourth Psalms, for instance. How perfectly they put it all. The great problem in life is, in a sense, how to lay oneself down to rest and sleep. 'I laid me down and slept,' said the Psalmist (Ps. 3:5). Anybody can lie down, but the question is, can you sleep? The Psalmist describes himself surrounded by enemies and by difficulties and trials, and his mighty testimony is that in spite of that, because of his trust in the Lord he lay down, and slept, and he woke safe and sound in the morning. Why? Because the Lord was with him and was looking after him.

That is the theme of so much of the Bible in the Old Testament and in the New that it is obviously a subject of supreme importance. I sometimes feel that perhaps nothing provides such a thorough test of our faith and of our whole Christian position as just this matter. It is one thing to say that you subscribe to the Christian faith; it is one thing, having read your Bible and abstracted its doctrine, to say, 'Yes, I believe all that, it is the faith by which I live.' But it is not always exactly the same thing to find that faith triumphant and victorious and maintaining you in a state of joy when everything seems to have gone against you and has well nigh driven you to despair. It is a subtle and delicate test of our position because it is such an essentially practical test. It is far removed from the realm of mere theory. You are *in* the position, you are *in* the situation, these things *are* happening to you, and the question is, what is your faith worth at that point? Does it differentiate you from people who have no faith? That is obviously something of very great importance not only for our peace and comfort but also, and especially at a time like this, from the whole standpoint of our Christian witness. People today tell us that they are realists and practical. They say that they are not interested in doctrine, and are not very interested in listening to what we say, but if they see a body of people who seem to have something that enables them to triumph over life, they become interested at once. This is because they are unhappy, and frustrated and uncertain, and fearful. If, when in that condition themselves, they see people who seem to have peace and calm and quiet, then they are ready to look at them and to listen to them. So that both from the standpoint of our own personal happiness and our maintenance of the joy of the Lord, and also from the standpoint of our witness and our testimony in these difficult days, it behoves us to consider very carefully what the Apostle has to say in these masterly statements about the way to deal with the tyranny of circumstances and conditions.

The matter seems to divide itself up quite simply. First of all he tells us what we have to avoid. There are certain things we must avoid, says the Apostle – 'Be careful for nothing.' That is a negative injunction – something to avoid. Now let us be clear about the term 'careful'. 'Be careful for nothing,' says the Authorised translation, but you will find another translation even better: 'Be anxious for nothing,' or 'Be anxious about nothing.' 'Careful' means 'full of care', that means anxiety, harassing care, nervous solicitude, tending to brood or to ponder over things. It is the word our Lord used in the Sermon on the Mount – you remember that section in the sixth chapter of Matthew: 'Take no thought . . .' It means do not be over-anxious, do not brood and ponder, do not meditate overmuch upon, do not have this nervous solicitude about the thing. That is the meaning of the term.

It is important, in passing, that we should understand that the Bible nowhere teaches us not to make ordinary provision for life, or not to use commonsense. It does not encourage laziness. You will remember that Paul in writing to the church at Thessalonica, said: 'If any would not work, neither should he eat' (2 Thess. 3:10). 'Careful' here, therefore, does not refer to wise forethought, but must be interpreted as anxiety, this harassing, wearying, wearing care. That is the thing the Apostle tells us we must avoid at all costs.

But you notice that he does not stop merely at that negative injunction. There is a very profound piece of biblical psychology here. The Apostle shows us how we tend to get into this state of nervous, morbid, brooding anxiety. You notice that he tells us it is all due to the activity of the heart and mind – 'The peace of God, which passeth all understanding, shall keep your hearts and minds through Christ Jesus.' It is the heart and the mind that tend to produce this state of anxiety, this morbid care and solicitude.

This is a profound piece of psychology, and I am emphasising it because later on we shall see how vital it is, in applying the Apostle's remedy to ourselves, that we should grasp and understand his psychological explanation of the condition. What Paul is saying, in other words, is that we can control many things in our lives and outside our lives, but we cannot control our hearts and minds. 'This condition of anxiety,' says Paul, 'is something which, in a sense, is outside your own control, it happens apart from you and in spite of you.' And how true that is to experience. Recall any occasion when you were in this condition of anxiety. Remember how it could not be controlled. You were lying awake and you would have given the whole world if you could only sleep, if you could but stop the heart and the mind from going on working, from revolving and thinking and so keeping you awake. But your mind would not let you sleep, your heart would not let you sleep. The heart and the mind are outside our control. Here is profound psychology indeed, and the Apostle does not hesitate to use it. Here, once more, we come across the wonderful realism of the Scriptures, their absolute honesty, their recognition of man as he is. So the Apostle tells us that in this way the heart and the mind, or, if you prefer it, the depth of one's being, tends to produce this state of anxiety. Here the 'heart' does not only mean the seat of emotions, it means the very central part of one's personality. The 'mind' can be translated by the term 'thought'. We have all, alas, experienced this condition and we know exactly what the Apostle means. The heart has feelings. If a dear one is taken ill, how the heart begins to work! Your concern, your very love for the person, is the cause of the anxiety. If you thought nothing of the person you would not be anxious. There you see where the heart and the affections come in. Not only that – the imagination! What a prolific cause of anxiety is the imagination. You are confronted with a situation, but if it were merely that, you would probably be able to lie down and go to sleep. But the imagination comes in and you begin to think, 'What if this or that should happen? Everything is fairly under control tonight, but what if by tomorrow morning the temperature should be up, or what if this condition should arise and lead to that?' You go on thinking for hours, agitated by these imaginations. Thus your heart keeps you awake.

Or, then, not so much in the realm of imagination but more in the realm of the mind and of pure thought, you find yourself beginning to consider possibilities and you put up positions and deal with them and analyse them and you say, 'If that should take place we shall have to make this arrangement, or we shall have to do that.' You see how it works? The heart and the mind are in control. We are the victims of thoughts; in this condition of anxiety we are the victims. The heart and the mind, these powers that are within us and which are outside our control, are mastering us and tyrannising over us. The Apostle tells us that this is something which at all costs we must avoid. I need not dwell upon the reason for that. I think we must all know it from experience. In this state of anxiety we spend the whole of our time reasoning and arguing and chasing imaginations. And in that state we are useless. We do not want to speak to other people. We may appear to be listening to them as they speak in conversation, but our mind is chasing these possibilities. And so, alas, our testimony is useless. We are of no value to others and above all we lose the joy of the Lord.

But let us hurry to the second principle. What have we to do in order to avoid that inner turmoil? What does the Apostle teach us here? This is where we come to that which is peculiarly and specifically Christian. If I do nothing else I trust that I shall be enabled to show you the eternal difference between the Christian way of dealing with anxiety and the psychological way or the commonsense way. Some may think that I am rather hard on psychology but let me indulge in a little apologia. Psychology, I believe, is one of the most subtle dangers in connection with the Christian faith. People sometimes think that they are being sustained by the Christian faith when what they have is merely a psychological mechanism; and it breaks down in a real crisis. We do not preach psychology, we preach the Christian faith.

Let me show you, then, the difference between the Christian way of dealing with anxiety and this other method. What does the Apostle tell us to do when we are threatened by anxiety? He does not just say, 'Stop worrying.' That is what commonsense and psychology say: 'Stop worrying and pull yourself together.' The Apostle does not say that for the good reason that to tell a person in that condition to stop worrying is useless. Incidentally, it is also bad psychology. If you happen to be a strong-willed person you can hold these things from the conscious mind with the result that they then go on working in the unconscious mind. That is what is called repression – a condition which is even worse than anxiety. But not only that, it is so idle to tell the average person to stop worrying – that is why I say Paul's 'psychology' is so important. It is the very thing he or she cannot do. They would like to, but they cannot. It is like telling a hopeless drunkard to stop drinking. He cannot, because he is helplessly in the grip of this lust and passion. In the same way the Bible does not say, 'Do not worry, it may never happen.' This is a popular psychological slogan and people think it is very wonderful – 'Why worry, it may never happen?' But if anyone says that to me when I am in this state, my reaction is: 'Yes, but it *may* happen.' That is my problem. What if it does happen? That is the essence of my problem, so it does not help me to say it may never happen.

Another negative is this. People tend to say to those wretched people who are anxious and worried, 'You must not worry, it is wrong to worry, and all the worry in the world will not make any difference.' Now that is perfectly true, it is sound commonsense. The psychologists in their turn say, 'Do not waste your energy. The fact that you are worrying is not going to affect the position at all.' 'Ah, yes,' I say, 'that is all right, that is perfectly true; but, you know, it does not get at the source of my trouble for this good reason. I am concerned with what *may* happen. I agree when you put it to me that worrying is not going to affect the position, but the position remains and it is the position that is causing me this anxiety. What you say is perfectly true, but it does not deal with my particular situation.' In other words, all these methods fail to deal with the situation because they never realise the power of what Paul calls 'the heart' and 'the mind' -- these things that grip us. That is why none of the psychology and commonsense methods are finally of any use.

What, then, does the Apostle say? He puts his remedy in the form of a positive injunction: 'Let your requests be made known unto God.' That is the answer. But now, here, it is of vital importance that we should know precisely and in detail how to deal with this. The Apostle says, 'Let your requests be made known unto God.' 'Alas!' says many a sufferer. 'I have tried, I have prayed; but I have not found the peace you speak of. I have not had an answer. It is no use telling me to pray.' Fortunately for us, the Apostle realised that also, and he has given us particular instructions for the carrying out of his injunction. 'Be careful for nothing; but in every thing by prayer and supplication with thanksgiving let your requests be made known unto God.' Is the Apostle just tumbling out one word after another, or is he speaking advisedly? I can show you that he is indeed speaking advisedly as he shows us how to let our requests be made known unto God.

How are we to do that? First he tells us to pray. He differentiates between prayer and supplication and thanksgiving. What does he mean by prayer? This is the most general term and it means worship and adoration. If you have problems that seem insoluble, if you are liable to become anxious and overburdened, and somebody tells you to pray, do not rush to God with your petition. That is not the way.

Before you make your requests known unto God, pray, worship, adore. Come into the presence of God and for the time being forget your problems. Do not start with them. Just realise that you are face to face with God. The idea of being face to face is inherent in the very word 'prayer'. You come into the presence of God and you realise the presence and you recollect that presence – that is the first step always. Even before you make your requests known unto God you realise that you are face to face with God, that you are in his presence and you pour out your heart in adoration. That is the beginning.

But following prayer comes supplication. Now we are moving on. Having worshipped God because God is God, having offered this general worship and adoration, we come now to the particular, and the Apostle here encourages us to make our supplications. He tells us that we can take particular things to God, that petition is a legitimate part of prayer. So we bring our petitions, the particular things that are now concerning us.

We are now coming nearer to letting our requests be made known. But wait, there is still one other thing – 'by prayer and supplication with thanksgiving'. That is one of the most vital of all these terms. And it is just here that so many of us go astray when we are in this condition with which the Apostle is dealing. I trust it is unnecessary that I should digress to point out that in connection with these steps the Apostle was not merely interested in liturgical forms. What a tragedy that people should take an interest in the form of worship in a mere liturgical sense. That is not what the Apostle is concerned about. He is not interested in formality, he is interested in worship.

Thanksgiving is absolutely essential for this reason: if, while we pray to God, we have a grudge against him in our hearts, we have no right to expect that the peace of God will keep our heart and our mind. If we go on our knees feeling that God is against us, we may as well get up and go out. No, we must approach him 'with thanksgiving'. There must be no doubt in our heart as to the goodness of God. There must be no question or query; we must have positive reasons for thanking God. We have our problems and troubles but there on our knees we must ask ourselves: 'What can I thank God for?' We have to do that deliberately and it is something that we can do. We must remind ourselves of it. We must say, 'I may be in trouble at the moment, but I can thank God for my salvation and that he has sent his Son to die on the cross for me and for my sins. There is a terrible problem facing me, I know, but he has done that for me. I thank God that he sent his Son, our Lord Jesus Christ, into the world. I will thank him for bearing my sins in his own body on the tree, I will thank him for rising again for my justification. I will pour out my heart in thanksgiving for that. I will thank him for the many blessings I have received in the past.' We must just work out with our mind and with all our energy the reasons for thanking and praising God. We must remind ourselves that he is our Father, that he loves us so much that the very hairs of our head are all numbered. And when we have reminded ourselves of these things we must pour out our heart in thanksgiving. We must be in the right relationship to God. We must realise the truth concerning him. Therefore we must come into his presence with a loving, praising, worshipping, adoration and confident faith and then make our requests known unto him. The prayer that Paul advocates, in other words, is not a desperate cry in the dark, not some frantic appeal to God without any real thought. No, we first realise and recollect that we are worshipping a blessed, glorious God. We worship first and then we make our requests known.

Then the next principle is the gracious promise of God to all who do this. We have seen what we have to do, we have been instructed how we are to deal with it, and now comes the gracious promise to those who do what the Apostle has just been telling us. This is, of course, the best of all, but we must learn how to look at it. Have you noticed the promise, have you noticed its character, have you noticed that it does not even mention the things that are worrying you? That is the peculiar thing about the Christian method of dealing with anxiety. Does the Apostle say, 'In all things – these things that are worrying – make your requests known and God will banish and remove them all?' No, Paul does not say that. He does not mention them, he just says nothing about them. To me that is one of the most thrilling things about the Christian life. The glory of the gospel is that it is concerned about us and not about our circumstances. The final triumph of the gospel is seen in this, that whatever our circumstances, we ourselves can be put right and maintained. It does not mention our condition, it does not talk about these things that are harassing and perplexing, it does not say a single word about them. They may or they may not happen, I do not know. Paul does not say that the thing feared is not going to take place, he says that we shall be kept whether it happens or whether it does not happen. Thank God, that is the victory. I am taken above circumstances, I am triumphant in spite of them.

That is the great principle. We all tend to be tyrannised by circumstances because we depend upon them, and we would like them to be governed and controlled, but that is not the way in which the Scripture deals with the situation. What the Apostle says is this: 'Make your requests known unto God, and the peace of God which passeth all understanding, shall keep your hearts and minds.' He will keep you absolutely safe from these things which are keeping you awake and preventing your sleep. They will be kept outside, and you will be kept in peace in spite of them.

Again, I would point out that never does the Apostle say that if we pray, our prayer in and of itself will make us feel better. It is a disgraceful thing that people should pray for that reason. That is the psychologists' use of prayer. They tell us that if we are in trouble it will do us good to pray – very good psychology, thoroughly bad Christianity. Prayer is not auto-suggestion.

Neither does he say, 'Pray, because while you are praying you will not be thinking about that problem, and therefore you will have temporary relief.' Again, good psychology but bad Christianity.

Neither does he say, 'If you fill your mind with thoughts of God and Christ these thoughts will push out the other things.' Once more, good psychology but nothing to do with Christianity.

Neither does he say, and I say this advisedly, 'Pray, because prayer changes things.' No, it does not. Prayer does not 'change things'. That is not what the Apostle says, that is again psychology and has nothing at all to do with the gospel. What the Apostle says is this: 'You pray and make your requests known unto God, and God will do something.' It is not your prayer that is going to do it, it is not you who are going to do it, but God. 'The peace of God, which passeth all understanding' – he, through it all, 'shall keep your hearts and minds through Christ Jesus.'

I must say a word about that expression 'keeping' your hearts and minds. It means garrisoning, guarding – a number of words can be used. It conjures up a picture. What will happen is that this peace of God will walk round the ramparts and towers of our life. We are inside, and the activities of the heart and mind are producing those stresses and anxieties and strains from the outside. But the peace of God will keep them all out and we ourselves inside will be at perfect peace. It is God who does it. It is not we ourselves, it is not prayer, it is not some psychological mechanism. We make our requests known unto God, and God does that for us and keeps us in perfect peace.

What shall we say of this phrase: 'The peace of God, which passeth all understanding'? You cannot understand this peace; you cannot imagine it; in a sense, you cannot even believe it; yet it is happening and you are experiencing it and enjoying it. It is God's peace that is in Christ Jesus. What does he mean by that? He is telling us that this peace of God works by presenting the Lord Jesus Christ to us and reminding us about him. To put it in terms of the argument of the epistle to the Romans: 'If, when we were enemies, we were reconciled to God by the death of his Son, much more, being reconciled, we shall be saved by his life' (Rom. 5:10).

'All things work together for good to them that love God, to them who are the called according to his purpose.' 'He that spared not his own Son, but delivered him up for us all, how shall he not with him also freely give us all things?' (Rom. 8:28, 32). 'I am persuaded, that neither death, nor life, nor angels, nor principalities, nor powers, nor things present, nor things to come, nor height, nor depth, nor any other creature, shall be able to separate us from the love of God, which is in Christ Jesus our Lord' (Rom. 8:38, 39). The argument is that if God has done that supreme thing for us in the death of his Son upon the cross, he cannot forsake us now, he cannot leave us half-way, as it were. So the peace of God that passeth all understanding keeps our hearts and minds through, or in, Christ Jesus. In that way God guarantees our peace and our freedom from anxiety.

I end with a word on the last principle, which is the all-inclusiveness of the promise. 'In nothing be careful' – 'Be careful for nothing, but in all things . . .' It does not matter what they are, there is no limit in it. Beloved Christian, whatever it is that is tending to get you down, tending to make you a victim of this anxiety, this morbid care, harassing and spoiling your Christian life and witness, whatever it is, let it be known unto God in that way, and if you do so it is absolutely guaranteed that the peace of God which passeth all understanding shall guard, keep, garrison your heart and mind. That mighty turmoil of heart and mind within you will not affect you. Like the Psalmist, you will lay yourself down and you will sleep, you will know this perfect peace. Do you know this, have you got this peace? Is this another bit of theory or does it actually happen? I assert that nearly two thousand years of Christian history – the story of the Christian Church – proclaim that this is a fact. Read the stories of the saints and the martyrs and the Confessors. And, you get the same evidence in contemporary stories. Recently I read of an experience told by John George Carpenter, until a few years ago the General of the Salvation Army. He tells how he and his wife had to part with their daughter, a lovely girl, of whom they were so fond and proud and who had dedicated her young life to foreign mission work in the East. Suddenly she was taken ill with typhoid fever. Of course, they began to pray, but John Carpenter and Mrs Carpenter somehow felt, although they could not explain it, that they could not pray for that child's recovery. They went on praying but their prayer was – 'Thou canst heal her if thou wilt' – they could not positively ask God to heal her, only – 'Thou canst if thou wilt.' They could get no further. They went on like that for six weeks and then this beautiful girl died. The very morning she died John Carpenter said to Mrs Carpenter, 'You know, I am aware of a strange and curious calm within.' And Mrs Carpenter replied, 'I feel exactly the same.' And she said to him, 'This must be the peace of God.' And it was the peace of God. It was the peace of God keeping the heart and mind quiet in the sense that they could not upset the person. There they were, they had made their request known in the right way, and to their amazement and astonishment – they were almost chiding themselves because of it – this amazing calm and peace had come to them. They could not understand it, and that was the only explanation – 'It must be the peace of God.' It was. Thank God for it. You and I cannot explain these things, they overpower us; but he is almighty. With prayer and supplication and thanksgiving, therefore, let your requests be made known unto him, and he, through his peace in Christ, will keep your heart and mind at rest and in peace.

Chapter 15

The Hebrew and the Greek mind

> Finally, brethren, whatsoever things are true, whatsoever
> things are honest, whatsoever things are just, whatsoever
> things are pure, whatsoever things are lovely, whatsoever
> things are of good report; if there be any virtue, and if
> there be any praise, think on these things (Phil. 4:8).

We come, in these words, to the last of the series of exhortations which the Apostle Paul addresses to the members of
the church at Philippi. The word 'finally' indicates quite
clearly that the Apostle is finding it very difficult to end this
letter. He so loves the members of the church at Philippi, his
attachment to them is so great because of the special
relationship that exists between them, and the whole character of the church is such that the Apostle feels drawn to
them in an exceptional manner, and he has thoroughly
enjoyed writing this letter to them. He finds it difficult,
therefore, to finish it, and yet he must, and so, apart from
certain further remarks of a more personal character, he
brings the letter to an end with this general exhortation.
Now these words are probably very familiar to all of us. In
the days when people used to put framed texts upon their
walls, you would often find this verse facing you. It is one
which is often quoted, and yet I suggest that perhaps no
words which were written by the Apostle Paul are so open
to misunderstanding. They have frequently been misunderstood; and have been the attacking ground of a great discussion which has gone on in the Christian Church almost
from the beginning. Therefore I feel that as we look at this

verse nothing is so important as the question of our approach to it.

There are certain verses in the Bible of which it can always be said quite truthfully that our approach to them is vital and determines our exposition. For those who are interested in this matter of exegesis and exposition, that is a very important principle. It is always dangerous to take a verse in isolation; no verse should be taken out of its context, but that is especially so with regard to some verses. For instance, it would be possible to approach this verse by taking the different words and terms that the Apostle uses and giving their exact meaning, and then to regard that as an adequate interpretation. But I want to try to show you that that is quite inadequate with a verse like this, and that here, especially, our whole approach to the statement is of supreme significance. In other words, the question that arises at once is this: What exactly is the Apostle Paul talking about here? And that immediately introduces us, as I have already reminded you, to the great discussion that has obtained from the very earliest days of Christianity, and has divided Christian people into two groups.

The problem which is posed for us by this particular text is the whole problem of the relationship between Christianity and culture. Now I am sure that many, if not most, Christian people, are interested in that question, because it is of very real significance and importance. Indeed, it behoves us to arrive at some decision with regard to this whole matter because it really is one of the most urgent and relevant problems confronting the Christian Church at this very moment.

We can put this in its setting by approaching the subject historically. If you go far back into history, you will find that the problem raised here is the difference between the Hebrew mind and the Greek mind – it is as old as that! In the ancient world two ways of thinking confronted men and women – the Hebrew outlook upon life, and the Greek outlook, and they were very different. In a sense, the fight that you find in the Bible – and you certainly find it in the subsequent history of the Christian Church – is this conflict between the Hebrew and the Greek, these two attitudes with regard to life. Let me note briefly some of the characteristic differences between the two outlooks.

Now the Hebrew always tends to be active; the Greek, on the other hand, tends to be abstract. The Hebrew believes in salvation by deeds and by actions, while the Greek believes in salvation by ideas. The Old Testament, which is the quintessence of the Hebrew outlook, is the story of God doing things – that is the Hebrew concept of salvation. Not ideas about salvation, not thoughts, not concepts, but God acting, God intervening, that is the Hebrew emphasis, whereas to the Greek everything tends to be a matter of ideas. Salvation is an idea, something that you work out in terms of thought, by passivity and contemplation – it is salvation by thoughts and ideas.

Then another important distinction is that the Hebrew is characterised by emotion and passion, whereas the Greek, I would say, is characterised by sentimentality and control. I think you will see the importance of these distinctions.

If you look at the great Hebrew prophets, whose writings we have in the Old Testament, you will find that they are full of emotion, full of movement, full of rugged strength, tearing asunder, blasting with force and with power. The Greek, on the other hand, does not like passion or emotion; at least, he likes controlled emotion which becomes sentimental; everything must be very orderly. The Greek does not stress power and might so much as beauty and order, arrangement and control. To put it, perhaps, in a word, the essential difference between the Hebrew and the Greek is the difference between the prophetic and the educative.

Now you see the importance of this at the present time. There are people in the Church who say that what we need is a great teaching ministry; but there are others who say that what we need, above everything else, is a prophetic ministry. They say it is not enough to present ideas by teaching – no, you need something more profound and fundamental and the prophetic note is the note that is needed. You can see that the decision of the Church with respect to

these two things will affect her ministry. In this you also see
the difference between those modern men and women who
just need to have ideas presented to them and those who
need the prophetic power that will blast and rend and convict and lead to conversion – the mighty activity of God.
That is the essential background to this verse that we are
looking at now.

So there you have, right away back in history, the difference between the Hebrew and the Greek. But the moment
the Christian Church came into being, the problem became
very acute, the moment this gospel was preached in Europe
and in the Greek areas of the world, the great fight began.
The tendency was for the Greek outlook, the philosophical
outlook, to impose itself upon the essentially Hebrew idea
of salvation, and to control and modify it. That is why you
find a man like the Apostle Paul going out of his way, in
writing to the church at Corinth, to say that he does not
preach Christ 'with the wisdom of words, lest the cross of
Christ should be made of none effect' (1 Cor. 1:17). He is
warning the people against philosophy, against this science
of learning, this Greek conception.

Now the authorities are all agreed in saying that for the
first three or four centuries the Christian gospel had to fight
for its very life against Greek philosophy: the idea of turning
the gospel with its activity, with its prophetic emphasis, into
just another, though perhaps the best and the greatest and
the most perfect, of the philosophies. But let us come down
the ages and see how this fight was continued. You see it
showing itself clearly in the sixteenth and seventeenth centuries, especially, first of all, in the sixteenth. I am referring
to the conflict between the Reformation and the Renais-
sance, for the two things came together at that time – the
revival of learning and the revival of religion – and there was
a great fight between them. In a sense, it was represented by
two people: Martin Luther and Erasmus. On the one hand,
Luther the prophetic preacher of the gospel, believing the
Hebrew idea; on the other hand, Erasmus with his ideas on
teaching and with his knowledge and culture. It is very

interesting to read the correspondence between these men, because there you will see a great elaboration of this question.

Then move on to the seventeenth century where you find the same thing once more, and here it is the conflict between Puritanism and Anglicanism – I mean Anglicanism in a general term. It was a fight between the Puritan idea of worship, which was simple, direct and immediate and which emphasised emotion, trembling in the presence of the Holy God, and being subject to the activity of God; there was a conflict between that, and the idea of worship that lays emphasis on forms, ceremonies, ritual, beauty of diction and language, ornate buildings and the Greek concept of beauty and goodness, as well as truth. And this great fight beween the Hebrew and the Greek in terms of Puritanism and Anglicanism has persisted throughout the centuries. You find it in the last century in a striking manner. In the eighteenth century, as a result of the evangelical awakening, the Hebrew idea came into the ascendancy with revival, conversions and God doing things. Ah, yes, but in the last century, as the result of the so-called 'Enlightenment' and a new interest in the Classics and in learning and in knowledge, the Greek idea began to percolate back, and its influence upon the interpretation of Scripture has been most profound. Indeed, the vast majority of theological ideas today show the decided influence of the Greek outlook upon salvation. Think of the men during the last century, men such as Emerson, Ruskin, Matthew Arnold and people like that, they are typical Greeks, and over against them you have the evangelicals with their Hebrew emphasis, and these two viewpoints are ever fighting against each other.

I call your attention to this because it is my profound conviction that the state of the Church today, in this and in most other lands, is entirely to be attributed to the fact that the Greeks have gained the ascendancy, that the old idea of the prophetic message is being pushed into the background, and the idea of worshipping God in terms of ideas and thoughts is gaining ground. You must not talk about conversion – that was all right in prophetic times, but there is no longer any need to be converted. No, you just absorb the idea, and, in this way, the whole world is going to be saved. That is the Greek conception in contra-distinction to the Hebrew.

And, of course, we are face to face with this self-same thing at the present time. But today it is a fight between Christianity and what is called Western, or European culture. Now it behoves us to examine this matter seriously and carefully. Is it the business of the Church to contend for that culture? I am not expressing any opinion on modern-day culture other than that it is very good, but I must ask whether it is the business of the Church merely to preach that type of culture, or whether it is the job of the Church to preach the prophetic Hebrew gospel, the activity of God, the need of conversion?

Are we simply standing for the propagating of certain values which have been useful in life and conduct, or are we to preach doom and judgment? Are we to call upon God, to repent and humble ourselves, and thus have personal dealings with God? That is the question, and you see it is of vital moment to the whole future of the Christian Church.

Now all this arises because of the eighth verse of Philippians 4. When we look at this verse, the question that we ask at once is this: What is Paul saying? Is he, just for once in his life, and for the only time in his writings, suddenly taking the Greek view? Is Paul just telling these Philippian people, 'Now, then, familiarise yourselves with Greek culture and spend your time in thinking about these things'? That is the question. You can see that our approach to this verse matters supremely, because this is the favourite verse of those who advocate the Greek outlook. If you ever have a discussion with them on the relationship between Christianity and culture, I can assure you that they will produce this verse – it is the only one they can produce – and they say that here the Apostle Paul is putting before us this Greek idea.

They are, however, in one difficulty, and it is interesting to notice how they all have to grant it – Paul uses the word *virtue*: 'Finally, brethren . . . if there be any virtue . . .' and immediately they begin to write their notes: 'Now,' they say, 'this is striking. That word virtue was a pagan word, and isn't it remarkable that this is the only time that the Apostle ever used it?' They have to acknowledge that Paul knew all about Greek culture, he was a man well-versed in these things, he was a cultured man, and yet they have to admit that in all his writings this is the only place where the Apostle uses this word. It was something the Greeks believed in and it was the basis of their philosophy. Greek philosophy was nothing but a constant appeal to men to exercise virtue, it was a moral appeal. But Paul uses the word just once, here, and that is why they are in difficulties.

But the question that arises for us is what exactly does the Apostle mean in this verse? There are a number of ways in which people traditionally have approached and interpreted this verse. The first is what I would call the sentimental approach and interpretation. Certain people who read these words, or see them upon the wall, say, 'How beautiful!' And they never get any further; it is the aesthetic approach. They say as they read verse 8 aloud to themselves, 'How wonderful!' I need not stay with this. If there is one thing with which the Apostle must never be charged it is with sentimentality. Sentiment, passion, yes; emotion, yes; but sentimentality, never – it is utterly foreign to the essential Christian character.

The second approach is what I would describe as an interpretation in terms of what is called 'the science of thought'. This is important, because it does seem to me that far too often, as Christian people, we confuse this so-called 'science of thought' language with the message of the Christian gospel. What it says is that you must fill your mind with beautiful thoughts, with poetry, good literature or music. That is the appeal of the gospel. If we fill our minds with these beautiful, lovely, uplifting thoughts and ideas, we shall be saved and emancipated from everything that tends to be unworthy and to drag us down.

You are familiar with this; you see it in the books and journals. We are told that last thing at night we must make sure that we have beautiful thoughts in our minds; it will not only help us to sleep, it will help our whole life and outlook, and we will wake up feeling fresher and brighter. 'Surround yourself,' people say, 'with beauty in poetry, literature and music, and in various other ways, and as you go on doing this, you will gradually become a better and better person.' Now there are Christian people who use this verse in that way, fondly imagining that that is what the Apostle is advocating: we must fill our minds with these wonderful things, and as we do so we will gradually be achieving salvation. That is the science of thought or mind culture, and it is a typical Greek outlook – it is excellent psychology, but an abuse of the Christian gospel.

And then there is what I might call the semi-Christian interpretation of this verse. It appeals to those who do believe that salvation is only possible in terms of the death and resurrection of our Lord, but who also believe that this type of thing has come as an addition and supplement to the gospel, and that it will help us perfect our salvation. This view says that the way to avoid sin and to live a good life, the way to be happy and to maintain our joy, is just to take these good and beautiful and true ideas and think about them, meditate upon them and surrender ourselves to them. Then, as we do so, we will become better people.

But the answer to all that is an eternal 'No!', and that for two main reasons. First of all there is a general reason, and then a specific reason indicated by Paul in verse 8 itself. First, these views are a misinterpretation of the whole of the New Testament teaching. The New Testament never asks us to contemplate ideas, it always calls upon us to look at the Person. That is the essential difference between the gospel and philosophy, between the Hebrew and the Greek. I would remind you once more that there was nothing that Paul was so afraid of as that the doctrine of the cross should be turned into a philosophy – and how easy it is to do it! To maintain, for example, that 'death is essential to life', or that there is 'a principle of sacrifice in life', is to turn the doctrine of the cross into a philosophical idea, and it is exactly the same with the resurrection. Have you not noticed, as you come to Eastertime, how people start sentimentalising about 'life', saying how the seed that was sown has died and that now the life germ has come out of death, and that there you see resurrection as a principle of life because you see it everywhere? And the glorious fact of the resurrection of Christ is philosophised in that way into a general principle of 'resurrection'.

Now that is something which the New Testament never does. The New Testament is concerned about facts, it is concerned about a Person, Paul said of him, '. . . that I may know him, and the power of his resurrection . . .', not a general principle of rising in life. No, the eternal Son of God was literally born as a babe in Bethlehem; it is not an idea, it does not belong to Greek mythology, it happened. He suffered and endured, he literally staggered up to Golgotha, he was nailed to the tree – these are not ideas. They happened! See him, look at him. He died and was buried, a stone was rolled to the mouth of that grave, but it was removed and he emerged. He came out literally in the body, he showed himself again. All along we are exhorted to consider him, and to consider these facts, while we are told that what he has done is all sufficient.

'But,' says someone, 'surely if that is all true, doesn't this other idea help? Isn't it still a good idea, and won't it help with my salvation if I fill my mind with beautiful words and thoughts and music?' No, that is the cloven hoof of the devil, that is where the devil comes in. The gospel of Jesus Christ needs no assistance, it needs no supplement, nothing can save a man but what God has done in Christ. If the whole of Greek culture and the Greek outlook failed to save the world, if it failed in the greater thing, do we need to call in its assistance in the lesser thing? Out upon the suggestion! 'But of him are ye in Christ Jesus, who of God is made unto us wisdom, and righteousness, and sanctification, and redemption' (1 Cor. 1:30). He is the life, I do not need you plus. He is the beginning and the end, he is all and in all and in him dwelleth all the fulness of the godhead bodily.

do not need Greek culture, I do not need science of thought, I have all in him. I will admit no assistance, no supplement.

And, of course, it is not a mere theory. I think I can show you clearly that the history of the last hundred years proves my contention. We have heard a great deal about this other idea during that time. We have not preached the prophetic gospel; we have not stressed the need for repentance and conversion and an utter humiliation before God; we do not like the term 'vile sinner', we are too polite! We work on the Greek idea, but what has it led to? You see what happens when we call in the assistance of culture to help us? Look at the modern world, look at the life lived by men and women, look at the moral muddle throughout the whole world. No, the very idea must be dismissed; people like to be told to fill their minds with beautiful thoughts, so to use this verse in the Greek sense is a danger to men and women because it panders to their pride.

Then, as I have tried to show you, it detracts from the glory and perfection of the work of Christ upon the cross. I can put that in terms of one particular illustration in order to show you the difference between these two things which we have been discussing together. Take the problem of dealing with fear, or the problem of dealing with unworthy thoughts, perhaps the problem of jealousy. Now the person who is troubled about one of these things is afraid of being alone, he is afraid of what will happen. The Greek idea believes in what is called subjugation. Here you are, alone, and you begin to be fearful, so at once you start thinking about things that are beautiful, lovely and pure, and as you are filling your mind with these thoughts you forget your fear, you have got it under control. So in that way you are harnessing that fear, you are attaching it to something higher, and as you do this, you get rid of your fear or these unworthy thoughts, and instead you have these beautiful and lovely ones.

Now that is not the New Testament method of dealing with the problem and for this good reason: it means that you are not facing yourself or the temptation honestly. While the Greek method tells you not to think about it, the Christian method tells you to look it straight in the face. The Christian, the gospel method, never tells you to avoid thinking about sin, it tells you to face it, and to think about it. And here is the essence of the whole matter and that is why, by nature, people prefer the Greek to the Hebrew. The Christian way of dealing with fear is like this. It comes to you and it says, 'Do you say that you, as a Christian, are afraid like this? Do you say that you, who believe that God loved you and sent his only begotten Son to die on the cross for you and rose again to justify you, do you say you cannot trust him with your little life? Do you say the God who has done the greater thing is not going to look after you?' The gospel does not say, 'Now think beautiful thoughts and forget the others.' The gospel comes to you and says, 'Are you as a Christian harbouring thoughts like that? Did Christ die in order that you should go on thinking in that way and living in that way? Face yourself,' says the gospel, 'look at your own imperfections, and then look into the face of Christ upon that cross and ask God to have mercy and compassion upon you.' That is the Christian method, not science of thought, but looking at yourself in the light of Christ and what he has done for you, bringing that sin, that foul, ugly sin immediately to him, facing it and yourself in his holy presence, and believing truly and absolutely and implicitly in his power.

In view of all this, I would suggest to you that what Paul was saying to the Philippians was this: Your whole thinking and all your actions must be controlled by the gospel. He was still concerned about their joy and peace, and this is his last word about it. In effect, he says, 'If you want to know that peace of God that passeth understanding, if you want to experience the joy of the Lord, then, in addition to what I have told you negatively, remember this positively: your whole life and thought and your actions must be controlled by the gospel. You must not think things that are incompatible with it.' And then he puts it in a positive form. The things we are to think about must be compatible with the gospel. They must be true, true in that ultimate sense, they must be serious, they must be reverent. Christians are essentially serious people because they have seen themselves as lost sinners saved only by the death of Christ on the cross, and those who have seen that must be profoundly, fundamentally serious. I do not say that they are solemn but I do say that they are serious and reverent; there is a seriousness in their whole outlook upon life. They must be just, and their thoughts must be pure, clean and unadulterated; lovely, in the sense that they will lead people to look at and love them; of good report, well spoken of; of virtue, moral excellence; of praise, moral approbation from the practice of the truth.

That is what the Apostle says. As Christian people we must see to it that the whole of our life, our very thoughts and ideas, everything, are under the mighty control of the risen Lord. Every thought must be brought into subjection to him. As we read in 2 Corinthians 10:5, we must bring everything into captivity to Christ; Christ must control our minds and the whole of our thinking. So let us beware of the subtle danger of confusing the general culture, which is good in and of itself, with the glorious gospel of God in Jesus Christ. Let our whole life be a tribute and a testimony to our Redeemer's praise.

Chapter 16

How to know God's peace

> Those things, which ye have both learned, and received,
> and heard, and seen in me, do: and the God of peace shall
> be with you (Phil. 4:9).

Let me remind you again that these two verses, the eighth
and ninth, constitute the Apostle's final exhortation to the
members of the church at Philippi, and we have seen that
they are particularly comprehensive. The eighth verse,
which we considered in our last study, stresses mainly the
thought of the Christian, the realm in which thinking should
be exercised, the way in which the gospel limits intellectual
life, and it defines the things about which the Christian life
should meditate. Then here in this ninth verse we come to
the other great section of the exhortation, and this is the
more practical part. Here Paul is concerned to emphasise
what the gospel has to say to us in the realm of conduct and
of action.

Here, then, in this final exhortation, we are reminded of
some fundamental principles with regard to the gospel
which we can never and, indeed, must never forget. The
Apostle is here, in a sense, giving a summary of everything
he has been trying to say. It is as if he were saying, 'I have
now gone into the details, I have dealt with these particular
problems, I have tried to visualise the temptations that you
may meet and all I have been saying to you can be put like
this: let your whole life be dominated in this way by the gospel, and then all will be well with you.' And that, I would
say, reminds us of two fundamental principles with regard to

the gospel. The first is that the gospel is not something which we add to our lives, it is rather, something which should entirely dominate them.

We must constantly repeat this, because I believe that a most subtle danger, which tends to assail us all, is the danger of making our Christianity some kind of addition to our lives, instead of seeing that the New Testament teaches everywhere that the gospel controls the whole of life. There is to be nothing in the life of the Christian that does not come under the control and domination of the gospel. In other words, in this exhortation the Apostle is reminding us that all our thinking, all our intellectual activity, must, to use his words in 2 Corinthians 10:5, be subjected to, or made captive to, the Lord Jesus Christ.

Now the life of man on earth can be divided into these two categories. Our whole existence here is a matter of thinking and of doing; and the Apostle teaches us that in both respects we are to be controlled by the gospel. He has given us the characteristics of the gospel in the realm of thought; the gospel is concerned only with things that are honest, things that are just, things that are pure and lovely and of good report, everything that belongs to the moral excellence and everything deserving of praise. And here, in conduct, it is exactly the same – 'These things which ye have both learned, and received, and heard, and seen in me, do': – your thinking and your acting are to be dominated entirely by the gospel of Jesus Christ.

The Christian life, therefore, is not merely a modification of the natural life, it is a new life, and Christians do not merely add something to their lives, they are people who have been changed at the centre, they are entirely different. Now we need not stay with this, but this, surely, is something which is basic in the New Testament teaching. 'If any man be in Christ, he is a new creature' (2 Cor. 5:17), not an improved creature, nor a renovated creature, but a new creature, a new creation; he is altogether different, his entire life is something that should present a striking contrast to those who are not Christian. Christians do not think in the same way, they do not live in the same way; there is this new power and purpose on the very throne of their being, dominating their activity and thinking, that covers the whole of their lives. All that is suggested by this great exhortation.

Then the second great principle is what the Apostle here shows us very plainly with regard to the New Testament doctrine of holiness. The New Testament teaching of holiness, or sanctification, is never presented as a law. This is something that tends to lead us astray. There is always the danger of turning New Testament holiness into moralities, but the two things are entirely different. The New Testament never gives a list of rules and regulations, it never tells us to do, or not to do, various things, that is the law. But the New Testament does not do that; holiness, it tells us, is rather something which is not only essential, but is inevitable if we truly desire to enjoy the blessings of the Christian gospel. I am never tired of putting it like this. The New Testament doctrine of holiness is an appeal to our Christian commonsense; it is an appeal to our reason. It does not come, as it were, in the form of a dictator saying, 'Do these things!' No, it rather comes and says, 'If you really want to enjoy the fulness and the blessings of the gospel of Christ, then there are certain things that you must do.'

That is why we must realise that there is no need to denounce people who are not living the holy life. The New Testament seems to me to be sorry for them. There is no need to denounce Christians who are not doing their utmost to live the Christian life, because, poor things, they are suffering enough as it is. They are missing the greatest things the gospel has to give. The New Testament regards as pathetic these people who claim that they desire the blessings of the gospel and yet are not doing the one thing that is essential to receiving them. They are deceiving themselves, they are foolish; is that not the term which our Lord himself used – the foolish man who built his house upon the sand? That is the New Testament way of proclaiming this doctrine of holiness and of sanctification. It comes to us with this great appeal, and tells us, 'Here are the blessings that are possible, but if you desire to receive them, you must pay attention to what always accompanies them.'

In other words, the New Testament blessings are always conditional. This is just another way of saying that one of the most important words in verse 9 is the last 'and': 'These things which ye have . . . seen in me do; *and* the God of peace shall be with you', that is, 'If you do this, then that will follow.' That is the New Testament way of offering these blessings. Indeed, search your Bible from beginning to end and you will find that all the promises of blessing are conditional. In the Old Testament, was that not true of the Children of Israel? That was the blunder which they made; they forgot that all that God had promised to Abraham, and their receiving the land and dwelling in it, was conditional. This was expressed in one of the commandments – 'Honour thy father and thy mother: that thy days may be long upon the land which the Lord thy God giveth thee' (Ex. 20:12). God promised the Children of Israel that they should possess that land only so long as they obeyed his commandments and lived life in accordance with his holy will. Read again about the two Mounts, the Mount of blessing and the Mount of cursing (Deut. 11:29). So long as the people obeyed the Lord they were blessed, but when they disobeyed they were cursed. And you remember how those foolish people thought that as they were the people of God, nothing could disturb them, but they forgot that the promises are always conditional. Or read also the preamble to the Ten Commandments in Exodus 19. It is all there, always this 'if', so if the condition is not observed, we have no right to expect God's blessing.

Then when you come to the New Testament, you find exactly the same thing. Take the Beatitudes from the Sermon on the Mount: 'Blessed are the meek . . . Blessed are the poor in spirit' and so on. These are the people who are blessed; yes, there is always the condition: you must be meek and poor in spirit; you must hunger and thirst after righteousness if you want to be filled. We are not told that we shall be filled because we are Christians, no, we have to hunger and thirst, and then we shall be filled, and blessed. And now we find this great exposition of that principle here in the ninth verse of this last chapter of Philippians.

So let us look at this statement, and analyse it into its component parts. The subject divides itself quite simply. The first principle taught here is the vital importance of practice, or of action and conduct. It is this little word *do*. You have heard these things, says Paul, you have learned them, and you have seen them in me; yes, but you must do them. Here you are, beloved Philippians, facing your uncertain future and here am I, a prisoner in Rome. I may never see you again, I may be put to death tomorrow, I do not know. But I do know that if you live this life, if you practise these things, then you have nothing to fear at all, the God of peace shall be with you, and nothing can ever harm you. You see the perfection of the Apostle's method? In verse 8 he has dealt with the realm of thought. Ah, but the Apostle knows the subtle danger that is always confronting us, the danger of being content with theoretical knowledge, the danger of being satisfied with doctrine only, the danger of failing to put into practice that which we know.

Let me underline again the emphasis which is placed upon this doctrine from the beginning to the end of the Bible. Was that not the whole trouble with the Pharisees? They were resting upon their knowledge of the law, and they felt that they knew it all so well; but the trouble with them was that they did not practise it. They were teachers, yes, but it is not enough to know these things, you must put them into operation. Or, take Paul's great demonstration of this principle in Romans 2. 'The trouble with the Jews,' Paul says, 'is that they think that because they are the people to whom the law was given, all must be well. But,' says Paul, 'the knowledge of the law does not save, it is the practising of the law that puts a man right with God, and they are relying upon their knowledge without the practice. You foolish men,' he continues, 'you are relying upon the fact that you are aware of God's commandments, but you must practise them.' That is his way of showing how the Jews are guilty, before God, of not receiving the salvation of Jesus Christ.

James says the same thing: The man who knows these things, but does not practise them is like a man who looks at his face in a mirror, and when he has turned away immediately forgets what he has seen. James shows that it is the man who looks into the perfect law of liberty, and 'continueth therein' who is going to be blessed (Jas. 1:22–27). Nothing is more dangerous for us than to be content with a mere superficial acquaintance with God's law. Our Lord says, 'If ye know these things, happy are ye if ye do them' (John 13:17). Ah, yes; you are not going to be happy merely because you know them; rather, happy are you if you put them into practice, and live them out in your daily life.

Or take that great warning in Matthew 7, the picture of the two houses, the house on the rock and the house on the sand. What do they represent? 'Whosoever heareth these sayings of mine, and doeth them . . .' says our Lord, 'I will liken him unto a wise man, which built his house upon a rock' (Matt. 7:24). But the man who builds his house upon the sand is the man who hears these sayings of Christ but does not do them. He has heard what the gospel has to offer him and he is aware of it, but he does nothing about it, and the foolish man imagines that all is well. But when trial comes, that house is utterly demolished. He has not done these things, he has been content with a theoretical knowledge, an academic acquaintance. So the Apostle in this last exhortation is warning the Philippians against that dread and terrible error. 'I have been with you,' says Paul in effect, 'and you have known and received certain things from me. Not only have you heard me speak, you have seen them enacted in my life, and I beseech you to put them into practice. Do not be content with a mere acquaintance with these things, live them out in your daily life, then the God of peace shall be with you and only then.'

Now it seems to me that two main difficulties arise at this point. I feel that many of us are missing so much in the Christian life because we just have not put this apparently obvious principle to the proof, and I think that this is so for two reasons. One is, of course, the very delight that some of us, by nature, tend to take in theoretical knowledge and truth. There are still some people who enjoy reading philosophy, theology and things of that kind. In my opinion, the consideration of reality and truth is the highest intellectual process of which man is ever capable. Look at the great doctrine expounded in this truth! Yes, but the greatest danger with such people is that they are content with that theoretical interest. You can be a great student even of the Bible and live a life that is utterly contrary to it. There are many such people, alas! There have been many whose chief hobby in life has been the dissection and analysis of the Bible. They were interested in its numerics and various other things, but they were rather hard and harsh, and often failed in some of the elementary principles of the Christian life. I mention this because we are so often told that this is the main cause of the modern turning away from the gospel. People say, 'I don't want to be like that Victorian whose head was so full of theology and an understanding of the Scriptures but who failed so tragically in his daily life,' and this criticism is often justified. This danger does face that type of individual. It is the masterpiece of Satan to make us put theory and practice into separate watertight compartments, to make men so interested in the Book that they forget to apply its teaching. What you have seen, says Paul, practise!

The second difficulty is this. There are some people who seem to miss the blessing of the gospel of salvation because they always think of it in terms of some experience, something which has to happen to them. They spend their lives waiting for an experience. Many wait for certain meetings, because they have heard of people who have been to such meetings and who have received great blessings, and they say, 'That is what I want. I will go and get this great blessing which the gospel has to give. The thing to do is to go to that meeting and then it will happen to me.' But such waiting for experiences is a denial of this teaching; you need wait for nothing. Begin to practise the plain teaching of the Scriptures; it is not an experience to be received. You may, of course, suddenly see this truth in a meeting; that is quite all right – the message may come home to you there. You may have specific experiences, you may have some emotional feeling, there are many such things, but the teaching of the New Testament is that without the practising of the precepts, we are not entitled to expect any of the promises. The Holy Spirit, said the Apostle Peter to the first people who listened to him, is given to them that obey God. Without that obedience we have no right to expect the blessings of the Holy Spirit.

But now let us come to something still more practical and immediate. If I say that without practice we cannot expect the God of peace to be always with us, what is it that we have to practise? Paul puts it quite simply: 'Those things, which ye have both learned, and received, and heard, and seen in me, do.' That is not egotism; the Apostle Paul was entitled to speak like that. 'Thank God,' says Paul, in effect, 'I have known these blessings of the gospel, and if you want to know them, then practise the things which you have learned and seen in me.' He does not hesitate to tell them to live the kind of life that he had lived in their presence. And that is a very valuable principle for us. We are to discover what we should do both by reading the Scriptures themselves and also by looking at the example of the saints.

Now here is something that to me is not only of great importance but also of great interest. I have often observed, when I have read the biographies of saintly, godly men and women, that they always conform to a pattern. The saints are remarkably alike. If you read the life of any one of them, you will always find that their life was based on certain very simple principles. The saintly life is always a very simple life, it is the ungodly whose lives are complicated. Sin always brings complications. It did at the very beginning, when man sinned and lied to cover his sin; and the moment men and women come back to God and live godly lives, their lives conform to a very simple pattern.

Thus, if you look at Paul, if you look at any one of the

saints who have ever adorned the Church, you will find that
there are certain simple things which they never fail to practise and to which they pay the most rigorous attention. Let
me just note them. You may think, as I mention them, that
they are almost puerile, and yet, as we examine ourselves, I
think we must admit that it is because we fail in these simple
things that we miss so much in the Christian life. Here, then,
are some of the principles by which the saints lived. First
and foremost, came their attitude to God. The first characteristic always of the saints was that they desired to live to
his glory. That, of course, expresses itself in a desire to
know God better. You have seen me, said Paul to the
Philippians, and what was the big characteristic in my life?
It was my great ambition to 'know him, and the power of his
resurrection, and the fellowship of his sufferings.' Do you
not see standing out in my life this great desire to glorify
God and to know him better?

Can we say that that is the chief thing in our lives? We
have many interests, many of them quite necessary and perfectly legitimate, but as we examine ourselves can we say
that this stands out above everything else, that our highest
ambition is to know God better, that our greatest endeavour
in life is to live to the glory of God? Take any of the saints –
Paul, Augustine, Luther, Calvin, Wesley – look at them,
and you will see that this is the dominating feature of their
lives. Yes, but let us be quite practical, how can we test
whether this is true of us? Well, it always expresses itself in
various practical ways, and the most obvious is that the
saints read as much as they could of God's revelation of
himself. 'These things, which ye have seen in me, do.' What
are they? First and foremost, reading the text book. If you
would know God, then go to God's revelation. If you want
to know him you cannot avoid it. Spend your time with the
Scriptures, long to understand them; say, as Peter puts it,
that as a newborn babe you thirst for the pure milk of the
word that you may grow thereby (1 Pet. 2:2).

Then, next, obviously, is prayer. If you like a person you
want to spend as much time as you can with that person. If

we want to know God better, surely we need to spend time talking to him. How much time do we spend in prayer, in secret, in public, in praying about these things, in talking to God about our own unworthiness, asking him to reveal himself more and more? 'These things do' – if you want the God of peace to be with you, it is a matter of doing, not waiting for experiences. You just start reading your Bible, and then you go on and begin to pray. You may say, 'But I can't pray.' Then talk to God about it. Tell him it is your desire to know him better and to spend time with him. Is it not obvious? Do these things, says Paul.

Furthermore, the attitude of the saints towards themselves inevitably follows. They realise their sinfulness, and therefore they humble and humiliate themselves and do their utmost to mortify their imperfections – you will find this in the biography of any saint. So how do they do this? By spending time in self-examination, which is one of the most difficult things to do in this busy world. But if a man would humble and humiliate himself before God, he must make time to examine himself and his life. He must examine it in the light of Scripture, and in the light of the lives of the saints. He must see where he fails; he must constantly survey his own heart, bringing out the hidden things and dealing with them. Self-examination – how the saints have concentrated upon that!

What else? The next thing is their attitude towards the world in which they find themselves. This again is inevitable. The saints have always regarded this world as a sinful place, opposed to God and opposed to the highest interests of the soul. They have, therefore, done their utmost to avoid its influence, its selfishness and worldly lusts, and they have broken with such things. I am not enunciating this as a law, I am just telling you what you can see in the lives of Paul and all God's saints. They have always seen that the world is opposed to our highest and best interests – that it is always dragging us down, and having seen that, they have renounced it, cost what it may.

What is their attitude towards those who are not Christians? It is to see them as victims of sin and Satan, and the saints have therefore felt sorry for them, and have spoken to them about these things. They have tried to enlighten them, to warn them of the danger to their souls; they have not hesitated, at the risk of being persecuted and laughed at, to remonstrate with them and to try to appeal to them to see the truth of God as it is in Christ Jesus.

So, to sum it all up, the saints have always regarded life as but a journey, a pilgrimage. They have regarded themselves as people travelling through this wilderness to God and to glory, and their eye has ever been upon that. Everything that stands between them and that, everything that has been opposed to that, has been avoided; they have concentrated on this one thing – godliness.

Now I have merely summarised the teaching of the Bible, you will find it in many places. Paul, for instance, in writing to Titus, sums it all up by saying that we are taught this: '. . . denying ungodliness and worldly lusts, we should live soberly, righteously, and godly, in this present world; looking for that blessed hope, and the glorious appearing of the great God and our Saviour Jesus Christ . . .' (Tit. 2:12–13). That is it – that is what we are to practise.

So we have seen the importance of practice and of what we have to practise and now, finally, let us look at the reward of such practice. Here it is – do these things: 'and the God of peace shall be with you'. Does anyone feel that I have been too narrow, that this is a very narrow kind of life and that it is hardly worth living? 'Avoid this, read the Bible, pray – isn't that an apology for life?' But this is what the gospel says, 'Those things . . . do: and the God of peace shall be with you.' So is the price too great? My dear friend, no one can decide that for you, you decide that for yourself. All that I would say is that if you want the God of peace to be with you, then do these things. That is what Paul had been doing, that is what the saints have always done. 'Is there any difference,' asks someone, 'between the peace of God spoken of in the seventh verse and God's peace here in this ninth verse? Verses 6 and 7 say ". . . let your requests be made known unto God. And the peace of God . . . shall keep your hearts and minds . . ."; but here Paul says, "the God of peace shall be with you".'

There is no essential difference. In verse 7 you have the particular application, but in verse 9 you have a general statement: 'Live this life,' says Paul in effect, 'and God himself will always be with you and he is the God of peace'. Peace is his great characteristic. There is peace in the love of God because he is holy; he is a God of peace and he wants to be at peace with you. That is the whole meaning of the gospel, that is why Christ came. Men and women had become miserable because they had rebelled against God and God sent Christ to make peace. The meaning of the cross is that God is making peace with his enemies, who have rebelled against him, making it possible for them to be at peace with him. Christ has blotted out our sin and therefore we can be at peace with God. And, too, he makes me at peace with myself, because as he removes sin out of my life, the stress and the strain and the struggle go and I find a strange peace. He makes me live at peace with others and he enables me to be in a state of peace whatever my circumstances and conditions and surroundings may be.

That is the promise and oh, what a gracious and glorious promise! Walk in the light in that way, says Paul, and God will be walking with you. That is the picture. It is exactly like Enoch of old: 'Enoch walked with God' (Gen. 5:24), and God walked with him. So here is Paul's promise to the Christians to whom he was writing: You walk in that way and the God of peace will be with you. Difficulties may arise, but he will quench them. Whatever happens he will ever be with you. 'Those things, which ye have both learned, and received, and heard, and seen in me, do: and the God of peace shall be with you.' In life, in death, always, his promise is: 'I will never leave thee, nor forsake thee' (Heb. 13:5).

Is he that to you? Do you know him? Have you found him by your side in the days of trouble? During illness and disease, trouble and unhappiness, is he with you? What a wondrous possibility! But that is the condition: Do these things and then, if you do, he will indeed be with you always.

Chapter 17

Learning to be content

> But I rejoiced in the Lord greatly, that now at the last your care of me hath flourished again; wherein ye were also careful, but ye lacked opportunity. Not that I speak in respect of want: for I have learned, in whatsoever state I am, therewith to be content. I know both how to be abased, and I know how to abound: every where and in all things I am instructed both to be full and to be hungry, both to abound and to suffer need (Phil. 4:10–12).

We have, in the words of Philippians 4:10–12, one of those portions of Scripture which always makes me feel that there is a sense in which the only right and proper thing to do after reading them in a church service is to pronounce the benediction! One trembles at the very approach to such exalted, noble words, recalling as they do one of the high-water marks in the Christian experience of this mighty Apostle to the Gentiles. Yet it is our business, though we approach them thus with fear and trembling, to try to analyse and expound them. With the end of the ninth verse in this chapter the Apostle has reached the end of the particular exhortations which he was anxious to address to the members of the church at Philippi. He has really finished with his doctrine, but he still cannot close the letter. There is one other thing he must do, and that is he must express his profound gratitude to the members of the church at Philippi for the personal gift which they had sent to him, while he was held in prison in Rome, by the hand of their friend and brother, Epaphroditus.

That is one of the reasons why Paul was writing the letter at all. The Philippian church had sent him some gift. We are not told what it was, whether it was in money or in kind, but they had sent him some gift by their emissary Epaphroditus. Epaphroditus is now going back to them, and Paul sends the letter with him. Having finished with his doctrine, he wants to thank them for this expression of their love and solicitude for him in his suffering and his imprisonment. That is what Paul proceeds to do in these ten verses running from verse 10 to verse 20. There is nothing, I always feel, about this great epistle, which is more interesting than to observe in detail the way in which the Apostle does everything; and the way in which he offers his thanks to the members of the church at Philippi is full of instruction and of interest. It is quite clear that this question of thanking the members of the church at Philippi for their gift and for their kindness presented the Apostle with a problem. You would have thought that there could surely be no problem in thanking people who have been kind and generous, and yet to Paul it is obviously a problem. It takes him ten verses to do this thing. You often find him dealing with a mighty doctrine in a verse or two, but when it comes to just thanking the members of the church at Philippi for their goodness and kindness, it takes him ten verses. You notice also how he goes on repeating himself. 'Not that I speak in respect of want,' and later on, 'Not because I desire a gift.' There is a kind of argument and he seems to find it difficult to find the right words.

Paul's trouble was something like this. He was very anxious to thank the church at Philippi for their kindness. But at the same time he was equally anxious, if not more anxious, to show them that he had not been waiting impatiently for, or expecting, this expression of their kindness, and still more that he was in no sense dependent upon their goodness and generosity. In that way he finds himself confronted with a problem. He has to do these two things at one and the same time – he has to express his thanks to the members of the church at Philippi, and yet he has to do it in a way which will not in any sense detract or derogate from the reality of his experience as a Christian man, dependent upon God. That is why it takes him ten verses. It was the problem of a Christian gentleman, sensitive to the feelings of others. And what a great gentleman this Apostle was, how concerned about the feelings of others. As a gentleman he is anxious to express his profound gratitude and to let them know that their kindness really did move him very deeply, and yet he is concerned, on the other hand, to make it abundantly clear to them that he had not been spending his time wondering why they had not thought of his needs, and suffering because they had not sent him something there in prison. He wanted to make it perfectly clear that that had never been his condition at all, and what we have in these ten verses is the Apostle's method of resolving that particular problem.

Now the thing we have to grasp about Christian truth is that it is something that governs the whole of our life. The Christian gospel dominates the entire life of the Christian. It controls his thinking, as we see in verse 8, it controls his actions, as we see in verse 9. And now, in these ten verses, we see how a Christian, even in such a matter as returning thanks for a kindness, does so in a way which is different from the way of a person who is not a Christian. The Christian cannot do anything, not even in a matter like this, except in a truly Christian manner. So here the Apostle, at one and the same time, shows his indebtedness to his friends, but his still greater indebtedness to the Lord. Paul was always jealous for the reputation of the Lord, and he was afraid that in thanking the Philippians for their gift he might somehow give the impression that the Lord was not sufficient for him. He must keep that first. He loves these Philippians very dearly and he is profoundly grateful to them. But he loves his Lord still more, and he is afraid lest in thanking them he might somehow give even a suspicion of a suggestion that the Lord was not sufficient for him, or that he had been depending upon the Philippians in an ultimate sense.

So he sets out in this mighty passage, with its staggering and astounding affirmations, to show the primacy of the Lord and the all-sufficiency of the Lord, while at the same time showing his gratitude and his indebtedness and his love towards the Philippians for this manifestation of their personal care and solicitude for him. The essence of the matter is found in verses 11 and 12. Here we have the doctrine – 'Not that I speak in respect of want: for I have learned, in whatsoever state I am, therewith to be content. I know both how to be abased, and I know how to abound: every where and in all things I am instructed both to be full and to be hungry, both to abound and to suffer need.'

We must now look at this great doctrine which Paul announces in this way. There are two big principles here. The first, of course, is the condition at which the Apostle has arrived. The second is the way in which he has arrived at that condition. They constitute the subject matter of this tremendous statement.

Let us first look at the condition to which the Apostle has attained. He describes it by the word that is translated here as 'content' – 'I have learned in whatsoever state I am, therewith to be *content*.' It is important that we should get at the precise meaning of this word. Our English word 'content' does not fully explain the Greek. The word Paul uses really means that he is 'self-sufficient', independent of circumstances or conditions or surroundings, 'having sufficiency in one's self'. That is the real meaning of this word which is translated 'content'. The affirmation made by the Apostle is that he has arrived at a state in which he can say quite truthfully that he is independent of his position, his circumstances, his surroundings and of everything that is happening to him. Now that that was no mere rhetorical statement on the part of the Apostle is made very clear in the records that we have of this man and of his life in different parts of the New Testament. There is, for instance, an interesting example of it in Acts 16 which describes Paul's first visit to Philippi where the recipients of this letter lived. You remember how he and Silas were arrested and beaten and thrown into prison with their feet made fast in the stocks. Their physical conditions could not very well have been worse, yet so little effect did that have upon Paul and

Silas that 'at midnight Paul and Silas prayed, and sang praises unto God' (Acts 16:25). Independent of circumstances, 'content in whatsoever state I am'. That is what you find also in the famous passage in 2 Corinthians 12, where Paul tells us how he learned to be independent of 'the thorn in the flesh'; he was self-sufficient in spite of it. You remember also how he exhorts Timothy to take hold of this principle by saying: 'Godliness with contentment is great gain' (1 Tim. 6:6). 'There is nothing like it,' he says in effect. 'If you have that you have everything.' Paul was an old man by then and he writes to the young man Timothy and says: The first thing you have to learn is to be independent of circumstances and conditions – 'Godliness with contentment'. These are but a few of many similar illustrations to which we might call attention.

The teaching of the New Testament, however, not only affirms that this was true of Paul, it makes it very clear that it is a condition into which we should all, as Christian people, enter. You remember how our Lord makes this point in Matthew 6:34 – 'Take therefore no thought for the morrow.' Be not over-anxious and worried about food, and clothing and things of that kind. That is the glorious, mighty independence of what is happening to us, that we should all know and experience. It is self-sufficiency in the good sense.

But it is most important that we should have a clear understanding in our minds as to what this means. The word 'content' tends to provoke certain misunderstandings about what the Apostle is teaching. You can so interpret this statement by Paul as more or less to justify the charge that the Christian gospel is nothing but 'the opium of the people'. There is a tendency on the part of large numbers of people today to feel that the Christian gospel has been a hindrance to the forward march of mankind, that it has been a drag on progress, that it has been nothing but 'the dope of the people'. They say that it is a doctrine which has taught people to put up with all kinds of conditions whatever they may be, and however disgraceful and unjust. There has been a violent political reaction against the gospel of Jesus Christ because people have so misinterpreted this kind of text as to put it this way:

> The rich man in his castle,
> The poor man at his gate,
> God made them, high or lowly,
> And order'd their estate.
>
> C.F. Alexander

Now that is just rubbish and a blank denial of what the Apostle teaches here. Yet how often has it been interpreted like that. It is a matter of great regret that one who could have written the hymn, 'There is a green hill far away' should have been guilty of such a violation of the teaching of the Bible – 'The rich man in his castle, the poor man at his gate'. Were men meant to be like that and to stay like that for ever? The Bible never teaches that; it does not say that men and women should be content to remain in poverty, that they should never endeavour to 'better' themselves. There is nothing in the Bible that disputes the proposition that all people are equal in the sight of God and that all are entitled to equality of opportunity. Grievous harm has been done to the Church of Christ because a statement such as this in our text has been misinterpreted in that way.

Neither does it mean mere indifference to circumstances. That is but the negative resignation of a pagan stoicism, and is far removed from the Christian position. What, then, does it mean? The Apostle says here that he is not mastered or controlled by circumstances. If you can improve your circumstances in fair and legitimate ways, by all means do so; but if you cannot, and if you have to remain in a trying and difficult position, do not be mastered by it, do not let it get you down, do not let it control you, do not let it determine your misery or your joy. 'You,' says the Apostle, 'must come into the state in which, whatever your conditions, you are not controlled by them.' That is what he affirms of himself. 'Whatever my condition or circumstance,' he says in effect, 'I am in control. I am master of the situation, I am not mastered by the situation. I am free. I am at liberty. I do not depend for my happiness upon what is happening to me. My life, my happiness, my joy and my experience are independent of the things that are going on round about me, and even of the things that may be happening to me.' I would remind you again that Paul was actually in prison, probably chained to a soldier on his right and another on his left, when he uttered these words, yet even in that condition he can say that he is independent of circumstances. 'My life,' says Paul, 'is not controlled and determined by what is happening to me; I am in a state and condition in which I rise right above them. These things are not the determining factors in my life and experience.'

Now that is his claim, and he was most anxious to emphasise the fact that it is an all-inclusive claim. Observe his words again. Having made the general statement, he now amplifies it: 'I know both how to be abased, and I know how to abound: every where and in all things I am instructed' – again he goes back to it – 'both to be full and to be hungry, both to abound and to suffer need.' He was anxious to make the all-inclusiveness of his claim perfectly clear. Let me put the opposites in series. He knows how to be abased, he knows how to be hungry and to suffer need; on the other hand, he knows how to abound, how to be full and to have plenty. It would be interesting to discuss the relative difficulty of these two things. Is it more difficult to have a contented mind when abased, or when abounding? I do not know whether we can ever answer the question. They are both extremely difficult and one is as difficult as the other. Can I be abased without feeling a sense of grudge, or without being worried? Can I suffer the need of food and clothing, can I be abased in my profession or office or work, can I somehow or other be put down and still remain in spirit exactly as I was before? How difficult it is, to take second place, to be hurt, to be insulted, to see others suffering in the same way, to suffer physical need or pain – to know how to be abased, how to be hungry, how to suffer need in some respect. One of the greatest tasks in life is to discover how to suffer any or all of those things without feeling a sense of grudge, without complaint or annoyance or bitterness of spirit, to discover how not to be worried or anxious. Paul tells us that he has learned how to do that. He has experienced every kind of trial and tribulation and yet he is unaffected by them.

Then take the other side. 'I know how to abound,' says Paul. 'I know how "to be full", I know how to enjoy plenty.' What a difficult thing this is. How difficult it is for the wealthy person not to feel complete independence of God. When we are rich and can arrange and manipulate everything, we tend to forget God. Most of us remember him when we are down. When we are in need we begin to pray, but, when we have everything we need, how easy it is to forget God. I leave it to you to decide which is the more difficult. What Paul says is that in either of these positions he is perfectly free. Poverty does not get him down, riches do not carry him away and make him lose his hold. He says that he is not dependent upon either, that he is self-sufficient in this sense, that his life is not controlled by these things, that he is what he is apart from them. Whether he is 'to abound' or to 'suffer need', it does not matter.

But he is not content with that, he goes still further and says, 'In all things, everywhere', which means in everything and in all things, every single thing in detail, all things together. Now Paul divides it up like this quite deliberately. He wants to say that there is no limit to what he can do in this respect – 'In every single, particular thing I am like that.' Then he adds: 'Now I will put them together – in all things, whatever may happen to me, I am self-sufficient, I am not dependent upon them, my life and happiness and joy are not determined or controlled by them.'

That, according to the Apostle, is the way to live, that is Christian living. It is good for us to face this mighty statement. We are living in days and times of uncertainty, and it may well be that the first and the greatest lesson we have to learn is how to live without allowing circumstances to affect our inner peace and joy. And yet perhaps there was never a time in the history of the world when it was so difficult to learn this lesson as it is today. The whole of life is so organised at the present time as to make it almost impossible to live this self-sufficient

Christian life. Even in a natural sense, we are all so dependent on the things that are being done for us and to us and around and about us, that it has become most difficult to live our own lives. We switch on the wireless or the television and gradually become dependent upon them, and it is the same with our newspapers, our cinemas, our entertainments. The world is organising life for us in every respect and we are becoming dependent upon it. There was a good illustration of that in the early days of the last war when the blackout regulations were first imposed upon us. We used to hear of something which was described as the 'boredom of the blackout'. People found it almost impossible to spend a succession of nights in their own homes doing nothing. They had become dependent on the cinema, the theatre and various other forms of entertainment, and when these things were suddenly cut off they did not know what to do with themselves. That is the very antithesis of what Paul is describing here. But increasingly it is becoming the tendency in life today; increasingly we are becoming dependent upon what others are doing for us.

This, alas, is not only true of the world in general, it is becoming true also of Christian people in particular. I would suggest that one of the greatest dangers confronting us in a spiritual sense is that of becoming dependent upon meetings. A kind of 'meetings mania' is developing, and there are Christian people who seem to be always at meetings. Now meetings are undoubtedly of great value. Let nobody misunderstand me and imagine that I am saying that you should only go to a place of worship on a Sunday. Meetings are excellent, but let us beware lest we become so dependent upon meetings that one day, when we find ourselves ill and laid upon our bed we do not know what to do with ourselves. We can become too dependent even on Christian meetings – even on a Christian atmosphere. A man was discussing with me the other day what is referred to as the 'leakage' that takes place among the members of certain Christian organisations mainly concerned with young people. There is a very real problem here. While they are in the atmosphere of the Christian organisation these young people are keen and interested, but in a few years' time they have become lost to the Church. What is the cause of the leakage? Very frequently it is that they have become too dependent upon a particular fellowship, so that when they go out into the world, or move to another district where they are no longer surrounded by all this Christian fellowship, they suddenly flag and fall. That is the kind of thing against which the Apostle is warning us. We must beware of the danger of resting on props, even in Christian service and witness. The Apostle therefore exhorts us to get into that state in which we shall be independent of what is happening around and about us even in these things. We must cultivate this glorious self-sufficiency.

Professor Whitehead uttered a great truth when he said in his definition of religion, 'Religion is what a man does with his own solitude.' You and I, in the last analysis, are what we are when we are alone. I confess that in a sense it is easier for me to preach from a pulpit than it is to sit alone in my study; it is probably easier for most people to enjoy the presence of our Lord in the company of other Christians than when alone. Paul would have us enjoy what he himself was enjoying. He had a love for the Lord that rendered him independent of all that was happening, or that might happen – in everything, in all things, wherever he might be, whatever was happening, he was content. Abased or abounding, in need or plenty, it did not matter, he had this life, this hidden life with Christ.

Let us consider briefly the second matter which we find here, namely, how the Apostle reached this condition. Here again he makes a very interesting statement. You notice that he says: 'I have learned,' or better, 'I have come to learn.' I thank God that Paul said that. Paul was not always like this any more than any one of us. He had 'come to learn'. He has another interesting word also. He says: 'Everywhere and in all things I am *instructed* both to be full and to be hungry.' The authorities are all agreed here in saying that what he really says is, 'I have been initiated', 'let into the secret', 'let into the mystery'.

Paul says that he has come to learn how to be in this condition. Now there are many intimations in the New Testament that this was particularly difficult for him. Paul was sensitive, proud by nature, and, in addition, he was an intensely active being. Nothing could have been more galling for such a man than to lie in prison. He had been brought up a Roman citizen, but here he is enduring bondage, not spending his life among great intellectual people, but among slaves. How does he manage it? Ah, he says, I have come to learn, I have been let into the secret, I have been let into the mystery.

How did he come to learn? Let me try to answer that question. In the first place, it was by sheer experience. I need only direct your attention to 2 Corinthians 12, especially verses 9 and 10 about 'the thorn in the flesh'. Paul did not like it. He struggled against it; three times he prayed that it might be removed. But it was not removed. He could not reconcile himself to it. He was impatient, he was anxious to go on preaching, and this thorn in the flesh was keeping him down. But then he was taught the lesson: 'My grace is sufficient for thee.' He came to a place of understanding as the result of sheer experience of the dealing of God with him. He had to learn, and experience teaches us all. Some of us are very slow to learn, but God in his kindness may send us an illness, sometimes he even strikes us down – anything to teach us this great lesson and to bring us to this great position.

But it was not by experience alone. Paul had come to learn this truth by working out a great argument. Let me give you some of the steps of the argument which you can work out for yourself. I think that the Apostle's logic goes something like this. He said to himself:

1. Conditions are always changing, therefore I must obviously not be dependent upon conditions.

2. What matters supremely and vitally is my soul and my relationship to God – this is the first thing.

3. God is concerned about me as my Father, and nothing

happens to me apart from God. Even the very hairs of my head are all numbered. I must never forget that.

4. God's will and God's ways are a great mystery, but I know that whatever he wills or permits is, of necessity, for my good.

5. Every situation in life is the unfolding of some manifestation of God's love and goodness. Therefore my business is to look for each special manifestation of God's goodness and kindness and to be prepared for surprises and blessings because, 'Neither are your ways my ways, saith the Lord' (Isa. 55:8). What, for example, is the great lesson that Paul learned in the matter of the thorn in the flesh? It is that 'When I am weak then am I strong.' Through physical weakness Paul was taught this manifestation of God's grace.

6. Therefore I must not regard circumstances and conditions in and of themselves, but as a part of God's dealings with me in the work of perfecting my soul and bringing me to final perfection.

7. Whatever my conditions may be at this present moment they are only temporary, they are only passing, and they can never rob me of the joy and the glory that ultimately await me with Christ.

I suggest that Paul had reasoned and argued it out like that. He had faced conditions and circumstances in the light of the Christian truth and the Christian gospel, and had worked out these steps and stages. And having done so he says: Let anything you can think of happen to me, I remain exactly where I was. Whatever may happen to me, I am left unmoved.

The big principle that emerges clearly is that Paul had learned to find his pleasure and his satisfaction in Christ and always in Christ. That is the positive aspect of this matter. We must learn to depend upon him and in order to do that we must learn to know him, we must learn to have communion with him, we must learn to find our pleasure in him. Let me put it plainly – the danger with some of us is of spending far too much of our time even in reading about him. The day may come, indeed will come, when we shall not be able to read. Then comes the test. Will you still be happy? Do you know him so well that though you become deaf or blind this fount will still be open? Do you know him so well that you can talk to him and listen to him and enjoy him always? Will all be well because you have always been so dependent upon your relationship to him that nothing else really matters? That was the Apostle's condition. His intimacy with Christ was so deep and so great that he had become independent of everything else.

Finally, I believe that what most helped him to learn this lesson was his looking at the great and perfect example of Christ himself. 'Looking unto Jesus . . . who for the joy that was set before him endured the cross, despising the shame' (Heb. 12:2). Paul 'looked unto him' and saw him and his perfect example. And he applied it to his own life. 'While we look not at the things which are seen, but at the things which are not seen: for the things which are seen are temporal; but the things which are not seen are eternal' (2 Cor. 4:18).

'I have come to learn in whatsoever state I am therein to be self-sufficient and independent of circumstances.'

Christian people, can you say that, do you know that state? Let this become first with us, let this become our ambition, let us strain every nerve and do everything we can to get into this blessed state. Life may force it upon us, but even if circumstances do not, the time is bound to come, soon or late, when earth and every earthly scene will pass away, and in that final isolation of the soul we shall be alone, facing death and eternity. The greatest thing in life is to be able to say with Christ himself at that hour: 'And yet I am not alone, because the Father is with me' (John 16:32).

May God in his infinite grace enable us all to learn this great and vital lesson, and to this end let us offer frequently that prayer of Augustus Toplady:

> While I draw this fleeting breath,
> When mine eyelids close in death,
> When I soar through tracts unknown,
> See thee on thy judgment throne,
>   Rock of ages cleft for me
>   Let me hide myself in thee.

Chapter 18

The final cure

I can do all things through Christ which strengtheneth me
(Phil. 4:13).

Here again we are confronted by one of those staggering statements which are to be found in such profusion in the epistles of this great Apostle to the Gentiles.

Nothing is more misleading, as one reads the letters of the Apostle Paul, than to assume that when he has finished the business which he set out to do, he has at the same time finished saying great and mighty things. We should always keep an eye on his postscripts. You never know when he is going to throw in a gem. Anywhere, everywhere, in the introduction to his letters, in the postscripts to his letters, there is generally some amazing insight into the truth or some profound revelation of doctrine.

We are here, in a sense, looking at the postscript of this letter. The Apostle finished the business at the end of verse 9 and he is now just offering his personal thanks to the members of the church at Philippi for their goodness to him personally, for the gift which they had sent. But, as we have already seen, the Apostle could not do that without being involved at once in doctrine. Anxious as he is to thank them, he is still more anxious to show them, and to show to others, that his sufficiency is in Christ, and that whether he is remembered or forgotten by men, he is always complete in the Lord. And it is in that connection that we come to this thirteenth verse.

I say that this is a staggering statement – 'I can do all things through Christ which strengtheneth me.' It is a statement that is characterised at one and the same time by a sense of triumph and by humility. Paul sounds at first as if he is boasting, and yet when you look at his statement again, you find that it is one of the most glorious and striking tributes that he has ever paid anywhere to his Lord and Master. It is one of those paradoxical statements in which the Apostle seems to have delighted; indeed, it is the simple truth to say that Christian truth is always essentially paradoxical. It exhorts us at one and the same time to rejoice, to make our boast, and yet to be humble and to be lowly. And there is no contradiction, because the boast of the Christian is not in himself but in the Lord.

Paul was very fond of saying that. Take, for instance, the statement: 'God forbid that I should glory, save in the cross of our Lord Jesus Christ' (Gal. 6:14), or again: 'He that glorieth, let him glory in the Lord' (2 Cor. 10:17). There is the exhortation on the one hand for us to be boasting; yes, but always boasting in him.

Now this statement belongs to that particular category and perhaps the best way for us to approach it is to give an alternative translation. The Authorised Version is, in a sense, quite correct, but it does not really bring out the particular shade of meaning the Apostle was anxious to convey. It says: 'I can do all things through Christ which strengtheneth me.' But I suggest that a better translation would be: 'I am strong or made strong, for all things in the One who constantly infuses strength into me.' The authorities agree that the word 'Christ' should not appear in this text, and we need not boggle at that. Paul actually put it like that. What the Apostle is really saying is not so much that he can do certain things himself, as that he is enabled to do certain things, indeed all things, by this One who infuses strength into him. In other words, we have in this verse the ultimate and the final explanation of what Paul has been saying in the preceding verses. There, you remember, he says – 'I have learned, in whatsoever state I am, therewith [therein] to be content. I know both how to be abased, and I know how to abound: every where and in all things I am instructed both to be full and to be hungry, both to abound and to suffer need.' We have seen that there the Apostle is saying that he has come to learn. He was not always able to do this. Paul had had to learn how to be content in every state, how to be self-sufficient, how to be independent of circumstances and surroundings. He had had to learn, indeed he goes on to say that he had been 'initiated' into the secret of how to do this. That is the meaning of 'I have been instructed', and we have seen some of the ways in which the Apostle had been led. We have seen that he had come to this knowledge by experience, by logical reasoning out of his Christian faith and by cultivating a personal, intimate knowledge of the Lord, looking to him and his glorious example.

But it is here, in this thirteenth verse, that we have the ultimate explanation. The real secret, says Paul, which I have discovered, is that I am made strong for all things in the One who is constantly infusing strength into me. That is his final explanation. Now I need scarcely remind you that that is the point to which the Apostle always returns. Paul never works out an argument without coming back to it. That is the point to which he always brings every argument and discussion; everything always ends in Christ and with Christ. He is the final point, he is the explanation of Paul's living and his whole outlook upon life. And that is the doctrine which he commends to us here. In other words, he is telling us that Christ is all-sufficient for every circumstance, for every eventuality and for every possibility. And, of course, in saying that, he is introducing us to what in many ways we may describe as the cardinal New Testament doctrine. The Christian life, after all, is a life, it is a power, it is an activity. That is the thing we so constantly tend to forget. It is not just a philosophy, it is not just a point of view, it is not just a teaching that we take up and try to put into practice. It is all that, but it is something infinitely more. The very essence of the Christian life, according to the New Testament teaching everywhere, is that it is a mighty power that enters into us; it is a life, if you like, that is pulsating in us. It is an activity, and an activity on the part of God.

The Apostle has already emphasised that in several places in this very epistle. Let me remind you of some of them. In the first chapter he says that he is 'confident of this very thing, that he which hath begun a good work in you will perform it until the day of Jesus Christ' (verse 6). 'I want you,' says Paul in effect, 'to think of yourselves as Christians in that way. You are the people in whom God has started to work; God has entered into you, God is working in you.' That is what Christians really are. They are not just men who have taken up a certain theory and are trying to practise it; it is God doing something in them and through them. Or listen again in the second chapter, verses 12 and 13: 'Work out your own salvation with fear and trembling. For it is God which worketh in you both to will and to do of his good pleasure.' It is of his own good pleasure that God is working in us both to will and to do – our highest thoughts, our noblest aspirations, our every righteous inclination is from and of God, is something that is brought into being in us by God himself. It is God's activity and not merely our activity, and that is why Paul tells us in chapter 3:10 that his supreme ambition in life is: 'That I may know him, and the power of his resurrection . . .' All along he is interested in this question of the power and of the life.

You find Paul saying exactly the same thing in other epistles. What is Paul's great prayer for the Ephesians? He prays that they might know 'the exceeding greatness of his power to us-ward who believe, according to the working of his mighty power, which he wrought in Christ, when he raised him from the dead' (1:19–20). He goes on in Ephesians 2:10 to say that we are 'his workmanship, created in Christ Jesus.' You remember also the great statement at the end of the third chapter: 'Unto him that is able to do exceeding abundantly above all that we ask or think, according to the power that worketh in us.' Now, that is characteristic New Testament doctrine, and if we have not grasped it we are surely missing one of the most glorious things about the Christian life and position. The Christian, essentially, is a man who has received new life. We come back again to what I am never tired of quoting, namely, John Wesley's favourite definition of a

Christian. He found it in that book by Henry Scougal, a Scotsman who lived in the seventeenth century, and in the very title – *The life of God in the souls of men*. That is what makes a Christian. The Christian is not just a good, decent, moral man; the life of God has entered into him, there is an energy, a power, a life in him and it is that that makes him peculiarly and specifically Christian, and that is exactly what Paul is telling us here.

Let me begin by putting this negatively. The Apostle is not telling us in this great verse that he has become a Stoic. He is not saying that as the result of much self-culture, he has developed an indifference to the world and its surroundings, and that as a result of discipline he has at last been able to see that he can do all things or bear all things because of this culture. It is not that. Let me remind you that the Stoic could do that. Stoicism was not only a theory, it was a way of life for many people. Read the lives of some of the Stoics and you will find that as a result of this outlook they had developed a kind of passive indifference to what might happen in the world. You may have heard or read of the Indian fakirs, men who have so developed the power of the mind that they control their physical bodies, and by concentration on mind culture can develop an immunity or indifference to what may be happening to them and round and about them. It is also the great principle which characterises many Eastern religions, such as Hinduism and Buddhism. All those religions are basically religions which are designed to help people to die to circumstances and surroundings, and to develop an indifference to the world that is round and about them, to go through this life and world unaffected by circumstances. Now the point I want to make is that the Apostle is not teaching some such doctrine. Paul is not telling us that he has become like the Eastern mystics, he is not saying that he has developed this stoical philosophy to such a point that nothing can affect him.

Why am I so concerned about this negative emphasis? The reason which compels me is that all such teaching is really hopeless, all those religions are finally pessimistic. Stoicism, in the last analysis, was profound pessimism. It really came to this, that this world is hopeless, that nothing can do any good, that the thing you have to do therefore is to get through life as best you can and just refuse to let yourself be hurt by it. The Eastern religions are, of course, entirely pessimistic. They regard matter in itself as evil, they regard the flesh as essentially evil; everything, they say, is evil, and the only thing to do is to get through life with a minimum of pain and to hope that in some subsequent reincarnation you will be rid of it altogether and at last be absorbed and lost for ever in the absolute and the eternal, ceasing to exist as a separate personality.

Now that is the very antithesis of the Christian gospel, which is not negative but positive. It does not regard matter as essentially evil nor the world as essentially evil in and of itself in a material sense. But we reject the negative view *in toto*, supremely because it fails to give the glory and the honour to the Lord Jesus Christ. That is the thing about which Paul is most concerned. Paul wants us to see that his victory is based upon his association with Christ. In other words, we come back to our original definition once more – to be a Christian is not only to believe the teaching of Christ and to practise it, it is to be so vitally related to Christ that his life and his power are working in us. It is to be 'in Christ', it is for Christ to be in us. Now these are New Testament terms – 'in Christ', 'Christ in you the hope of glory'. They are found everywhere in these New Testament epistles.

We can put our doctrine in this form. Paul is saying that Christ infuses so much strength and power into him that he is strong and able for all things. He is not left to himself, he is not struggling alone and vainly against these mighty odds. It is a great power from Christ himself which is entering, and has entered, into his life, and it is there as a dynamo, as an energy and strength. 'In this,' says Paul, 'I am able for anything.'

Now this is surely one of the most glorious statements Paul ever made. Here is a man in prison, a man who has already suffered a great deal in his life, a man who knows what it is to be disappointed in so many ways – persecuted, treated with derision and scorn, even disappointed sometimes, as he tells us in the first chapter, in his fellow-workers. There he is in prison, in conditions calculated to produce dejection in the stoutest heart, facing perhaps a cruel martyrdom – yet he is able to send out this mighty challenge: 'I am able to stand, to bear all things in the One who is constantly infusing strength into me.'

I am anxious to put this doctrine like this at the present time. There are those who feel that at a time like this, it is the business of the Christian preacher and the Christian Church constantly to be making comments on the general situation. There are many people who say: 'Are you dealing only with matters of personal experience while the world is as it is? Is it not remote from life? Have you not read your newspaper or even heard the report on the wireless? Don't you see the whole state of the world? Why don't you make some pronouncement on the world situation or on the state of the nations!' My simple answer to such talk is this. What I, or a number of preachers, or the entire Christian Church, may say about the whole situation will probably not affect it at all. The Church has been talking about politics and the economic situation for many years but with no noticeable effect. That is not the business of Christian preaching. The business of Christian preaching is to say to the people: In this uncertain world, where we have already experienced two world wars within a quarter of a century, and where we may have to face yet another and things that are even worse, you must ask yourself, 'How am I going to face it all? How can I meet it all?' For me to give my views on international politics will not help anybody; but thank God there is something I can do. I can tell you of something, I can tell you of a way which, if you but practise and follow it, will enable you, with the Apostle Paul, to say, 'I am strong, I am able for anything that may happen to me, whether it be peace or war, whether it be freedom or slavery, whether it be the kind of life we have known for so long or whether it be entirely different, I am ready for it.' It does not mean, I must repeat, a passive, negative acquiescence in that which is wrong. Not at all – but it does mean that whatever may come, you are ready for it.

Are we able to speak the language of St Paul? We have already known certain tests and trials, and more may well be coming. Can we say with this man that we have such strength and power that whatever may come we are ready for it? The Apostle had power that enabled him to bear anything that might happen. How are we to obtain this power?

There is a great deal of confusion concerning this, and all I want to do is to try to lessen that confusion.

Many people spend the whole of their lives in trying to obtain this power, and yet they never seem to have it. They say: 'I meet other Christians who have this, but I never seem to get it.' Or, 'I would give the whole world if I could only get this power into my life. How can I get this power?' They spend their life trying to obtain it and yet they never do. Why is this? I think the main trouble is due to a failure on their part to recognise and to realise the right respective positions of the 'I' and the 'him', or the 'One', who is mentioned by the Apostles. 'I can do all things,' or 'I am able for all things through the One who is constantly infusing strength into me,' or, to put it in the words of the Authorised Version, 'I can do all things through Christ which strengtheneth me.' Now there is the crux of the whole matter – the right relationship and the correct balance between 'I' and 'Christ'.

There is a great deal of confusion at this point. The first cause of confusion is an emphasis on that 'I' only. In a sense, I have already dealt with that. It is what the Stoic does, it is what the Hindu or the Buddhist does, it is what all these people who go in for 'mind culture' are constantly doing. And we have seen that this is inadequate. But perhaps the final reason for its inadequacy is that it is a type of teaching that is possible only for people who have a strong will power and who have time to cultivate this will power. Indeed, I agree entirely with what Mr G. K. Chesterton said was his main objection to the simple life, namely, that you have to be a millionaire in order to live it. You need the time, and if you are a working man you have neither the leisure nor the opportunity – you have to be a millionaire before you can live the simple life. Is it not exactly the same, or indeed more so, with this other teaching? If you happen to be born a highly intellectual person and have the time and the leisure you can give your days and your weeks to concentration and to the culture of the mind and spirit. That is no gospel for the person who has neither the leisure nor the energy, and especially not for those who have not the intelligence. We must not over-emphasise the 'I'.

That is one error, but there is another, which is at the other extreme. As there are some who over-emphasise the 'I', there are those who tend to obliterate the 'I'. Let me put it in terms of something which I read in a religious journal. This is their definition of a Christian. The Christian, said that article, is:

> A mind through which Christ thinks,
> A voice through which Christ speaks,
> A heart through which Christ loves,
> A hand through which Christ helps.

My reply to that in terms of my text is – nonsense. And it is not only nonsense but a travesty of Christian teaching. If the Christian is a mind through which Christ thinks, a voice through which Christ speaks, a heart through which Christ loves and a hand through which Christ helps, where is the 'I'? The 'I' has vanished, and 'I' has been obliterated, the 'I' is no longer present. The teaching represented by that quotation is that the Christian is a man or woman whose personality has gone out of existence, while Christ is using his various powers and faculties. Not using him but using his voice, using his mind, using his heart, using his hand. But that is not what Paul says. Paul says: 'I can do all things through Christ which strengtheneth me.' Or listen to him elsewhere. You remember what he says in Galatians 2:20: 'I live; yet not I, but Christ liveth in me.' Is there in these verses an obliteration of the 'I'? 'I live, yet not I, but Christ liveth in me: and the life I live in the flesh, I live by the faith of the Son of God, who loved me, and gave himself for me.' The 'I' is still there.

We must, therefore, if we are to be just to this doctrine, safeguard the true position. The Christian life is not a life that I live myself and by my own power; neither is it a life in which I am obliterated and Christ does all. No, 'I can do all things through Christ.' I wonder if I can best put this by telling you of how an old preacher, famous in the last century, once put it when preaching on this very text. Those old preachers used sometimes to preach in a very dramatic way. They would have a kind of dialogue with the Apostle in the pulpit. So this old preacher began to preach on this text in this way: 'I can do all things through Christ which strengtheneth me.'

'Wait a minute, Paul, what did I hear you say?'

'I can do all things.'

'Paul, surely that is boasting, surely you are just claiming that you are a superman?'

'No, no, I can do all things.'

Well, the old preacher kept up the dialogue. He questioned Paul and quoted every statement made by Paul in which he says that he is the least of all saints, etc. 'You are generally so humble, Paul, but now you say, "I can do all things," haven't you started boasting?'

And then at last Paul says: 'I can do all things through Christ.'

'Oh, I am sorry,' said the old preacher, 'I beg your pardon, Paul. I did not realise there were two of you.'

Now I think that puts it perfectly. 'I can do all things through Christ.' 'There are two of you.' Not I only, not Christ only, but Christ and I, two of us.

Very well, then, let us put the doctrine like this. What is the right way to approach this question of power? How can I get this power which Paul tells us was being infused into him and which made him strong and able to stand and bear all things? May I suggest an analogy? I do so with hesitancy and trepidation because no analogy is perfect, and yet to use one can help us to arrive at the truth. What is vital, in this connection, is the matter of the approach, or, if you prefer a military term, the strategy. Never is the strategy of 'the indirect approach' more important than it is here. You know that in military strategy you do not always go straight at the objective. Sometimes you may appear to be going in the opposite direction but you come back. That is the strategy of the indirect approach and that is the strategy that is needed here.

Let me put it, then, in terms of an illustration. This question of power in the Christian life is like the question of physical health. There are many people in this world who spend most of their lives in seeking health. They spend their time and money going round from Spa to Spa, from treatment to treatment, from physician to physician. They are seeking health. Whenever you meet them they begin at once to talk about their health. The big thing in their lives is this question of health, and yet they are never well. What is the matter? Sometimes the trouble is due to the fact that they forget first principles, and the whole explanation of the state they are in is that they eat too much, or take too little exercise. They are living an unnatural life, and because they eat too much they produce certain acids and these acids produce conditions that call for treatment. They have to be told to eat less or to exercise more, or whatever it may chance to be. Their problem would never have arisen were it not that they had forgotten the first principles, the fundamental rules of life and living. Because of this, they develop an unnatural situation and a condition that needs treatment. Now I suggest that that is analogous to this whole subject of power in one's life as a Christian. Health is something that results from right living. Health cannot be obtained directly or immediately or in and of itself. There is a sense in which a man should not think of his health at all. Health is the result of right living, and I say exactly the same thing about this question of power in our Christian lives.

Or let me use another illustration. Take the question of preaching. No subject is discussed more often than power in preaching. 'Oh, that I might have power in preaching,' says the preacher and he goes on his knees and prays for power. I think that that may be quite wrong. It certainly is if it is the only thing that the preacher does. The way to have power is to prepare your message carefully. Study the word of God, think it out, analyse it, put it in order, do your utmost. That is the message God is most likely to bless – the indirect approach rather than the direct. It is exactly the same in this matter of power and ability to live the Christian life. In addition to our prayer for power and ability, we must obey certain primary rules and laws.

I can therefore summarise the teaching like this. The secret of power is to discover and to learn from the New Testament what is possible for us in Christ. What I have to do is go to Christ. I must spend my time with him, I must meditate upon him, I must get to know him. That was Paul's ambition – 'that I might know him'. I must maintain my contact and communion with Christ and I must concentrate on knowing him.

What else? I must do exactly what he tells me. I must avoid things that would hamper. To use my illustration, if I want to be well, I must not eat too much, I must not get into an atmosphere that is bad for me, I must not expose myself to chills. In the same way, if we do not keep the spiritual rules we may pray endlessly for power but we shall never get it. There are no short cuts in the Christian life. If in the midst of persecution we want to feel as Paul felt, we must live as Paul lived. I must do what he tells me, both to do and not to do. I must read the Bible, I must exercise, I must practise the Christian life, I must live the Christian life in all its fulness. In other words, I must implement what Paul has been teaching in verses eight and nine. This, as I understand it, is the New Testament doctrine of abiding in Christ. Now the word 'abiding' makes people become sentimental. They think of abiding as something passive and clinging, but to abide in Christ is to do what he tells you, positively, and to pray without ceasing. Abiding is a tremendously active thing.

'Well,' says the Apostle, 'if you do all that he will infuse his strength into you.' What a wonderful idea. This is a kind of spiritual blood transfusion – that is what Paul is teaching here. Here is a patient who has lost much blood for some reason or another. He is faint and gasping for breath. It is no use giving him drugs because he has not enough blood to absorb them and use them. The man is anaemic. The only thing you can do for him is give him a blood transfusion, infuse blood into him. That is what Paul tells us the Lord Jesus Christ was doing for him. 'I find I am very feeble,' says Paul, 'my energy seems to flag and sometimes I feel I have no life blood in me at all. But, you know, because of this relationship, I find he infuses it into me. He knows my every state and condition, he knows exactly what I need. Oh, how much he gives me! He says, "My grace is sufficient for thee," and so I can say, "When I am weak then am I strong." Sometimes I am conscious of great power; there are other times when I expect nothing, but he gives everything.'

That is the romance of the Christian life. Nowhere does one experience it more than in the Christian pulpit. There is certainly romance in preaching. I often say that the most romantic place on earth is the pulpit. I ascend the pulpit stairs Sunday after Sunday – and I never know what is going to happen. I confess that sometimes, for various reasons, I come expecting nothing; but suddenly the power is given. At other times I think I have a great deal because of my preparation; but, alas, I find there is no power in it. Thank God it is like that. I do my utmost, but he controls the supply and the power, he infuses it. He is the heavenly physician and he knows every variation in my condition. He sees my complexion, he feels my pulse. He knows my inadequate preaching, he knows everything. 'That is it,' says Paul, 'and therefore I am able for all things through the One who is constantly infusing strength into me.'

That, then, is the prescription. Do not agonise in prayer, beseeching him for power. Do what he has told you to do. Live the Christian life. Pray, and meditate upon him. Spend time with him and ask him to manifest himself to you. And as long as you do that, you can leave the rest to him. He will give you strength – 'as thy days, so shall thy strength be' (Deut. 33:25). He knows us better than we know ourselves, and according to our need so will be our supply. Do that and you will be able to say with the Apostle: 'I am able [made strong] for all things through the One who is constantly infusing strength into me.'

Chapter 19

All our need supplied

> Not because I desire a gift: but I desire fruit that may
> abound to your account. But I have all, and abound: I am
> full, having received of Epaphroditus the things which
> were sent from you, an odour of a sweet smell, a sacrifice
> acceptable, wellpleasing to God. But my God shall supply
> all your need according to his riches in glory by Christ
> Jesus (Phil. 4:17–19).

In these verses we have the final statement that the Apostle
has to make with regard to this question of the gift that has
been sent to him by the members of the church at Philippi
while he is a prisoner in Rome. They have sent him the gift,
obviously a large and generous one, through Epaphroditus,
and now that Epaphroditus is going back to Philippi, the
Apostle is anxious to convey his thankfulness. We have
already considered what he has to say about this matter, and
we have seen the profound theological implications that are
involved. We have emphasised his great concern that the
Philippians, much as he loves them, should not imagine that
he is finally dependent upon them. That is his difficulty, how
to thank them profusely without giving the impression that
he is dependent upon them, and how to thank them without
detracting from the glory of God, and we have seen how he
contrives to do that. But here we come to the end of his
statement and once more we see clearly how anxious he still
is that the Philippians should hold this matter in the right
perspective; that is why he goes on repeating himself. He is
jealous for the honour, the glory and the reputation of the

Lord, and he is anxious that they should know that he finds his complete fulness in Christ – there must be no mistake about that.

Yet he is also anxious that they should realise that he deeply appreciates their thoughtfulness for him. As he tells them this, he pays them a very great compliment. He says they are the only people who have sent him a gift. We cannot stay with this – it is a great subject in and of itself – but we must remember how careful the Apostle was that no one should ever think that he preached the gospel in order to make money. You will find him dealing with that subject in 2 Corinthians 11, as indeed he has already dealt with it in 1 Corinthians 9. Suggestions were being made that he went around to make money, that he was commercially minded. In fact, Paul was so concerned about the gospel, and above all about the Lord himself, that he refused any payment from them, but went on working with his own hands as a tent-maker, in order to support himself so that no one could ever say that he was making money out of the cross of Christ.

Now this is a great subject, and we should realise how many of the troubles of the Christian Church have arisen because the Church has not always remembered the apostolic pattern. The Church became very wealthy and powerful in a worldly sense, but she lost her spiritual power. Someone wisely pointed out that as long as the Church could say, 'Silver and gold have I none,' she could repeat the miracles of the Apostle Peter, but when the day came that she had much silver and gold, then she became a worldly power, a secular institution using Christian terminology, and she ceased to function as the power of God among men. I only touch upon that in passing. The point I am emphasising is that the Apostle here reminds the Philippians that in view of the fact that that is his method and the way in which he lives, he does greatly appreciate the gift they have sent. For some reason, the other churches did not realise his sufferings, but twice over the Philippians had sent him a gift and he appreciated it profoundly. But then he is a little bit unhappy about it – 'notwithstanding ye have well done' – this reminder that they had done it once again; then: 'not because I desire a gift' – back he comes to it once more. It was a wonderful thing for them to do, but God forbid that they should think or imagine that he had been unhappy until their gift came, or that he could not get on without it. Even if he could, that did not lessen their generosity, but it does establish again the fulness of the supply that is to be found in God through our Lord and Saviour Jesus Christ. In other words, the great thing the Apostle is anxious about here is that the Philippians should be quite clear in their minds about this whole question of the satisfaction of our needs as Christian people while we are here on earth.

Now he has some very interesting things to say about this. Take the phrase 'giving and receiving' in verse 15. The Philippians have given, and Paul has received, and Paul goes on to enunciate three principles in connection with Christian generosity, Christian benevolence, Christian charity, or the principles of charity in the lives and conduct of Christian people. The first is that our generosity is always a very thorough test of the real value of our Christian profession. Paul loved this church at Philippi because they were such excellent Christian people, and they proved that by sending gifts to him.

Let us reconstruct the picture. These Philippians were Gentiles, the Apostle Paul was a Jew; you remember the animosity that there was between Jew and Gentile, the bitterness and hatred on both sides, the Jew regarding the Gentile as a dog and the Gentile regarding the Jew almost as a barbarian because he did not know any philosophy. Then this Jew comes to preach in Philippi and these people are converted and become a church. Later they hear of the Apostle's need, and they immediately send him a gift, and they do that twice. There is only one explanation of that, says Paul, it is their Christian love, their understanding of the gospel and what it means. They love this man because he has brought them something that is of greater value than the whole world. Here is a man who has brought them peace with God and a new love and understanding and joy, this joy which he goes on repeating. They owe everything to him, and, therefore, when they realise that he is in need and is suffering, they must do something about it, their very Christian love makes them do it.

Now that is something that we find emphasised very frequently in the New Testament. The Apostle teaches the Corinthians how to do this and we find the same teaching, in that famous parable spoken by our Lord when he went into the house of a man called Simon the Pharisee. A woman who was a sinner came and fell at his feet. She washed his feet with her tears and wiped them with the hairs of her head, and anointed them with ointments, while Simon the Pharisee had done nothing for him. Then our Lord, realising Simon's disapproval of the whole incident, told the story of the two debtors who had been forgiven their debts, and he showed how the one who had been forgiven the greater debt loved the creditor most. 'In the same way,' says our Lord in effect, 'that woman shows that she realises what I have done for her.' We express our love and understanding by what we do, and I think the principle is self-evident. If we really believe the gospel, then we must believe that nothing is more important in the world today than the propagation of that gospel; that should be our greatest concern. That is why it has always seemed to me to be a contradiction of New Testament teaching to have to appeal for funds, either for local churches or for the missionary cause. No, this matter puts us under judgment; people who really believe and love the Lord are those who know something of that constraining power which makes them say, 'I can do no other.' 'For God loveth a cheerful giver' (2 Cor. 9:7).

That, then, is Paul's first principle. The second principle – we must be careful how we put it, and yet the Apostle puts it quite distinctly – is that Christian charity and benevolence is a marvellous investment. 'Not because I desire a gift,' says the Apostle in verse 17, 'but I desire fruit that may abound to your account.' Now this is a very striking statement. Paul puts it like this: I am profoundly grateful to you for these gifts that you have given to me, but, you know, what really pleases me most is not the benefit I have derived myself, but the way in which I can see that your account, your deposit account, has been mounting up as the result of this; I am pleased because of the interest that is going to accrue to your account – 'he that hath pity upon the poor lendeth unto the Lord' (Prov. 19:17).

Again, this is a principle which is taught in several places in the New Testament. In Luke 16:9 our Lord says, 'Make to yourselves friends of the mammon of unrighteousness; that, when ye fail, they may receive you into everlasting habitations.' His teaching is: 'Make right use of your money, or the wealth that you may have received in this world. Use it in such a way, and do so much good with it, that you will be laying up for yourselves friends in heaven, so that when you fail, there will be people there to receive you.' In other words, you are doing this now, yes, but you are preparing for yourself in the future. You cannot exercise Christian charity and benevolence without unconsciously benefiting yourselves at the same time.

The Apostle Paul says the same thing in 1 Timothy 6 where he tells Timothy to exhort those who are rich in this world to use their wealth for the good of others. Why? 'Laying up in store for themselves a good foundation against the time to come, that they may lay hold on eternal life' (vv.17–19). You appear to be giving, but in this marvellous, mysterious manner you are laying up, you are getting interest which will be put to your deposit account, says Paul. We must handle this matter carefully. The Apostle is not exhorting the Philippians to be benevolent *in order* that they may build up an account, and our Lord is not teaching that in the parable in Luke 16. This is a glorious doctrine – you can do nothing as a Christian but that it has an ultimate repercussion, and the glory of this benevolence is that though you are apparently giving, you are going to receive.

The third principle on this subject is that though, in a sense, the Philippians had given their gifts to Paul, in reality they had been giving them to God. That is the message of the eighteenth verse: 'I have all, and abound: I am full, having received of Epaphroditus the things which were sent from you, an odour of a sweet smell, a sacrifice acceptable, wellpleasing to God,' Now that is the most glorious and wonderful thing of all. 'This gift of yours to me,' says Paul in effect, 'is not only something that I have received, it is like a sweet smell in the sight of God.' The Children of Israel were told to take offerings to God of a 'sweet smelling savour' and this is a wonderful picture of that – it is the pleasant odour that comes up from the offering. God descended to the level of the understanding of the Israelite people, and spoke in this anthropomorphic manner in order that he might describe the pleasure he derived as the people brought their offerings. We all know how pleasant it is to smell the aroma of a flower, and these gifts were like that to God. Paul says that these particular gifts to him personally have emitted that delightful odour, the aroma of this beautiful act has been wafted right up into heaven, and God, on his eternal and everlasting throne, has been well-pleased with it.

This is the supreme principle with regard to this whole matter of giving and receiving. Our Lord has established this once and for ever in the story of the woman with the two mites which make a farthing. She dropped them into the box and few people saw her or knew anything about it. Great gifts were being given, yes, but she gave all she had, and that little act was wafted to heaven and God saw it. It is exactly the same with all Christian giving. Anything we may do to help a Christian cause, or to help Christians individually, any act that we may perform for Christ's sake, because we have been animated and moved by our love to him, though we may think we are doing it only to that person or cause, any such act is taken right up out of that level and is something that God sees and blesses. Thus Paul is saying to these people that in reality it is not so much that they have given a gift to him, as that they have taken their sacrifice, their sweet smelling savour, to God and he has received it, and he loves his people because of it.

Have we not felt, as we have considered these statements of the Apostle, that that is the way in which the Christian Church should be operating? Is it not tragic to think that churches have to have sales of work and fêtes, and have to call in the world and its entertainments, in order to maintain the cause of Christ, and that they have to call in important people who are not spiritual, just in order to increase the funds? It is a tragedy that we do not realise that the Christian teaching with regard to giving and receiving is that we do it all in the sight and presence of God; it is to him like a sweet smelling savour.

But there is something else to add which, in a sense, is still more important. What the Apostle is concerned about finally is that these Philippians should thoroughly understand that in the whole matter of living the Christian life, they must avoid any morbid, sinful anxiety with regard to the whole question of how they are to live and what is going to happen. And here Paul lays down this amazing principle in the nineteenth verse: 'But my God shall supply all your need according to his riches in glory by Christ Jesus.' How does Paul come to say that? He is thanking them for what they have done for him, he was in need and they had superabundance, and he sends them that message. 'Philippian people,' says Paul in effect, 'at the moment I am in prison. You are out of prison and able to help me, and I am very grateful for it. But the day may come when you yourselves may not be able to give. The position may be reversed, and you may be the ones in need. But do not worry, whatever your state or position may be, "my God shall supply all your need". That is my position. I have told you that I have learned in whatsoever state I am therein to be content, and you must learn the same thing. And the secret of it all is that "my God shall supply all your need according to his riches in glory by Christ Jesus."'

Here, then, unmistakably, is the great New Testament teaching with regard to the whole vexatious subject of how as Christian people, we are to live in this world and what our attitude should be to the very necessities of life itself. It is one of the most remarkable things the Apostle has ever said, coming in the same category as his other statements which we have already considered: 'I have learned . . .' and, 'I can do all things through Christ.' Our Lord teaches this self-same thing in Matthew 6, in the Sermon on the Mount: 'Take therefore no thought for the morrow . . .'; do not spend so much of your time in considering what you shall eat or drink . . . 'Consider the lilies of the field . . . sufficient unto the day is the evil thereof.' That teaching is repeated many times. And it is what the Apostle is repeating at this point in his letter to the Philippians.

I do not know how you feel, but I can never read words like these without feeling, and I say it deliberately, that the main trouble with us as Christian people is that we are such fools. How we rob ourselves of the riches of grace! How, with our worldly wisdom, we put our little limits upon what God offers us, and oh, how we rob ourselves of so much of the joy of salvation, and the glory of Christian living! Take a man like Paul. Was there ever a happier man than this? Take many another saint who has adorned the Christian Church. These people appear at first sight to be so reckless and yet how wonderful their lives have been! Well, this is the great doctrine and you can find it in the Old Testament as well. David at the end of his life said, This is my testimony, 'I have never seen the righteous forsaken, nor his seed begging bread'. That is the Old Testament counterpart of this statement of Paul's.

So, then, let us analyse it. Here is a promise made by God to his people that our every need shall be supplied. Let us consider first of all the greatness of the promise, or, if you like, the greatness of the supply. What is my position as a Christian? According to Paul, my position is that God is concerned about me – *my God*. What have I to draw upon? God is in charge, God is there handling the resources. But Paul has not done with that; he describes it further. He calls it 'his riches in glory', or, 'his glorious riches'. What is the wealth of God? No one can answer the question: 'The earth is the Lord's, and the fulness thereof' (Ps. 24:1). This subject is sometimes handled in Scripture with an element of what I do not hesitate to call divine humour and irony. You read Psalms like the forty-ninth or the fiftieth and you see how God speaks to the people, some of whom thought that their sacrifices to God were going to benefit him, and the reply is, 'For every beast of the forest is mine, and the cattle upon a thousand hills' (Ps. 50:10)! God is the owner of everything; he brought everything into being out of nothing. What is the wealth of God? It is equal to his glory, which is absolute and eternal. 'His riches in glory.' I would commend to you, as an interesting, fascinating and moving study, to go through these epistles of Paul and make a note of the parallel statements to this. For example, 'Unto him that is able to do exceeding abundantly above all that we ask or think' (Eph. 3:20) – that is it! You cannot describe it. The riches of his grace, the riches of his glory are illimitable.

But you can see, even then, that Paul feels that that is not enough, he must add to it: 'My God shall supply *all* your need' – there is no limit, it does not matter what it is. And yet I think we must be careful, as we interpret that, lest we wrest the Scriptures to our own destruction. It is literally true to say that with God all things are possible and that God can and will supply all our needs. Yes, but you and I are not always the best authorities as to the state of our need. He does not say, 'My God shall supply all your luxuries,' but, 'My God shall supply all your *need*,' and what you and I need, and what we think we need, are not always exactly the same. No, we are not promised luxury, but all our need; whatever it may be, my God shall supply it, there is no limit in that sense.

But the Apostle uses still another word to convey this benevolence: the word 'supply'. Now it is very interesting to note that in the original Greek the word translated here as 'supply', is the word which is translated in the previous verse as 'I am full' – 'I have all things and abound.' So that what Paul is saying is this: my God shall satisfy to the full all your need according to his riches in glory by Christ Jesus. God will fill you to the very brim with everything that he sees you truly and really need.

That, then, is just a glance at the greatness of the promise. I wonder, Christian people, whether we realise as we should, and are as conscious as we might be, of the fact that this promise applies to us. This is certain, this is without any equivocation at all, this is what is promised to God's people. He, with all that wealth, is behind us, and he knows all our need.

But let me mention, in the second place, what I must call the limitation to the promise. 'My God shall supply all your need according to his riches in glory by [in] Christ Jesus.' Yes, there is a very definite limit to this promise. The statement about God supplying all our needs is not made to the world at large, it is not made to everybody; it is a particular statement, a particular promise, and it is limited by Christ Jesus. It almost sounds contradictory for me to say that it is limited in Christ Jesus. Is there any limit to Christ? No, there is not – and yet there is! Paul means that God's largesse and beneficence come through a particular channel and that channel is Christ Jesus. I know that God makes his sun to rise upon the evil and upon the good, and upon the just and the unjust; that is common grace and God's general beneficence. But this is a particular promise; it is something personal and individual that comes only through the channel of Christ Jesus – all the treasures of the riches of God's grace come only through him.

This is a fundamental of the whole of the New Testament teaching, so it means that unless and except we are in this particular relationship to God, this promise does not apply to us. This promise is only made to those who, having seen their desperate plight and condition and lost estate, have run to Christ and given themselves to him, and are being incorporated into him, and are members of his body. It is made to no one else; the promise is confined to Christians, to those who are in Christ Jesus in this relationship, who are connected to the channel, who are recipients of the grace of God in salvation. So there is a very definite limit to the promise in and of itself; it is illimitable, but it is confined to the channel of Christ, what he has done in his life and death and resurrection. He is calling his people unto himself and it is for them, and for them alone.

So we have seen the greatness of the promise, and the limitation of the promise, and that in turn brings me to the last principle, which is the certainty of the promise. 'My God shall supply . . .' There is no doubt about it, it is not contingent, it is not uncertain, it does not say, 'perhaps', 'maybe'. No! 'My God *shall*.' 'As certainly as I am writing to you,' says Paul in effect, 'this will happen to you. I know, I am certain, these are his terms.' Now Paul does not say that he knows exactly how God is going to do it, and we do not know either. 'God moves in a mysterious way, His wonders to perform.' You read the story of men like George Muller, and you see the kind of way in which God works, but sometimes he takes away in order to give, and we have all, perhaps, had experience of that in some small way or other. He seems to empty before he fills, but he does it, and he will do it. It is certain. It is absolute.

What, then, are the arguments for the certainty? Let me note them. If you and I are in Christ, we are in a very particular relationship to God; if we are in Christ, we are partakers of the divine nature, we are members of the household of God, we are of his family and we belong to him. What a staggering statement, but it is the simple truth. If we are in Christ, then we are and 'heirs of God, and joint-heirs with Christ'. We are children in this amazing personal relationship; God has become our Father, and you remember the argument that our Lord himself deduced from that? He said, 'The very hairs of your head are all numbered' (Matt. 10:30), and further, 'If ye then, being evil, know how to give good gifts unto your children, how much more shall your Father which is in heaven give good things . . .' (Matt. 7:11). All these are astounding statements of the fatherly interest and concern of God in us. The analogy is there on the very surface. Just think how parents anticipate their child's need; the child does not have to ask, they are there watching, they see the need where even the child does not see it. And God is like that to us if we are in Christ; he is going to supply our every need because he is our Father.

But there is something even greater; there is that remarkable argument used by Paul in chapters 5 and 8 of his epistle to the Romans. It is one of those great logical arguments that is based on the proposition that if the greater is true, the lesser must inevitably follow: 'For if, when we were enemies, we were reconciled to God by the death of his Son, much more, being reconciled, we shall be saved by his life' (Rom. 5:10) – it is inevitable. Or, again, he says, in chapter 8:32, 'He that spared not his own Son, but delivered him up for us all, how shall he not with him also freely give us all things?' There is no need to argue; the God who sent his only begotten, his well-beloved Son to the cruel cross on Calvary, where his blood was shed and his body was broken, in order that we rebel sinners might be saved and pardoned and redeemed, God, who has done that for us, is not going to forsake us in lesser matters like food and drink and clothing and these temporal things. No. 'He which hath begun a good work in you will perform it until the day of Jesus Christ' (Phil. 1:6). The greater that he has already done is a guarantee that he will certainly do the lesser. 'My God shall supply all your need according to his riches in glory by Christ Jesus.' The blessed security of the Christian is not only in things spiritual, it is even in things material, if we obey these conditions. The promise of God is absolute.

Chapter 20

My God

But my God shall supply all your need according to his riches in glory by Christ Jesus. Now unto God and our Father be glory for ever and ever. Amen (Phil. 4:19–20).

The Apostle here, as we saw in our last study, is comforting the Philippians, and reminding them that their future is perfectly safe and secure. Whatever might happen to them, whatever experience they might be called upon to undergo, he is confident and assured that their supply will always be at hand because it will all be supplied in full by God himself. We considered the terms in which he puts that argument before them: the greatness of God and the illimitable character of his wealth and riches. We saw, too, that it all comes through Christ, and Paul is certain of it, because of the powerful argument that the God who has done the greater thing in the death of Christ, cannot leave them now, after they have been brought into the Christian life. Paul produces this argument in order to give the Philippians a sense of confidence and assurance.

In this study I am anxious to concentrate attention on the particular way in which Paul puts all this: '*My God* shall supply all your need . . .' He has already used the expression 'My God' in the third verse of the first chapter, where he says, 'I thank *my God* upon every remembrance of you;' and you will find that he uses this, or the similar expression, 'My Lord', in many other places as well.

Now this is something which was very characteristic of the Apostle. You cannot read any of his epistles, or any of his recorded speeches or sermons in Acts, without being impressed at once by the personal note which always came into every statement. This personal experience is always there, and he never writes without your being conscious of a warmth and a growing devotion. Whatever else may be said about the epistles, that, I think, must be granted by everyone. Obviously, the man is writing out of a rich personal experience – there is nothing academic and remote about these letters. They are not only pastoral, and you not only sense the love which exists between the Apostle and the people to whom he is writing, but also his every reference to God and our Lord Jesus Christ has a note of personal intimacy, devotion and love. Indeed, the juxtaposition of these two words, 'my' and 'God', remind us of what is, after all, the central feature of the Apostle's religious life, and the dominant characteristic of all the New Testament writers also. In other words, they are a perfect blend of doctrine and experience.

Now I think that a very good case could be made out for saying that most of the troubles which the Christian Church has experienced throughout her long history have been due to the fact that Christian people have not been careful enough to see that these two elements were present at the same time and the same place. Our tendency is to emphasise the one or the other, and often the one at the expense of the other. There are those who emphasise and stress doctrine: they talk about God, they are aware of the doctrine and the truth concerning God, that is their great interest. God is the subject of their constant study and research, the big theme that occupies their mind and attention, and they are aware, not only of the doctrine of God, as God is taught in the Bible, but also of how that doctrine has been elaborated by the Church in many a Council. They are learned, erudite and knowledgeable, and yet, somehow, you cannot help feeling that their interest and concern is purely academic and theoretical, that they are engaged in a kind of science. As one man takes a physical science and tries to discover truth concerning it, these men seem to have taken up, as their interest in life and the field of their scientific quest, the knowledge of God. The result is, of course, that they give the impression that they have what has been termed 'dry as dust' theology. The knowledge is there, the doctrine is there, the awareness of truth is there, but nothing more. Never do they give the impression that they are talking about 'my God'. The various truths appear almost to be abstractions and isolated concepts concerning some august and supreme being – doctrine and no more.

But, on the other hand of course, you have those who go to the other extreme. It is personal experience that receives the prominence and the emphasis. They tell you that they know no doctrine and, frankly, they are not interested. They have a lot to say about the 'dry as dust' theologians, who can argue with such cleverness and produce their casuistry, but who seem to be devoid of a personal knowledge in their hearts and minds and experience. These others talk of their experiences, what they have felt, what they have proved and known. The whole emphasis is upon themselves. They have got something; they certainly have had the experience, and they are talking out of it and about it, but their whole emphasis is on that and they say, 'It is no use talking to me about doctrine. Don't ask me to explain the doctrine of God, or the doctrine of the incarnation or the atonement. I don't understand these things, but I have felt and experienced something.'

I think you will agree with me that this is the tendency: either the one extreme or the other. But that is something which can never be said of this great Apostle, or any of the New Testament writers. The glory of their position is that the two things come together. God, yes; but also 'my God'. Doctrine *and* experience, the objective *and* the subjective. The grand statement of truth and yet the experimental, or, if you prefer it, the experiential knowledge of that truth.

So that is what the Apostle reminds us of in dealing with this question of the security of the Christian believer, and it is the ultimate ground of his assurance and confidence. You need not worry about the future, says Paul, '*my* God shall supply all your need according to his riches in glory by Christ Jesus.'

Here, then, surely, is a statement which deserves our very careful attention and analysis. Let me put it to you first and foremost by asking a question. Do we habitually speak of God as 'my God'? Do I, as a Christian, instinctively use that expression? Do I say from the depths of my being, 'My God, how wonderful Thou art'? Do I speak of *my* Lord Jesus Christ? Is this a natural expression of my religious life and of my Christian experience? Paul, as I will show you as we look at verses 19 and 20, does not confine this to himself. 'Our God' – for the Philippians and everyone else; he is 'our God and Father'.

There are, then, certain things we can deduce. Firstly, the Apostle speaks about a God whom he knows. This, perhaps, we can emphasise by putting it in opposition to a number of negatives. Paul's worship and religion were not superstition. It is possible for us to think that we are worshipping God and yet be guilty of superstition. Paul brings that charge against the citizens of Athens. 'As I walked about the streets of your city,' he said in effect, 'I observed that you are too superstitious and I have observed your altar to the Unknown God' (Acts 17). There are those who say with W.E. Henley, 'I thank whatever gods may be for my unconquerable soul.' They do not know God, but believe vaguely that there is a great Power. It is a religion of fear and dread, an awareness of something indefinable, tremendous, far away in the distance, somewhere. This numinous idea is not what characterises the worship and religion of the Apostle Paul. His is not a superstitious religion. God is a reality, a Person with whom he does business and with whom he has conversation and communion.

Secondly, let me put it like this: clearly, the God he speaks of is not merely the God of philosophy. This again is an important negative. There is, of course, the God of philosophy. There are schools of philosophy which would teach us and have us believe that the existence of God can be proved. There are those who arrive at God as a result of a number of arguments as elaborated by Thomas Aquinas. The philosophers themselves talk a great deal about God, but the God of the philosopher tends to be an abstraction, a sort of philosophic 'x' that is essential to the scheme and system. He is what they call the 'ultimate reality' or the 'absolute'. Oh, the pride of knowledge with which they tend to use the term! It is as if they think they are superior to the humble Christian who talks of 'my God'. Now that is the tendency of the philosopher. Let no one misunderstand me; I am trying to indicate the terrible danger of confusing this mere philosophical conception with the God of whom Paul speaks – 'my God', someone whom he knows.

Thirdly, the God of whom Paul speaks is not only the God of theology – and here I am trying to be scrupulously fair. Unfortunately, it is possible for us to speak of a God who is nothing but a theological conception. It is an advance and yet it is something very different from the God about whom the Apostle speaks in our text here. It is possible for us to be interested in the Bible because it is incomparably the greatest book in the world, and to a man of intelligence there can be no more fascinating study than the study of this book. Then you begin to read books about the Bible, and you come up against the greatest minds the world has ever known, incidentally, the greatest philosophers in this Christian era. But here they are, combining knowledge with a study of this book, and they elaborate this doctrine, and they talk about the God of revelation who has done this and that, but still you may only be dealing with an abstraction, with God who figures in this book much as one would deal with a character in a Shakespeare play. You have read the play so often that the character has almost assumed reality for you – and yet, of course, he has not. He is a fiction that Shakespeare conjured up in his mind and put in his play.

Now there is a terrible danger that God may be to us someone like that; essential to our theological system, but not someone we know. The theology of the Bible is a mighty intellectual concept, and the terrible danger is that God may only be a part of that scheme to us. No, that is not the God of whom the Apostle writes and so constantly speaks. Paul knows God. God is not merely some vague, indefinable

Spirit, breaking in and doing something terrifying and alarming; nor is he 'the ultimate' – someone who is essential to an understanding of the history of the Jews to whom Paul belongs. No, to Paul he is a reality, someone he knows – 'my God'. The God I know, the God of experience to whom I speak, who is more real than life itself. The Apostle Paul knew God. But we cannot stop at that.

Our second main deduction is that Paul loves God. This is not an exaggeration. Do you not detect it in the phrase 'my God'? He not only knows him, he is proud of him. He tells us something about the character of God. He does not tremble in the presence of God as he thinks of God's might and power and his illimitable sway. The reason is given in the next verse: to Paul God is also 'Father'. Here is another interesting theme – the frequency with which Paul refers to God as the 'God and Father of our Lord Jesus Christ'. This is an exposition of our Lord's statement, 'He that hath seen me hath seen the Father' (John 14:9). God is like that. He is the Father of our Lord Jesus Christ; he is our God and our Father; and the result is that Paul loves God.

Now we are used to these statements; they sound so simple, but how profound they are! The commandment is that we should love; not only that we should believe and accept a number of principles and statements, but 'Thou shalt love the Lord thy God with all thine heart, and with all thy soul, and with all thy might' (Deut. 6:5). Love God! How easy it is to slip over a phrase like this – 'my God'.

Do we love God? Or do we rather feel that he is someone who is set over against us, some great Power from whom we cannot escape, someone who seems to thwart us and prohibit us from doing the things we want to do? Is that our thought of God, or can we say that we love him? 'My God', in the sense of possessing, as the lover possesses the object of his love; one who is dear to us.

Thirdly, Paul also tells us something about the character of God. He is defining God here in contradistinction to other gods. Let us remember that the Apostle was writing to the Philippians, and until Paul went to Philippi they were pagans, apart from a few Jews and proselytes. They were, of course, polytheists. Even as in Athens, so they had pagan temples and altars in Philippi; they had been brought up in the atmosphere of polytheism and worshipped gods of silver, wood and stone. Reminding the Philippians once more of the great change in their lives, Paul says in effect, 'Let me remind you that you need not worry; I am basing my confidence on my God, not on the gods you used to worship.' God is not like the other gods that foolish people in their blindness are still worshipping, but 'my God'. Paul defines him and his characteristics. What are they? These are two things we must emphasise at this point.

In the first place, God is the only true and living God. Again, you will find Paul elaborating this in many places. In his address in Athens he tells the people that God is not someone who lives in temples of gold or silver (see Acts 17), he is not dependent upon man. God is the Eternal, the Creator, the Artificer and Sustainer of everything that is; glorious in holiness and power – 'my God'. Now that is something which we need to hold constantly in our minds. The God who is our Saviour, the Father of our Lord Jesus Christ, is also the Creator. This is where doctrine is so important. He exists from eternity to eternity. He has made everything out of nothing. He is the one to whom 'the nations are as a drop of a bucket, and are counted as the small dust of the balance' (Isa. 40:15). He is the only true and living God, the Creator. He is in that sense the 'absolute' and more of the philosophers. Paul, in other words, was anxious to remind them that this is not a superstitious belief, a figment of the imagination – 'the God of whom I am speaking is the living God'. He is a Person, and he has not only created everything and sustains everything, but everything is subject to his dominion and reign: 'The Lord reigneth.' This God of whom I am speaking will 'never leave thee, nor forsake thee' (Heb. 13:5).

Secondly, he is the covenanting God – the God of the covenants. If you read Deuteronomy 29, you will see that it is one of the places where this great idea of God covenanting himself to people is emphasised and elaborated. The God of whom I am speaking, says Paul, is not a God at whom you arrive through superstition or philosophy, but is based upon a revelation. God has been pleased to manifest himself, to tell us about himself, to reveal his great purpose with regard to men and women, to reveal his great plan of salvation. He has told us these things in such a way that I am entitled to speak of him as 'my God'.

Let me remind you of some passages: Genesis 17:8: 'And I will give unto thee, and to thy seed after thee, the land wherein thou art a stranger, all the land of Canaan, for an everlasting possession; and I will be their God.' That word 'their' is important. God is going to be 'their God' in a particular way.

Jeremiah 31:33: 'But this shall be the covenant that I will make with the house of Israel; after those days, saith the Lord, I will put my law in their inward parts, and write it in their hearts; and will be their God, and they shall be my people.' That is the great covenant. God made it originally with Abraham and went on repeating it until you come to Christ; then you get the New Testament elaborations of the same covenant worked out by Paul, for example in 2 Corinthians 6:16: 'For ye are the temple of the living God; as God hath said, I will dwell in them, and walk in them; and I will be their God, and they shall be my people.' Then there is a great exposition in Hebrews 8 where the author again refers to the new covenant – 'I will be to them a God, and they shall be to me a people' (Heb. 8:10). The Covenant of God! Now this is something of which our fathers used to talk a great deal, but which we, alas, have allowed to fall into desuetude. This covenant of God with his own people: I am going to confine myself to you, my people; you are the people of my peculiar possession; I will be your God in a sense that I am not going to be a God to anyone else.

Therefore, beloved Philippians, says Paul, have no concern or worry about your future.

But let me emphasise the other side. If God is a God who has committed himself to Paul, Paul has committed himself to God. He is the God to whom I have given myself, says Paul, and whom I acknowledge. I have covenanted myself to him. There are two sides, two parties to a covenant. God covenants himself to us, but we must covenant ourselves to God, and, says Paul, I have done so.

But lastly, Paul says 'My God' in order to tell them that God is a God whom he has proved. Paul not only knows him and loves him and is aware of his profound characteristics, but – 'My God shall supply all your need.' I know him, says Paul, I am not writing theoretically; I have staked my whole life, my everything on him. Once I came to know him truly, I gave myself to him. I staked everything, on him and on the truth concerning him, and, here Paul says, in effect, 'I have never been disappointed.' Never!

Read again 2 Corinthians 11 and 12 and Paul will tell you something about his experiences – beaten with rods, shipwrecked, misunderstood, maligned, starving, almost killed as a result of being stoned – and yet his statement is always that the Lord delivered him out of them all.

There is a glorious example of this in Paul's second letter to Timothy: 'At my first answer [trial] no man stood with me, but all men forsook me' (4:16). This mighty Paul, who had preached and done so much for others, who suffered so much, was on trial, and no man stood with him but all forsook him! 'I pray God,' he says, 'that it may not be laid to their charge. Notwithstanding the Lord stood with me, and strengthened me . . . and the Lord shall deliver me from every evil work, and will preserve me unto his heavenly kingdom' (vv. 16–18). 'I will never leave thee nor forsake thee'. Paul has proved that.

Philippians, says the Apostle, 'my God shall supply all your need.' That is the sort of God he is; I have tested him; I have proved him; he has never let me down, never failed. 'My God' – the God I know, the God I love, the God I can guarantee, the God I can vouch for, as it were, the God who never fails, the God who has said, 'And, lo, I am with you alway, even unto the end of the world' (Matt. 28:20).

So I ask the same question here that I put at the begin-

ning: Can you say 'my God'? Do you know him? Is he real
and living to you? Do you love him? Have you proved him
and tested him?

What enables us to have this experience? I cannot deal
with this in detail, so I merely mention it. All this has come
true for Paul because he has gone to God through Jesus
Christ. The Lord himself has said to him, 'I am the way, the
truth, and the life: no man cometh unto the Father, but by
me' (John 14:6). You can never know God except in Jesus
Christ. You may know the philosophical abstraction, the
logical concept, but the only people who really know God
are those who realise that they do not know him, and that
they can never arrive at that knowledge by themselves. And
in utter hopelessness and helplessness they cry out to God,
'I do not know you,' and then they believe that they are
simply asked to abandon themselves to God to take charge
of them. In utter helplessness they ask Christ to reveal God
and they go on asking until they are able to say 'my God'
through Jesus Christ.

Do what Paul did. Surrender to God, and, if you do, trust
him; then you will come to know him – and not without. The
Holy Spirit is given to those who obey God. If you obey by
coming to Christ, and giving yourself to him, he will give
you the Spirit of adoption whereby we cry, 'Abba, Father' –
'My God'.

Chapter 21

The fellowship of the saints

> Salute every saint in Christ Jesus. The brethren which are
> with me greet you. All the saints salute you, chiefly they
> that are of Caesar's household (Phil. 4:21–22).

In these verses the Apostle, in a kind of second postscript,
is just conveying the greetings of himself and his fellow-
workers and, indeed, of all the members of the church at
Rome, to the members of the church at Philippi. You will
find that this is something which he puts in practically all his
epistles. He not only writes for himself, he writes for all the
Christians who are with him wherever he happens to be.
But, what interests us in this additional postscript is the
extraordinary and beautiful picture which the Apostle gives
of the nature and life of the early Christian Church. It is not
his intention to do that, but in conveying his greetings, he
does incidentally – and, in a sense, almost of necessity – give
us this idyllic picture.

Now there are times when I feel, and feel very strongly,
that perhaps one of the greatest needs of the Church today
is the need to recapture this New Testament picture. You
cannot read the epistles and observe the character of the
Church at the beginning without being impressed at once by
the striking and strange departure from this pattern which
has taken place. We must admit that, in general, the Christian Church has become formal, set, and more or less life-
less. You read these New Testament passages and you get
these little glimpses, in the introductions and postscripts
especially, and you are given a picture of a very wonderful

fellowship, of a body of people meeting together to worship God, to consider our Christian gospel, and to share their experiences. The thing that stands out at once is the fellowship, the love, and this peculiar quality of intimacy and understanding. The New Testament itself describes the Church as the body of Christ, and is often at pains to remind us of the nature and relationship of the different parts. The New Testament Church was clearly a Church thrilling with life, with power and with fellowship and understanding. If you try to conjure up in your mind a meeting of the early Church, and contrast it with a typical meeting in a church today, you must be strangely impressed by the remarkable and extraordinary difference. When you think of the tendency in the Church to pay increasing attention to the building, to forms and ceremony and ritual, and to the development of a kind of hierarchy, offices and things of that kind, then does it not strike you that you cannot find it in the New

Testament? In the New Testament, the Church is primarily a fellowship, and there is an atmosphere of intimacy and love. There is an absence of formality and of that word which has, alas, been emphasised so much in the last hundred years – dignity. The form was apparently irrelevant. These people were concerned about the substance, and the result was that some of the churches met in houses; they met wherever they could, but because they were met together in this way and manner, it was a church.

So we are given just a glimpse into that in this brief second postscript. The things that strike us at once are the active nature of the fellowship and the spirit of unity. It does not matter what town they lived in, or what country, they all seemed to be one in the amazing love which they had for one another and in their interest and concern for one another. The Philippian Christians were concerned about the Christians in Rome; the people in Rome sent their greetings to the Philippian Christians; and it is the same in all the epistles. It does seem to me that this is a thorough test of our whole position as Christian people. Do we feel this special interest in other Christian people? Are we concerned to read about them? Are we concerned about their condition? Are we concerned about their sufferings?

I ask these questions at a time like this when we are finding ourselves back in a state which is strangely similar to that which obtained in the New Testament era. Do we ever give a thought to so many Christian people all over the world who are suffering, and who are not free to worship as we are? In the early Church what stood out was the interest the Christians had in one another. What was happening to the others? Were they suffering persecution? There was a great desire to help one another, and to help spread the gospel in all lands and amongst all peoples. This was a special feature of the lives of these early Christians. Thus, in sending their greetings to one another, they simply underlined and emphasised the point that the Church is indeed the body of Christ and that there is a peculiar unity among the members, as there is between the members and our great and glorious Head.

The word of salutation reminds us at once of that, but I want to go beyond that now, and concentrate attention on something additional. Paul makes a very significant statement here: 'Salute every saint in Christ Jesus . . . All the saints salute you, chiefly they that are of Caesar's household.' Now that is the striking thing at this point. The two phrases together give a picture of the Christian Church and of its members, but I feel that this particular phrase tells us something very special and additional about the Christian. In order that I may help you to retain the thought in your mind, let me suggest it in terms of the following proposition:

Firstly, what it means for anyone to be a Christian. Christians are saints.

Secondly, anyone can be a Christian.

Thirdly, one can be a Christian anywhere.

The first, then, is that we must be clear in our minds what it means for anyone to be a Christian. What is a Christian? The Apostle answers that question by his repeated use of this word *saint*, or *saints*. And again, of course, we see at a glance how the Church throughout the ages has tended to depart from the New Testament pattern. When we hear the word 'saint', do we not all instinctively think of a special type of church member, an exceptionally 'Christian' person? The Church, in her use of this term 'saint', has departed radically from the use made of it in the New Testament. Despite the Protestant Reformation, we think of the saint in terms of Roman Catholic teaching; we regard a saint as an unusual Christian who is canonised by a body of men because of some peculiar merits or outstanding virtues. So we would hesitate to call ourselves saints. We are far too fond of saying that we are 'far from being a saint', as if we were afraid that someone might regard us as saints!

This is a radical departure from the New Testament, for, according to New Testament teaching, every Christian, every member of the Christian Church, is a saint. Read the introductions to the epistles – 'to the saints that are in Rome . . . in Corinth . . .', 'called to be saints', every one of them. 'Salute every saint,' or, to put it in more modern language, 'Give my greetings to every single saint in the church.' In other words, the Apostle not only speaks of every single, individual member of the church at Philippi as a saint, but regards them as such. You cannot be a Christian without, at the same time, being a saint. So that clearly means that our definition of what constitutes a saint has somehow gone astray. A saint, according to the Bible, is someone who has been set apart, a holy person. As you read the New Testament, you will find references to the 'holy mount', and this refers to a mountain which was set apart by God and consecrated. There was no change in the constitution of the mountain as such, but God set it apart. The 'holy vessels', too, were vessels of the Temple which were consecrated; blood was poured upon them and they were set apart for use in the Temple.

That, then, is the key to the understanding of what the New Testament means by 'saint'. First and foremost, a saint is a person who has been called out of the world by the almighty God. We were born in sin and shapen in iniquity but then the grace of God in Jesus Christ came to us and apprehended us, sought us out, and set us apart. We are set apart as God's special, holy people; people whom God has marked out for himself. In such people God is taking a special interest – they are the people whom he is anxious to use for a very special purpose.

So that is the New Testament conception of a member of a church: someone who has been dealt with by God in a way that differentiates him or her from all those outside. It is very important that we should hold on to this primary and initial meaning of the word 'saint', and that in the first instance we should not think of what we do or do not do, but rather of what we *are*. And we are conscious, therefore, that, in spite of all our sinfulness and unworthiness, God has been dealing with us, God has disturbed us, there is something different in us from what was once true of us, or of the average person. If God is in my thoughts and if I want to serve him more truly, then I am a saint, because that is not true of the average person. The natural man cannot understand God, nor the things of the Spirit of God. The natural man is enmity against God. The majority of people are not concerned, so why are we? Is there any explanation except that God has done something to us? Christians, church members, saints, are people who are set apart by God for his great and glorious purposes. They are his special people.

And that, of course, leads us inevitably to say that the people who realise the truth of these things set out to live holy lives. The secondary meaning of 'saint' is one who is trying to live a holy and godly life, well-pleasing in God's sight. Now that is what is meant by being a Christian. The thing to emphasise is not so much what we are trying to do, but, rather, our awareness and consciousness of being separated by God. As the vessel was set apart, as the mountain was set apart, so we have been put into a different category. Christian men and women are special, exceptional people in this world; they cannot help it, because it is the action of God upon them, and so, with the New Testament Christians, we ought to rejoice in this fact and in our distinction, in the fact that we are set apart in this separate order, we are this separate group of people, here in this world of time. This is what it means for anyone to be a Christian.

Our second proposition is that anyone can be a Christian – and let no one misunderstand what I mean. I arrive at that conclusion in this way: 'Salute every saint in Christ Jesus,' says Paul. 'The brethren which are with me greet you. All the saints salute you, chiefly they that are of Caesar's household.' So I find that I have to deduce the following points: Jews and Gentiles can be Christians. It is the Apostle Paul who is writing, and he is a Jew. Who are his fellow-workers? One of them is 'Luke, the beloved physician', another is Demas, and in addition there are certain other people to whom he makes reference. In Rome some are Jews but many of them, most of them probably, are Gentiles and, indeed, dividing it up still further, some of these Christians were actually servants in Caesar's household. Some are slaves, some free men, some of them members of the so-called nobility connected to the very person of the Emperor himself. That is the nature and constitution of the Church – neither Jew nor Greek, bond nor free, male nor female, but all one in Christ Jesus.

That is why I maintain that anyone can be a Christian. It is not a matter of nationality; it is not a question of being born in a particular country nor of belonging to a certain tradition. Neither is it a matter of a particular psychological temperament. We are aware how certain people, claiming for themselves an unusual degree of intelligence, often maintain this, saying that being a Christian is a matter of temperament. Some people have, they say, 'a religious temperament' – (if not 'complex') – and they think that this whole matter can be easily dismissed in that way. If you have some particular bent or temperament, then you will be a Christian; if you have not, then you will not be a Christian, but do not worry about it.

The simple answer to that is to read any one of the epistles. Indeed, you need not go any further than to study the twelve Apostles, and immediately you will find that men of every conceivable temperament are to be found side by side in the Christian Church, all coming from different cultures, essentially different in themselves, and yet all together in the Church, rejoicing in the same hope. This is one of the most glorious characteristics of the Christian Church, for it is a reminder to us that, after all, what makes us Christians is what God does to us. We are Christians because of the action of God, and therefore questions of temperament or intelligence are quite irrelevant. The facts support this theory. In the Church there have always been people of every conceivable type and permutation and make-up, and they are still to be found today. There are still Jews and Gentiles in the Church; men and women of scientific and artistic outlook; men and women with various trainings and differing antecedents, from every conceivable culture. All over the world you still see it.

That is what makes the Christian Church the most romantic place on earth. You never know what is going to happen; because of this truth there is hope for all; no one is 'beyond the pale'. Now I am anxious to emphasise this: 'All the saints salute you, chiefly they that are of Caesar's household.' Who would ever have expected to find members of the Church in Caesar's household – in that Imperial household, subject to the life that was so characteristic of an ancient court? This was an amazing, almost an unbelievable thing. Do you remember, too, how we are told that even the disciples, the Apostles themselves, when they were told of the conversion of Saul of Tarsus were at first a little doubtful? 'Can it happen?' they said. Was Saul really and truly a Christian? But that is the very thing that the gospel does; 'Saints in Caesar's household'.

I had the privilege once of hearing the Home Director of the China Inland Mission giving a short account of a visit he had made to China, and I heard him say that of all the things he had seen in China, the most amazing was a church that he visited in a prison. Fantastic work had been going on, and a number of men had been converted, and so a church had sprung up among prisoners in a prison. I also had the privilege of listening to a German evangelical pastor who was visiting this country. He said that the most remarkable work in Germany today is going on among ex-S.S. men, who had been guilty of the most terrible atrocities. They had awakened to the horrors of their past life, and there were a great number of conversions among them. 'The saints in Caesar's household.'

Now I want to apply that by means of an illustration. In my pastoral experience, I sometimes have the following difficult problem to deal with: parents come to me because their child has become interested in, or is proposing to marry, somebody who is not a Christian. This person is not interested in Christianity, never observes the Sabbath, and so on, and the Christian parents feel it is the end of all things and utterly hopeless. But what I have to say to such people is this. When you are in the realm of the gospel no one is hopeless. It is not impossible. Saul of Tarsus – the last man you would have thought of – was converted. There are 'saints in Caesar's household'. Christian people, never allow yourselves to regard anyone as hopeless. The gospel is the power of God. If you have a problem like that, pray for the conversion of this other person. It happens. Slaves, free men, anybody, anywhere, can, by the grace of God, become Christians. Let us, then, as we remember this phrase about the saints in Caesar's household, always bear that in mind lest we be discouraged or even fall guilty of denying the gospel itself.

Lastly, one can be a Christian anywhere. 'All the saints salute you, chiefly they that are of Caesar's household.' I must emphasise that a little and qualify it. You can live as a Christian anywhere, voluntarily or involuntarily, without any limit. In other words, there is no need for special circumstances and conditions. Some people think that you cannot be a Christian unless you come out of the world, but that is the fundamental error of monasticism. The 'saints in Caesar's household' – Christians in the most difficult circumstances imaginable! There are people who, when they are converted, think that they must of necessity change their occupation or go from one house to another. The lesson here is that you can be a Christian anywhere, and you must not have the feeling that you need to have particular circumstances and conditions before you can practise the Christian life. We must witness to it wherever we chance to be. Those people belonged to the household of Caesar. They were servants and slaves, or maybe high ranking officials in Caesar's household. The gospel had taken hold of them in Caesar's palace and there they were, witnessing to the Christian life.

Let me apply this particularly to those who, in the words of our text, are 'saints that are in Caesar's household'. As Christians, we are all the same and it is the business of all of us to bear our witness wherever we may chance to be, but there are differences. We are in different places and in different circumstances, and the whole art of the Christian, if I may so put it, is to realise the special way in which we can witness in special places. Today there are people who are 'saints in Caesar's household'. I am thinking of school teachers, doctors, and sisters and nurses in hospitals, government officials and various other people. The Bible has a good deal to say on this subject. You remember Nehemiah, the cup-bearer to the King, and the story of Esther? If there was ever a 'saint in Caesar's household' it was Esther, and the same is true of Daniel and his companions. Special conditions, calling for certain special truths. As saints in Caesar's household, these people have to realise certain special things. Let me speak directly to any 'saint in Caesar's household' who may be reading this book now. You are confronted by exceptional dangers. The greatest danger is of being ashamed of the gospel because you are intelligent, and because you are among intelligent, intellectual people who are more prone to scoff than anyone else, and more likely to try to slight it. You may therefore find you are taking part in various Christian activities at home, but are doing nothing to witness where you happen to be working.

The next danger is that of compromising your principles, perhaps out of ambition, because you are anxious for success. There is nothing wrong in a righteous ambition, but if it once makes you compromise your Christian position, it is wrong. You must exercise exceptional care, for you are being watched very carefully. Probably you are being watched more carefully than anyone else. Irritability, bad temper, scamping work – all these things are being judged by others.

You have been placed where you are and you have exceptional opportunities. You find children under your care, or patients in a sick bed who are beginning to think about death and eternity – I need not elaborate. The Christian in an exceptional position has an exceptional opportunity.

So let me just add a word about the rules you must follow. In a way, there is but one rule: keep your loyalty to Christ always in the first position; if you do that, you can never go wrong. Loyalty to Christ first, always. Do your work as well as you can, because the better you do your work, the better Christian you are. Christian students, try to obtain your First; come out on the top of the list. It is a wonderful testimony for Christ. Loyalty to Christ first, then do all your work with all your might. Then be wise: 'as wise as serpents, and harmless as doves' (Matt. 10:16). Be wise in the way in which you introduce the gospel, and bear your witness. Do not be foolish; do not do it mechanically; do not make yourself a nuisance to people. Remember the uniqueness of the position, its exceptional character, and pray to God to give you his wisdom that you may testify truly.

Remember, always, that loyalty to Christ comes first; because of your very special position you may be tempted and tried beyond all others. It happened to the 'saints in Caesar's household' right at the beginning. It was they who had this first great test. There came an Emperor who claimed that he was a god and he demanded that everyone should say, 'Caesar is Lord,' and the first people who were asked to do this were the members of his own household. Officials came to them and said, 'You must say, "Caesar is Lord." We are not objecting to your being Christians, but in addition you must say, "Caesar is Lord."' And, to their everlasting and eternal glory be it said, they refused to say it. They said: 'There is but one Lord, the Lord Jesus Christ.'

Even if it meant being cast to the lions in the arena their loyalty to him came first. They went on doing their work in Caesar's household and then at that point, as Daniel and Esther, they took the risk. They lay down their lives for their Lord and Master. That is the rule to employ; we must be loyal to him to the ultimate limit, even if it should involve death.

But, lastly, let me say a word of encouragement to all 'saints in Caesar's household'. If you are true and loyal, then it will happen to you as with the early 'saints in Caesar's household'. Having thus gone on with their work, they eventually had to take their stand and thousands of them were massacred. But you remember what happened? The day came when Caesar himself became a Christian. How did it happen? It was because of what the Roman Emperors and their advisers had observed about these Christians. Just a handful of people at the first, but they were saints; they were God's people and they held it a supreme honour to be accounted worthy to suffer for his name's sake. That ancient world observed this, and eventually even Caesar himself became a Christian. 'The blood of the martyrs is the seed of the Church,' and men and women who stand thus for Christ and for truth can be certain that their witness will be honoured, and they themselves will be given the crown of glory and have a special reward in glory.

'The saints in Caesar's household' – exceptional dangers, but exceptional opportunities. The one absolute rule of loyalty to him, and an assurance that if you are loyal, your stand and your labour will never be in vain. Thank God for the privilege of being part of such a fellowship – the fellowship of the saints, the people of God.

Chapter 22

The grace of the Lord Jesus Christ

> The grace of our Lord Jesus Christ be with you all. Amen
> (Phil. 4:23).

We come now to the last of our studies in this great epistle
to the Philippians. Perhaps a better translation of our text is
the Revised Version which puts it: 'The grace of our Lord
Jesus Christ be with your spirit.' These are the last words;
they express the Apostle's final prayer for these people who
were so dear to him, and whom he loved so much in the
Lord. But it is very important for us to realise that this is no
mere formal ending to a letter; it was not just a casual,
expressive phrase used by the Apostle. I have often
emphasised this particular truth. Paul never wrote anything
in a casual manner, and if we have learned nothing else in
working through Philippians, it is good for us to have learnt
that nothing must be taken lightly in an epistle by this great
Apostle. His apparent asides are often packed with doctrine, his postscripts are full of truth and instruction. Unlike
us, who often end a letter with some formal expression
which we do not stop to consider, or use a meaning we are
not careful to weigh, Paul, when he uses an expression like
this, means exactly what he says. And here in this final
word, this final prayer, he really is offering what I do not
hesitate to describe as the most comprehensive prayer that
any person can ever offer on behalf of another.

You will find that the Apostle is very fond of this particular expression; he ends his letters to the Galatians and to

Philemon in the same way, and, with a slight variation, you will find this expression somewhere or other in most of his epistles, either in the remarks at the beginning, or in a final word of salutation like this. It is, then, something which the Apostle means literally, and in this one verse he sums up everything that he has been saying to the Philippians. You remember how often we have been made to realise that the Apostle's object is to encourage and strengthen these Philippians. He wants them to know the joy of their salvation; he himself knows what it is to thrill with this glorious experience, and to have a joy in the Lord which nothing can change and affect. Though he is in prison he still rejoices, and he wants them to rejoice. He may be allowed to live on, and he may visit them again, or he may be put to death, he does not know. But whether it is life or death, the one great thing is that the Philippians should so understand and grasp the truth, that they will have this joy – 'Rejoice in the Lord alway, and again I say: Rejoice.'

That is his theme, and it is for their sakes that he takes up these various questions, these various things that tend to rob us of joy, and he deals with them and explains them, and then he gives his positive exhortations. That is his whole object: he wants them to live at the full height of this wonderful salvation into which they have been brought by the Lord Jesus Christ. And what better way is there to express all that than in this very verse – 'The grace of the Lord Jesus Christ be with your spirit.' If that is so, if you have that salvation, then all these other things are included. So nothing greater can be desired or requested for any of us than that the grace of the Lord Jesus Christ should be present with us and controlling our spirits.

Thus, you see, we have here one of Paul's great, comprehensive statements, and all I want to do now is to look at it with you and, by splitting it up into its component parts, to see something of the all-inclusiveness of this petition.

'The grace of the Lord Jesus Christ': now there you have, first of all, a statement which, as we have seen, is so often found in Paul's letters. We often speak of Paul as the

Apostle of faith, and it is perfectly true, but I am not sure that a better term would not be 'the Apostle of grace'; it is his great theme and he can never get away from it. To follow this word right through the epistles and to observe the various things Paul has to say about it makes a most fascinating and interesting study. Of course, there is a sense in which the word baffles description and transcends understanding. Ultimately, grace is something which I feel, and it cannot be described accurately. Perhaps the nearest description we can give is that it is unmerited and spontaneous favour. That is what is really meant by grace in this instance: unmerited favour, something that arises spontaneously in the heart of God himself, something which man does not deserve at all, in any sense. Grace is not in any way a response to something that is good and noble in man; it is God looking upon man, blessing him in spite of what he is and in spite of what is so true of him. That is the essence of the biblical doctrine of grace. Though man had sinned against God, and rebelled against him and had been so utterly unworthy of God's blessing, God looked upon him, and in his infinite grace decided to bless him.

You notice how often at the beginning of these letters you find an expression like this: 'Grace, mercy and peace . . .' Now those are three very interesting words, and the old theologians used to be fond of discussing the question of the right order in which those words should come. They generally agreed in saying that though that is perhaps the best formal way in which to use them, actually, in the mind of God, the order should be: mercy, grace and peace. By that, they meant that God in heaven looked down upon earth and upon man, and saw man in his misery, his unhappiness and wretchedness as the result of sin. And the first thing that God felt was pity – that is mercy; he felt merciful towards man. And then, feeling mercy and pity, God decided that he must do something about it, and so grace came in. Man deserved nothing, nothing whatsoever, but in spite of that, God in his grace looked upon him and thus decided to shower upon him his love and favour. As near as we can ever get to it, that is the meaning of the word grace; it is unmerited, spontaneous, self-generated, not produced by anything outside God, but coming out of the being and the heart of God himself; the love of God expressing itself in this way towards man – grace.

Then in Paul's prayer we come to the words 'the Lord Jesus Christ'. Go again through this epistle to the Philippians and count up the number of times in which the Apostle uses this expression 'the Lord Jesus Christ', or 'Christ Jesus'; I find it astounding and amazing. From this alone it is clear that the very centre of Paul's religion, and his whole faith and Christian life, is the Lord Jesus Christ himself. Of course Paul worshipped God the Father, yes, but what Paul is out to teach everywhere is that were it not for the Lord Jesus Christ he would never have known the Father. Martin Luther was very fond of putting this point in this way. He used to say, 'I know no God but Jesus Christ.' Now he was not guilty of heresy there; what he meant was this: I cannot know God except in Jesus Christ. It is what our Lord himself said: 'I am the way, the truth, and the life: no man cometh unto the Father, but by me' (John 14:6). So he is the centre, he is essential, and the Apostle can never forget that fact.

Many times in the course of these studies we have emphasised this truth. Paul never forgot his experience on the road to Damascus. He had disliked the Lord, he had blasphemed him and felt that he was an impostor, and he had done his best to massacre and exterminate all the followers of Christ. And then he saw him, and from that moment the Lord Jesus Christ dominated the life of this man. Christ was at the centre of Paul's experience; Paul lived for him: 'To me to live is Christ, and to die is gain' – why? – that 'I may be with Christ; which is far better.' And his ambition was: 'that I may know him, and the power of his resurrection . . .' He looked for him and his glorious appearing. The Lord is coming out of heaven, as he has gone back into heaven, and he is going to change these bodies of ours and fashion them like unto his glorious body.

'I can do all things,' says Paul, 'through Christ which strengtheneth me' – Christ is always at the centre. And here, in his very last word, Paul gives him the pre-eminence again; he cannot speak a last word to anybody except in terms of Christ.

I just note these things in passing because they seem to me to remind us again of our whole position. Is the Lord Jesus Christ like that to us? In this prayer the Apostle is again enunciating his great doctrine – the Lord Jesus Christ – Jesus, Jesus of Nazareth. We are not concerned about philosophy or theory; our whole faith centres on a Person, someone who literally walked the face of this earth. 'We have not followed cunningly devised fables . . . but were eyewitnesses of his majesty' (2 Pet. 1:16). Our whole position depends upon someone who was born as a babe in Bethlehem, someone who lived in Nazareth and worked as a carpenter, a young man who went out preaching at the age of thirty, and did astonishing things for three years – Jesus.

And the whole teaching of Paul is that the person who appeared as a man amongst men is none other than the Lord God Jehovah, God the Son, the Lord Jesus Christ. Jesus is Lord, he is God, and he is also the Christ, the Messiah, the one whom God anointed and whom God set apart for the specific purpose of working out this great plan of salvation that mankind might be rescued and redeemed. Here, you see, in his final prayer and last word, Paul holds us face to face with the great central doctrine, the unique deity, the godhead, of Jesus of Nazareth; Jesus is Lord, Jesus is God, and he is the Messiah, the one who is set apart for the work. It meant his birth, his death, his resurrection; it meant shedding his own blood to purify man, that man might be reconciled to God. It is all here.

But now let us take it as a whole again: 'The grace of our Lord Jesus Christ.' What does Paul mean by this? Well, he uses this expression because, let me emphasise this again, the grace of the Lord Jesus Christ is the beginning and the end of our Christian salvation. There is no better way of expressing this, perhaps, than the way in which the Apostle put it in 2 Corinthians 8:9, which is one of the most glorious things the Apostle ever said: 'For ye know the grace of our Lord Jesus Christ, that, though he was rich, yet for your sakes he became poor, that ye through his poverty might be rich.' That is it, that is the perfect summary of the whole way of salvation. It is the grace of the Lord Jesus Christ that makes it all possible; if it were not for that we would have no faith or salvation. He, there in heaven and in glory, full of the glory of eternity and of the Father, came and made himself poor. We need not stay with this, we have already considered it all* in the second chapter of this great epistle – 'Let this mind be in you, which was also in Christ Jesus: who, being in the form of God, thought it not robbery to be equal with God: but made himself of no reputation, and took upon him the form of a servant, and was made in the likeness of men: and being found in fashion as a man, he humbled himself, and became obedient unto death, even the death of the cross.' That is the grace of the Lord Jesus Christ.

Now that is the beginning of our salvation, but it is also the continuation of our salvation, it is the whole basis of our perseverance in faith and it is the only thing that guarantees the ultimate end and consummation of our salvation. 'The grace of the Lord Jesus Christ' is responsible for the whole of our salvation from beginning to end. 'By grace are ye saved through faith; and that not of yourselves: it is the gift of God' (Eph. 2:8). Those are the Apostle's statements, so that this great verse, 'The grace of the Lord Jesus Christ' is a vitally important one for us to hold on to, because the Apostle means that we may experience all of God's gracious purposes with respect to us in Christ Jesus our Lord.

Having said that, let us come on to the second expression. 'The grace of the Lord Jesus Christ be with your spirit,' says the Apostle, and there, too, is something which is of real significance. Why does he say 'with your spirit'? It seems to me that the only adequate answer to that question

---

* See Volume 1, *The Life of Joy.*

must be put in this way. Our spirits are the highest part of
our natures; everything that is central and most important is
ultimately in the spirit. It is by our spirits that we are capable of communion with God. We are body, soul, spirit, and
the spirit is the highest – body is that which is animal, soul
that which links us to one another, but the spirit is a kind of
link between ourselves and God, even in spite of the Fall.
The spirit within us asks for that completion which God
alone can give; it is the very highest part of our being and
nature. The spirit of man is that in man which still, in spite
of sin and the Fall, marks us out from the animal and
reminds us that mankind was originally made in the image
and likeness of God. Ultimately, of course, it is true to say
that our spirit controls the whole of our life. So you see why
the Apostle prays very deliberately that the grace of the
Lord Jesus Christ might be with their spirits. If our spirit is
that which ultimately controls our whole life, how important
it is that the grace of the Lord Jesus Christ should be controlling it, and that is why the Apostle puts it like that.

Let me put it negatively. I say that our spirits are much
more important than anything else, so the condition of our
spirits is very much more important, for instance, than our
actions. Proverbs 16:32 puts this point very well: 'He that is
slow to anger is better than the mighty; and he that ruleth
[controls] his spirit than he that taketh a city.' What a profound word of wisdom that is! We very foolishly tend to
think that what one does is the most important thing, but
according to that ancient wisdom, and to the Apostle Paul
who was teaching the same thing here, the control of one's
own spirit is very much more important than anything one
may possess. There have been men in the history of the
world who have had great intelligence, some have been
kings, and princes, some military leaders, but because they
could not control their own spirits, they have ruined everything. More important than capacity and ability to do things
is this ability to be something, and especially this ability to
be in control of one's spirit, and to see that one's mind and
heart are in a true and correct state.

Or, to use another negative, it is more important for us to use our spirits correctly than it is for us to pay too much attention to the things that happen to us, and I have no doubt that that also is very much in the mind of the Apostle at this point. Here he is, writing to these Philippian people who are surrounded by troubles and problems. Yes, says Paul, many things may happen to you, but your own condition is of greater importance than those things because if your spirit is right, in a sense it does not matter what happens to you. Someone once said, 'It is not life that matters, but the courage that you bring into it.' Now I do not like that man's use of the word 'courage'; I prefer the way in which the Apostle puts it here. What ultimately matters in life is not so much the things that happen to us as the way in which we look at those things, so that if my spirit is right, then I am more or less independent of what is happening around and about me. Now that has been the major theme of the Apostle throughout this epistle. He is in prison, and in a sense everything is against him, but he is above it all because his spirit is right. 'The grace of the Lord Jesus Christ' is controlling his spirit.

We have been looking at that great phrase, 'The peace of God shall keep your hearts and minds' – and it is just the same thing. So that what the Apostle is saying in these last words is, in effect, 'I pray that the grace of the Lord Jesus Christ shall be with your spirit, because if he is there in his full grace, guarding your spirit, then whatever may happen to you, you yourself will be all right.'

Or let me put it like this. Is not a wrong spirit the cause of most of our troubles and problems in life? Look back across your life and consider the causes of unhappiness and pain and distress. Have we not honestly to admit to one another in the sight of God that we ourselves have created most of our problems and troubles? Evil thoughts and imaginations and desires – what havoc they play with us! A sense of wrong or a grudge, jealousy, envy – those are the things which distress and cause us trouble. How much unhappiness and wretchedness we would avoid in this life and world if only our spirits were sweet and pure. That is why the Apostle says, 'The grace of the Lord Jesus Christ be with your spirit.' There will be no evil thoughts, there will be no evil imaginations, there will be no jealousy and envy, there will be no sense of wrong or of grudge, there will be no tendency to complain against God, if your spirit is sweet and wholesome and pure. That is why Paul puts his special emphasis upon our spirits.

Finally, let me emphasise this in a third and last principle. What, then, does the grace of the Lord Jesus Christ do to us and to our spirits? Let me suggest these answers.

Firstly, the grace of the Lord Jesus Christ endues us with every one of the Christian graces. I can best explain this by quoting 2 Corinthians 8:7: 'Therefore, as ye abound in every thing, in faith, and utterance, and knowledge, and in all diligence, and in your love to us, see that ye abound in this grace also.' Paul is referring here to the grace of liberality, so when the grace of the Lord Jesus Christ is with you, you have all the graces of the Christian life, faith, hope, love, knowledge, understanding, and all these things. Now this is another way of saying, 'I pray that all the fruits of the Spirit may be manifested in your spirits.' If the grace of the Lord Jesus Christ is with our spirits, we will have knowledge, as Paul here tells us – knowledge of sins forgiven, knowledge of the gracious purpose of God with respect to us, and, after all, that is the greatest thing a man can ever know. What I am anxious for you to know at all times, says the Apostle to these beloved Philippians, is what God's purposes of grace are with respect to you, so that wherever you are you may always know that God loves you as your Father, that you are a child of God, that you are in the great purpose of God, and, finally, that you are in the plan of salvation and are ultimately destined to the glory which will go on, world without end. The grace of the Lord Jesus Christ endues us with every other grace, so having that, I have faith, I have hope, I have love, I have knowledge and understanding, and I begin to manifest these various fruits of the blessed Holy Spirit.

Then, secondly, the grace of the Lord Jesus Christ always restrains us. Those of you who are interested in the old theologians will remember that they always devoted a section to what they called 'restraining grace', and a vitally important thing it is – this grace of the Lord Jesus Christ that holds us back when we would rush forward into something which is wrong, or when our spirits tend to run away with us. Our Lord never manifested such faults – there was a calmness, a composure, a balance and a perfection of life in him, with the meekness, the humility, and all these things about which we read in the Gospels. So as his grace controls our spirits, he will restrain us in that way.

What else? Well, thirdly, the grace of the Lord Jesus Christ also animates, and stimulates us in our dealings with one another. That is why Paul wrote that great word which I have already quoted, 'For ye know the grace of our Lord Jesus Christ, that, though he was rich, yet for your sakes he became poor, that ye through his poverty might be rich' (2 Cor. 8:9). Paul was writing to those members of the church at Corinth who had not made a collection for the poorer saints. He said, in effect, 'As that is what Christ has done for you, do you not think that you ought to make yourself responsible for the poorer brethren?' The grace of the Lord Jesus Christ thus makes us love one another and consider one another. The Philippians had done it to Paul, and he prays that this grace may continue to lead and guide them.

Finally, the grace of the Lord Jesus Christ strengthens and sustains us, and Paul has written about this in the second chapter. Here were people, members of the church at Philippi, who, in a great trial and affliction, were abounding in joy. How did they manage it? The answer is that the grace of the Lord Jesus Christ strengthened and sustained them. The Philippians were passing through a period of very great trial, but they knew an abundance of joy, and out of their deep poverty, they were extremely liberal. It is the great theme of the New Testament. You find it most perfectly in 2 Corinthians 12, where Paul has been praying about his thorn in the flesh, and, you remember, having prayed three times that it might be removed, he learned this great lesson; Christ said, 'My strength is made perfect in weakness.' And that is what the Apostle is trying to tell these Philippians.

How does the grace of the Lord Jesus Christ strengthen and sustain us? It is by assuring us of his love, giving us perfect peace, enabling us to see beyond our problems to the glory that lies ahead. In Psalm 63 the Psalmist spoke those great words: 'Thy lovingkindness is better than life.' The man who can say that has conquered life. 'I may have trials in life,' he says, 'yes, I know that eventually they have to come, but they are only temporary and passing. But your lovingkindness will never go, will never leave me nor forsake me.' And Paul had proved that, whether in prison, or in shipwreck, or in persecution, the grace of the Lord Jesus Christ was always with him. It is something of which the world can never rob us. 'Thy lovingkindness is better than life.'

Or let me put it like this: the grace of the Lord Jesus Christ is sufficient for all things. Back we come again to Paul: he prayed three times that the thorn in the flesh might be removed, and the Lord answered him and said, 'My grace is sufficient for thee.' It is enough; yes, the thorn shall remain, but it does not matter, his grace will be enough, it will take you through. And that, it seems to me, is the supreme blessing in life. 'The grace of the Lord Jesus Christ be with your spirit.'

My beloved friends, we live in an uncertain world, an uncertain life; no one knows what is going to happen to any one of us. There are an almost infinite number of possibilities. Can we end our consideration of this mighty epistle on a grander note than this? Whatever may happen in life or in death; whatever may take place in any conceivable situation or circumstances, whatever may be your lot, the grace of the Lord Jesus Christ will be sufficient, it will hold you, it will sustain you, it will even enable you to rejoice in tribulation, it will strengthen you, establish you, hold you, keep you, answer your every need and take you through. Ultimately it will present you faultless, perfect, in glory in the presence of God. 'The grace of the Lord Jesus Christ be with your spirit. AMEN.'